THE MEMOIRS OF
EDWIN WATERHOUSE

THE MEMOIRS OF
EDWIN WATERHOUSE

A Founder of Price Waterhouse

EDITED BY
EDGAR JONES

B. T. Batsford Ltd · London

ISBN 0 7134 5579 9
Typeset by Latimer Trend & Company Ltd, Plymouth
and printed by Butler & Tanner Ltd, Frome, Somerset
for the publishers
B. T. Batsford Ltd
4 Fitzhardinge Street
London
WIH OAH

CONTENTS

THE MEMOIRS OF EDWIN WATERHOUSE   49

LIST OF ILLUSTRATIONS

Between pages 96 and 97

List of Illustrations

Maps and Figures

FOREWORD

Edwin Waterhouse was – by virtue of his professional expertise, standing and personality – an eminent Victorian, whose life and career have so far passed largely unrecognized. I hope this book will go some way towards recording his achievements.

It was in 1865 that Edwin Waterhouse joined S. L. Price, who had been in practice on his own account since 1849, to set up what became known as Price Waterhouse. Edwin became senior partner of the firm in 1887, a position which he held for nearly 20 years. He was also one of the early leaders of the Institute of Chartered Accountants in England and Wales, joining the Council in 1887 and serving as President in 1892–4.

I believe this book will appeal not only to those with an interest in the development of Price Waterhouse and the accountancy profession, but also to those with a wider interest in the social history of Victorian and Edwardian England. For within, Edwin writes about his long and varied life, covering such aspects as his family background, education and subsequent career, his Surrey estate and holidays and social events. His studied observations also give a unique view of the professional classes at work and play – and their attitudes and conventions.

My thanks are due to Gill Hill, a descendant of Edwin Waterhouse, for allowing us access to Edwin's memoirs and thus making this book possible; to Dr Edgar Jones for his painstaking editing of these and his research into Edwin's career and that of his contemporaries; and to John Barrett, a senior manager in my firm, for 're-discovering' the memoirs.

London 1988   Jeffery Bowman
                                                   Senior Partner,
                                                   Price Waterhouse

HOW THE EDWIN WATERHOUSE MEMOIRS WERE FOUND

When I was appointed as the first archivist to Price Waterhouse in July 1983 I was handed a file, for safe keeping, of extracts from the memoirs of Edwin Waterhouse. The extracts had been made in the 1930s, and only dealt with matters relating to the firm. I also established that no one within the firm knew of the present location of the memoirs, or whether in fact they were still in existence.

I then started on the task of examining, sorting and cataloguing the firm's private papers. One file I examined was concerned with the history of Price Waterhouse in the United States, and in it was a letter dated May 1948 which stated 'The Diary [sic], it seems, is now in a safe at Feldemore, E.W's old house, which is occupied by the Admiralty, and cannot at present be got out ...' (That 'Diary' turned out to be eleven volumes of memoirs – see plate 1.) This set me off on the trail for the memoirs.

Over the next few months I searched the indexes at the British Library, the manuscripts department of the British Museum, and the Historical Manuscripts Commission and also made numerous telephone calls to Record Offices in those areas of the country where I knew the Waterhouses had lived. But all to no avail.

I then arranged a meeting with a partner in the solicitors Waterhouse & Co. (which had been founded by Edwin's brother, Theodore) to see if he knew of the existence of the memoirs. He didn't, but he spoke to one of his fellow partners who made a telephone call; the upshot of which was that I got into my car and drove to the home of the daughter of Theodore Waterhouse, son of Edwin Waterhouse by

How the Edwin Waterhouse Memoirs were found

his second marriage. There in a cupboard were the memoirs. This was in March 1985.

John Barrett
Archivist,
Price Waterhouse

John Barrett joined Price Waterhouse in 1963 and prior to becoming the firm's archivist he was a senior audit manager in the Independent Business Group. His outside activities include being an official guide to the City of London.

Acknowledgements

First, I must thank Price Waterhouse for allowing me the opportunity to edit the manuscript memoirs and family papers of Edwin Waterhouse, and in particular Mr Jeffery Bowman, the Senior Partner, and Mr Richard Wilkes, the partner who took overall responsibility for the project. Without the initiatives taken by the firm and the funding which they provided, this collection would not have been published.

However, in the practical execution of this historical work, I have one person, above all others, to thank, Mr John Barrett, a senior manager of Price Waterhouse. He traced the whereabouts of the Waterhouse memoirs and ensured that they might be preserved, edited and then published. Throughout the two years of this exercise, he has been an unfailing source of encouragement, enthusiasm and information. I am sincerely grateful to him for his sustained effort.

I owe a considerable debt of gratitude to David and Gill Hill, who have allowed me to consult the various manuscripts on numerous occasions, and always been most hospitable and friendly. I have enjoyed visiting them and benefited from their knowledge of the Waterhouse family.

In addition, I am indebted to Carol Wood for typing the Introduction, text and footnotes, an arduous task which she has performed with infectious cheerfulness. I thank A. J. Knowler Ltd, who processed most of the black-and-white photographs, and to Maxwell Grizaard, who reproduced the remainder, for their professional expertise. I am grateful to the Headmaster of Belmont School for Boys for allowing access to the house and grounds of Edwin Waterhouse's former home.

Nicola Westbury very generously allowed me to consult her B. Arch. thesis on the 'Country Houses of Holmbury St Mary' and willingly discussed the findings of her research. Mr J. Petti of Waterhouse & Co., solicitors, provided information on the history of his firm and the Waterhouse family. I thank the following institutions and libraries for allowing me to consult their archives in the execution of this project:

Acknowledgements

the Bristol Central Library; British Library; Institute of Chartered Accountants in England and Wales; Liverpool Record Office; Manchester Central Library; Public Record Office, Kew, and the Royal Institute of British Architects Library.

EDGAR JONES
February 1988

Abbreviations used in the text

DBB	*Dictionary of Business Biography*
DNB	*Dictionary of National Biography*
ICAEW	Institute of Chartered Accountants in England and Wales
LNWR	London and North Western Railway
PRO	Public Record Office, Kew
PW	Price Waterhouse
RIBA	Royal Institute of British Architects Library
WWMP	Michael Stenton and Stephen Lees (Editors), *Who's Who of British Members of Parliament* (4 Vols, Hassocks, Sussex, 1976–81)
WwW	*Who was Who*

INTRODUCTION

Edgar Jones

'I have always felt that, with few exceptions, a man's personality or ego', wrote Nicholas E. Waterhouse (1877–1964) in 1961,

> is built up on the earliest reactions of his childhood and the manner in which he tackled its problems, quite as much as on heredity or the society in which he chanced to be born. In his earliest years he is a creature of instinct and quite capable of rebelling against behaviour which seems to him unnatural, and I think that, unless he is very docile, these characteristics will remain somewhere deep down within him always.[1]

Whilst many contemporary psychologists would not entirely agree with this interpretation of character formation, there remains a core of truth in this statement. Nicholas was the eldest son of Edwin Waterhouse and followed him into the accountancy firm of Price, Waterhouse & Co., becoming its senior partner in 1945.[2] Apart from periods of schooling at Winchester and further education at New College, Oxford, Nicholas kept in close contact with his father, visiting him regularly for both social and professional reasons until the latter's death in September 1917. Given that these views on the nature of personality came from one who knew Edwin deeply and extensively (and that the father–son relationship which existed between them had doubtless contributed to these beliefs), it is appropriate to begin this assessment of the life, career and achievements of Edwin Waterhouse with an account of his parents and childhood experience.

Family, Childhood and Education

Nicholas Waterhouse (1768–1823), grandfather of Edwin, was the only son of Ellythorp and Sarah Waterhouse of Liverpool.[3] Although

15

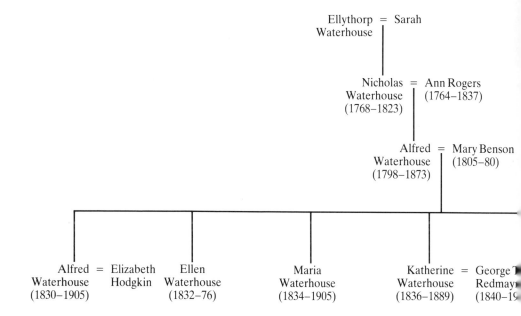

Ellythorp = Sarah
Waterhouse

Nicholas = Ann Rogers
Waterhouse | (1764–1837)
(1768–1823)

Alfred = Mary Benson
Waterhouse | (1805–80)
(1798–1873)

Alfred = Elizabeth   Ellen   Maria   Katherine = George
Waterhouse   Hodgkin   Waterhouse   Waterhouse   Waterhouse   Redmay
(1830–1905)   (1832–76)   (1834–1905)   (1836–1889) (1840–19

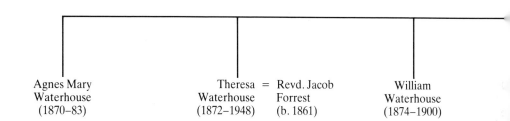

Agnes Mary   Theresa = Revd. Jacob   William
Waterhouse   Waterhouse   Forrest   Waterhouse
(1870–83)   (1872–1948) (b. 1861)   (1874–1900)

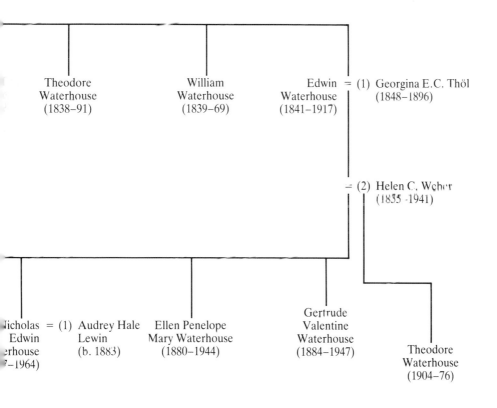

A simplified genealogical table of the Waterhouse family

Theodore
Waterhouse
(1838–91)

William
Waterhouse
(1839–69)

Edwin = (1) Georgina E.C. Thöl
Waterhouse   (1848–1896)
(1841–1917)

= (2) Helen C. Weber
       (1855–1941)

Nicholas = (1) Audrey Hale
Edwin   Lewin
erhouse   (b. 1883)
7–1964)

Ellen Penelope
Mary Waterhouse
(1880–1944)

Gertrude
Valentine
Waterhouse
(1884–1947)

Theodore
Waterhouse
(1904–76)

Ellythorp had received a comparatively sound education it had not provided him with entrepreneurial acumen and his shop for ready-made clothes in Pool Lane did not prosper. His early death left Sarah, aged 37, with three daughters and a son in circumstances of financial embarrassment.[4] A woman of great energy and strong Quaker principles, she was advised by her friends to continue with the business. Such was Sarah's determination that, by the time of her death, she had paid off her husband's debts and saved sufficient to provide each of her daughters with a dowry of £900. Meanwhile Nicholas, her only son, was thus enabled to inherit a small estate, worth £1300, which had been left to her by Nicholas and Bridget Clough, her parents.

In the 1780s the manufacture of fustians (a coarse, twilled cotton fabric) was an expanding industry, one of whose centres was Bolton. Desiring that her son should not fail in business as her husband had done, Sarah Waterhouse sent Nicholas there to be apprenticed in that trade.[5] He had been schooled to the age of fourteen in Everton, where he gained an appreciation of English prose and poetry. Like so many intelligent men whose tuition fell short of their abilities, Nicholas Waterhouse placed considerable emphasis on the value of education and 'used to remind his sons of their superior advantages, ascertaining their progress in Latin &c., and stimulating them in their studies'.[6]

On completing his apprenticeship in Bolton, Nicholas Waterhouse entered a cotton warehouse in Manchester, boarding with friends, Richard and Martha Routh, near neighbours of Daniel and Mary Rogers, the parents of Ann (1764–1836), who was to become his wife. Thomas Ellison in *The Cotton Trade of Great Britain* (1886) stated that Nicholas then returned to Liverpool and commenced business as a cotton broker in 1782, residing with his father at 28 Pool Lane.[7] Having been born in 1768, he would have been but fourteen and the evidence of his relatives suggests that Ellythorp Waterhouse had died before Nicholas set up on his own account. Nevertheless, it remains true that he acted as a selling broker for Messrs Rathbone and other leading importers in Liverpool, and as a buying broker for the major consumers in the nearby manufacturing districts. Around 1795 Isaac Cooke, who came from Manchester, entered the firm, and c.1803 became Waterhouse's partner. When Cooke retired in 1819, Nicholas introduced his three sons, Nicholas Junior (1795–1828), Daniel (1796–1861) and Alfred (1798–1873)[8] to the broking business, whose counting house was at 6 Exchange Alley.[9] In 1823, the year that Nicholas Senior died, their office in Liverpool was transferred to 1 Oldhall Street, where it remained throughout the nineteenth century.[10]

Introduction

Although Nicholas Waterhouse had been forced by his father's penury to serve an apprenticeship, he appears to have died a comparatively wealthy man. His daughter, Lucy Fowler (1803–69), Edwin's aunt, recalled that the gardens of his house in Everton had four glasshouses containing many curious and beautiful plants and fruits, much admired by those who attended parties there.[11] And his obituary in *The Liverpool Mercury* stated that Nicholas Waterhouse had become a man of standing in the city: 'one of the Society of Friends, of which, as well as society at large, he was a valuable and useful member . . . he was universally respected'.[12] Lucy Fowler, whose admiration of him was perhaps uncritical ('I do not remember in him a fault')[13] nevertheless could record that he 'was highly esteemed by those who knew him as a man of business for his integrity, uprightness and punctuality'.[14]

Having established himself in the broking business, in July 1829 Alfred Waterhouse married Mary Bevan (1805–80), by whom he had four boys and three girls, Edwin born on 4 June 1841 at 'Oakfield', Aigburth, being the youngest of them all. Little is known of Alfred's involvement in Nicholas Waterhouse & Sons. Presumably the office of senior partnership passed from Nicholas Senior to the eldest son, Nicholas Junior, and then to Daniel when the former died in 1823. A fourth brother, Rogers Waterhouse (1807–68), was admitted to the partnership around 1833–34 and he in 1859 served as president of the Cotton Brokers' Association.[15] In 1843 at the comparatively early age of 45 Alfred Waterhouse decided to resign from the firm. As his wife, Mary, related,

> my dearest Alfred is about going out of business, a step he has contemplated for years, but wishing to weigh so important a subject well, has not been precipitate about it. . . . In leaving the concern in which he has been brought up, and a partner since a very young man, my dear Alfred provides that our eldest boy [Alfred junior] shall be apprenticed to it, when his schooling is finished, if we wish it; and have a share on coming of age, should his habits be business-like, and his general conduct such as to render him a suitable partner.[16]

Trade disagreements with America had adversely affected his business, while a quarrel with other Quakers led to his father's resignation from the Liverpool Society of Friends.[17] Living in the suburb of Aigburth, Alfred Waterhouse had, in the words of his wife, been 'enabled to lay aside the desire for greater acquisition, and settle down contentedly on what, with the blessing, will doubtless be sufficient'.[18] Having determined to leave his home town, he eventually purchased a substantial house with impressive gardens near Reading, at Whiteknights (p. 65).

Descriptions of Alfred Waterhouse's personality are rare. Like his father, he appears to have been a man of integrity, hard working and honest. Perhaps the key to an understanding of the family environment into which Edwin Waterhouse was born was their membership of the Society of Friends. His relatives were all devout Quakers and Edwin himself recorded of his grandfather Nicholas: his 'bringing up had not endowed him with much softness of character and the narrowness of Friends' views did not bring him into sympathy [with] others'.[19] A rather harsh and unyielding attitude to many of the pleasures of life was also adopted by Edwin's father Alfred. Music and the 'lighter side of literature' were forbidden subjects[20] and alcohol was prohibited even to visitors,[21] while Edwin, on entering University College School, was cautioned against making friends with boys of different religions.[22] Something of this puritanism passed into Edwin Waterhouse's own household as his son, Nicholas recollected; visits to the theatre were discouraged;[23] children were urged to adopt Gladstone's habit of chewing each mouthful of food 32 times;[24] to prevent any impropriety resulting at a party 'any nooks, corners or comfortable seats suitable for sitting out were brilliantly lit, and any doors or windows leading to the gardens were closed and locked'.[25] William Waterhouse, younger brother of Nicholas, had been 'trounced' by Edwin when he discovered that the former had shared a Hansom cab with a lady unchaperoned on their way home from a dance, even though she was Miss Lidderdale, the daughter of the general manager of the Bank of England's Law Courts Branch, and who lived almost next door to the Waterhouses in London.[26]

The Waterhouse family's Non-conformity also found expression in homeopathic medicine.[27] A method of treatment devised by Samuel Hahnemann (1755–1843) at the end of the eighteenth century, homeopathy is based on the theory that small doses of a drug will cure symptoms that larger quantities would cause; the smaller the dose, he believed, the greater this paradoxical effect. Although the practice is unsupported by science, it represented, as Waterhouse himself observed, a humane alternative to the often brutal treatment prescribed by orthodox medicine.

Thus it was from a background of comparative affluence, commercial success and unyielding moral strictures that Edwin Waterhouse entered his teenage years. Having been educated up to the age of 15 by private tutors in his father's various homes, in September 1855 he and

Introduction

his brother, William (1839–69), were sent to University College School, Gower Street, London. It had a considerable reputation and, being open to all regardless of religious faith, attracted young men of ability from a variety of circumstances. The experience of attending both the school and subsequently University College itself proved invaluable to the shy and somewhat sheltered Edwin. The restricted nature of his parental upbringing was revealed in an incident recalled by Edwin himself. Given the eclectic spiritual tone of the establishment, his father had cautioned him 'not to make friends hastily' and 'to confine my attention within the walls of the school to my lessons'. 'Before long', however,

> a dear little Unitarian schoolfellow, Guy Paget, lodging at 'The Hall' close by the school, asked me to join his birthday party at tea. I was so shocked as having allowed our intimacy to grow to such a height as to render such an invitation possible, that I nearly fainted; I gave him an unintelligibly rude refusal. But we continued to be good friends and I do not think I ever suffered from the religious views of my schoolfellows.[28]

Not only did it broaden his knowledge and skills (he proved to be an able scholar winning prizes for Latin, chemistry, mathematics and moral philosophy, and took a good second-class B.A. degree, having studied Greek, Latin, English and mathematics with prizes in Greek and English) but also it introduced him to many members of a middle-class elite who in later life were to occupy important posts in government, administration, the professions and commerce. Amongst the friendships he formed in Gower Street and which later benefited his career were those with Herbert Cozens-Hardy, Farrer Herschell, Julian Goldsmid, Henry Peto, Henry Selfe Page Winterbotham and Henry Mason Bompas.

Just as William had been his companion at University College School, so Theodore (1838–91), the second eldest brother, was to be his guide at university. William had departed to spend some time in Manchester in the offices of his architect elder brother, Alfred (1830–1905). Having decided to become a solicitor, Theodore had been advised by his friend [Sir] Edward Fry (1827–1918) to take a degree, as it would broaden his education and reduce the period of his articles by two years. Theodore entered University College in January 1857 (Edwin following him there in October), and, though his schooling had been much interrupted by poor health, proved himself to be the ablest scholar of the four brothers. Being four years older than Edwin,

Introduction

Theodore exercised an important influence on the former's general education. 'Perhaps', recalled Edwin,

> I was a little too anxious to follow him, and leaned too much upon him for we were seldom apart out of classroom hours, and those of whom I saw most were his, rather than my, friends. I failed therefore to get into a separate circle of which my conversational powers might have been developed better than in the constant company of those to whom it satisfied and behoved me to act as a listener.[29]

Theodore Waterhouse generally took first place in college examinations, taking prizes in moral philosophy and the history of philosophy. Of the 50 who sat finals, 20 were failed, 20 awarded second (including Edwin) and ten gained first-class honours, although originally only three firsts were to be given, Theodore being among this select group. In December 1862 he returned to University College to win the Joseph Hume Scholarship, despite being unwell at the time of the examination, and two years later took it in jurisprudence, while also coming first in the Bachelor of Laws papers.[30] In recognition of his intellectual gifts, Theodore was elected a Fellow of University College London in 1867. 'I never knew anybody', wrote former student J. W. Richardson (1837–1908),

> who could compare with him for tenacity and accuracy of memory. If he looked up a word in a dictionary, he very deliberately noted its inflexions, its root, its gender, and its various meanings, and having once noted he seemed never to forget.[31]

Having both sat their finals in 1860, Edwin and Theodore moved to 60 (now 34) Park Street, near Grosvenor Square, where they remained until the former's marriage in 1869. Theodore served his articles with Messrs Clayton, Cookson & Wainwright of 6 New Square, Lincoln's Inn, and in February 1864 achieved second place (of 122 candidates) in the Incorporated Law Society's final examination.[32] In the following year he decided to set up his own practice and took an office at 10 Lincoln's Inn Fields.[33] Throughout this period of academic study and professional training, as Edwin himself acknowledged, Theodore served as an example to his younger brother: 'great were the advantages to me in having one so interested in my welfare for good as he always was, ready to help and advise me'.[34] However, just as Edwin was able to assist his eldest brother, Alfred, in the financial management of his architect's firm, so too could he teach Theodore. For the latter's partner, William Winterbotham, recalled of Theodore:

> He was exact and thorough in all his work, and rarely made a mistake; never did careless work himself and he was impatient of careless work in others. He was especially precise in all matters of account. He often said that the first thing a solicitor ought to learn is to keep accounts. For some years he kept the accounts of his business himself, not only entering up the cash-book and posting the ledger, but even making a fair copy of these books in his own hand; and for many years he made his own entries from day to day of the work done by him.[35]

Waterhouse & Co., the City firm of solicitors which he founded,[36] flourishes today – though not on the scale of Price Waterhouse, one of the largest accountancy practices in the world. Since Theodore never achieved the popular acclaim of his architect brother, Alfred, posterity has proved to have been less kind to him than other members of his family.

A Professional Career

Having served as an assistant in a financial investigation into the affairs of the Cambrian Railways Co. in 1867, Edwin encountered the company's chairman Sir Charles Jackson, who remarked, 'Mr Waterhouse, you will some day be a very eminent man in your profession'.[37] Initially, as Edwin himself recalled, he had no conception of accountancy or business and 'felt a dislike of the "city"' and of the 'pale and anxious faces which I saw on my infrequent visits there'.[38] Since both his elder brothers, Alfred and Theodore (William entering the family firm as a cotton broker), had entered the professions, Edwin toyed with the notion of becoming a doctor but concluded that, having no particular medical talents, this was a course of uncertain outcome. In the event matters were settled fortuitously. Having decided to leave Bristol to purchase a retirement home, Alfred Waterhouse Senior moved to Whiteknights, near Reading, where he became acquainted with three ladies, the sisters of William Turquand (1818/19–94), the eminent City accountant. It was soon arranged that Edwin would enter the offices of Coleman, Turquand, Youngs & Co., at Tokenhouse Yard – as an unpaid pupil – to learn about business in general from the standpoint of a public accountant. On the 7 January 1861, aged 20, Edwin began work.[39]

For two years Edwin followed the profession of an accountant under the overall supervision of Mr Weise, a partner. He studied book-keeping and the various ways in which insolvent businesses could be wound up, this being the principal activity performed by Coleman, Turquand, Youngs & Co. At the end of this period, there existing no qualifying examinations, Edwin was promised a salary during the coming year and in 1863, having completed the customary three years pupildom, he informed Turquand of his intention of setting up on his own. His employers offered to extend his contract so that he might gain more experience but Edwin, encouraged by the advice of his father and brother Alfred, determined to establish his own practice. On 24 February 1864, after a holiday in the Riviera and having been given £2000 by his father, he put up his brass plate at 11 Old Jewry Chambers in the City.[40]

Although there were rising numbers of accountants earning large fees in London, the problems of getting started were considerable. As the profession had yet to set up an institute from which members could obtain qualifications, business was commonly gained by personal contacts; the well-established firms, such as Colemans, Deloittes or Quilter, Ball & Co., maintaining a powerful hold over the most lucrative commissions. Accordingly, as his office diary for 1864 records, Edwin spent much of the first few weeks in practice writing to friends or acquaintances of his father for work.[41] Among those to whom he sent letters were: St Leger Glyn, Paul Bevan, Lewis Fry, J. W. Richardson, Edward Ashworth, William Fowler, J. W. Pease, Crewdson & Worthington and J. B. Braithwaite.[42] His letter book for the period reveals that Harmood Walcot Banner (1814–78), the Liverpool accountant,[43] was an early and very important contact, doubtless an acquaintance of his father or uncles there. On 2 April 1869 Edwin wrote to Messrs Harmood Banner & Sons:

> I need not say how happy I should be to undertake any work for such a firm as your own, and how much greater importance to a young man like myself the obtaining of such work is than the question of a large or small amount of remuneration for it. I should, of course, be very unwilling in my desire to obtain work to do business on terms which might be thought too low for a first class accountant, but under the present circumstances, I beg to leave the question of terms entirely in your own hands.[44]

Introduction

The approach proved to be a profitable one. Banner sub-contracted the audit of the Queen Insurance Co. in Leadenhall Street, London, to Waterhouse,[45] and this became one of his leading clients in the first year of his practice: of the 95 hours he worked to 26 June 1864, for example, it came second in the list arranged according to time employed ($18\frac{1}{2}$ hours).[46]

His principal client, however, in this embryonic period, was his elder brother Alfred Waterhouse. He spent some 40 hours on his accounts in April–May 1864,[47] checking and examining the architect's books for 1862–63 and drawing up a balance sheet and profit and loss account for the year ended April 1864. For the future, Edwin suggested 'a few alterations in the method of keeping the accounts, which', he believed, 'will add greatly to their efficiency and accuracy';[48] these included the application of 'a double entry system in supplementary ledgers'.[49] It was said that the managerial and financial controls and organization introduced by Alfred Waterhouse made his the most efficient architect's practice of the day and some of the credit for these innovations must have been due to Edwin, who continued to advise him on accounting matters.[50]

Other clients gained at this time included the British Ice Making Co. (an examination into the state of the business and which ultimately contributed to its successful second attempt at trading),[51] Sudlow & Co. in King Street (the dissolution of a partnership between J.J.J. Sudlow and R. Delatorre),[52] British Schools Savings Bank at Carshalton (preparation of a balance sheet and audit),[53] and John Fowler, the manufacturer of steam ploughs and agricultural equipment in Leeds, to whom Edwin wrote:

> my father has sent on to me a letter he has received from you in which you state that you think my assistance might be valuable to you in organizing and starting a system of accounts, specially adapted to the business of your works, as well as in taking charge of and generally superintending them for some months.[54]

His practice appears to have become reasonably well established during 1864, sufficient to have taken on a clerk, W. H. Hardy, previously the Under Secretary of University College,[55] having consulted Mr Weise in the matter.[56] However, during his visits to Leeds to plan 'a system of cost accounts',[57] he encountered William H. Holyland (1807–82), a principal clerk of Turquand, who was engaged in winding up the Leeds Banking Co. Holyland revealed that he was about to join his friend Samuel Lowell Price (1821–87), an accountant in Gresham Street (p. 216), in partnership and suggested that Edwin make a third in the arrangement. As he himself recorded,

> I have been doing very well for myself during the last few months, but the offer seemed to open out chances of quickly attaining a wider experience, whilst ensuring a more steady practice and affording me the advantages of assistance should I need it. After consulting my father and some business friends, I accepted the terms offered [to] me, and we arranged to put our names as a firm on the 1st May 1865.[58]

Thus, the firm of Price, Holyland & Waterhouse was founded with office at 13 (subsequently 44) Gresham Street on the first, second and third floors.[59]

Although not the eldest, S. L. Price, the most experienced of the three, became the senior partner. The son of Charles Price, a Bristol potter,[60] he had originally worked for Bradley & Barnard, public accountants, auctioneers and agents to assignees and creditors in bankruptcies, 30 Broad Street, Bristol.[61] At some point in the 1830s, probably 1836, Bradley, Barnard & Co. opened a London office at 2 St Swithins Lane,[62] and it seems that Price was sent there to take charge.[63] In 1847 their city office moved to 27 Gresham Street but was no longer mentioned in *Mathew's Bristol Directory* for 1849.[64] The explanation was the formation of a new partnership, Barnard, Thomas & Co., which moved to 5 Gresham Street. When W. E. Edwards (d. 1884) and S. L. Price established their accountancy firm they also occupied the same address.[65] The arrangement was not blessed with permanency, for an advertisement in *The London Gazette* (1850) gave notice that 'the partnership between W. Edwards and S. L. Price . . . was dissolved on 24 December 1849'. From then until May 1865 when he joined Holyland and Waterhouse, Price practised on his own at 5 Gresham Street.[66]

Whilst Price had almost 20 years experience as a public accountant to call upon when the firm of Price, Holyland & Waterhouse was formed, the same could not be said of William Hopkins Holyland. He was recorded in the *London Post Office Directory* for 1851 as being a warehouseman,[67] and between then and 1856 was in partnership with Rogers and Lowrey at 90–91 Watling Street.[68] His name is absent from the *Directory* in 1857 but re-appears in 1858 as an accountant at 25 Lincoln's Inn Fields.[69] It is possible that he had learned book-keeping whilst attending to the accounts of the warehouse business, but that his expertise or connections proved insufficient to sustain a practice for there is no further mention of him between 1859 and 1865, when it may be assumed he was employed as a principal clerk by Coleman, Turquand, Youngs & Co.

As the senior and most experienced partner, Price contributed £1000 to the firm of Price, Holyland & Waterhouse in 1865, Holyland and Waterhouse each investing £500. In addition, Edwin paid a premium of £1000 to Price and £250 to Holyland.[70] Their first year's profits were reported as being in excess of £7000 and that would have given Edwin an income of around £1750, which was a comfortable sum by mid-Victorian standards.

Edwin Waterhouse remained with the firm until his retirement in December 1905, becoming the senior partner in 1887 on the death of Price.[71] In October 1874 Price had suggested, in view of Holyland having retired from the partnership in March 1871,[72] that the style be altered to Price, Waterhouse & Co.[73] With the exception of the removal of the comma in 1940 as an economy measure and the dropping of the '& Co.' in July 1981, the firm's name has survived without change until the present day.

From its formation in 1865 until Edwin Waterhouse's retirement in 1905, Price, Waterhouse & Co. prospered. A measure of its success and importance within the profession may be obtained from the firm's fee income. In the year ended April 1866 the partnership earned £9138, increasing to an average of £14,450, per annum between 1870 and 1885 with peaks in 1870 (£18,070), 1876 (£17,135) and 1877 (£17,749). There was an appreciable rise in Price, Waterhouse's fees after 1889 (£20,824), and by the late 1890s they earned in excess of £40,000 per annum (1898 £43,979; 1900 £47,842; 1902 £55,360).[74]

In later years, when senior partner, as was then customary, Edwin Waterhouse took a lion's share of the profits; in 1896–97 when £35,897 was available for distribution among four partners, he received £21,000 (58.5%) and in 1898–99 the figures were respectively £38,015 and £18,274 (48%).[75] At his death Edwin left £257,136 gross and it would appear that the greater part of his fortune had been earned from professional fees rather than share dealing or other forms of financial speculation.

Among the firm's largest clients, and particularly those handled by Edwin Waterhouse, the most important was the London & North Western Railway Co., which in 1891–92 generated the highest single fee, £1199.[76] Edwin had originally been introduced to the officials of the L.N.W.R. at Euston, when a clerk to J. E. Coleman, who had been appointed to assist the shareholder auditors.[77] He must have established a sound working relationship with them and the accounts staff at

Introduction

Euston, for in November 1866, on the resignation of Coleman as professional advisor,[78] the auditors, Henry Crosfield and R. W. Hand, chose Price, Holyland & Waterhouse to succeed him.[79] This situation continued until May 1873, when the sudden death of Hand resulted in Edwin being elected as a temporary auditor.[80] Re-elected in January 1874,[81] he continued to serve in this capacity until being replaced by [Sir] Edward Lawrence (1825–90) in January 1876. Henceforth the appointment of a public accountant to assist the auditors appears to have been personal to Edwin rather than to his firm, an arrangement which was confirmed upon the death of Crosfield in 1882.[82] Edwin Waterhouse succeeded him at a special meeting held on 16 February of that year and continued to serve as joint auditor until his retirement in January 1913, when he was followed by his son, Nicholas.[83] The board of directors recorded their appreciation of his sustained contribution, adding that

> not only would the proprietors [shareholders] lose the services of a guardian of their interests who has shown conspicuous ability, but the directors would miss the presence of a friend whom they held in the highest esteem and with whom they had been associated for so many years.[84]

Railway companies, as some of the largest businesses in the Victorian economy, were among the most prestigious clients that an auditor could obtain, and the L.N.W.R., as one of the leaders in its field, was a particularly valued audit. Growth was generated internally and by take over and the audits of the acquired subsidiaries fell to Edwin Waterhouse; these included the Cambrian Railways, Birkenhead Railway, Lancaster & Carlisle, Chester & Holyhead, West London Extension[85] and the North London Railway.[86] Other railway audits obtained by Price, Waterhouse & Co. and supervised by Edwin included the South Eastern, Metropolitan and London, Brighton & South Coast Companies.[87]

Unlike the first generation of successful City accountants, such as Quilter, Ball, Harding, Coleman and Turquand, Edwin Waterhouse did not achieve prominence through insolvency work. Whilst responsible for winding up a number of major bankrupt businesses (the Royal Copper Mines of Cobre in Cuba, New British Iron Co. and the Land Securities Co.),[88] Waterhouse's expertise lay primarily in the field of auditing and investigations. The contrast, in part, reflected the great transformation which was affecting the leading accountancy firms in the second half of the nineteenth century. As limited liability companies (whose existence had been countenanced by the 1855 and 1862 Companies Act) became more secure and the shareholding public became more demanding of accurate information, so the need for liquidators declined and the accountant, who could assess the financial viability of an enterprise, found himself regular commissions. 'The duties, difficulties and responsibilities of our profession', Edwin remarked in his 1893 presidential address to the Institute of Chartered Accountants in England and Wales, 'more especially as auditors, are as yet hardly appreciated even by the commercial world, and yet the usefulness of our profession and the necessity of our employment becomes day by day more apparent.'[89]

In addition to the railway companies already mentioned, Edwin Waterhouse was appointed joint auditor to the National Provincial Bank of England (from 1880)[90] and to the London & Westminster Bank;[91] in the latter case the appointment was shared with Turquand. Following the failure of the City of Glasgow Bank in 1878, several of the large British banks decided to re-register with limited liability, and on revising their constitutions took the opportunity to appoint professional accountants to undertake the external audit. Other personal audits held by Edwin included the Wilts & Dorset Banking Co.,[92] Equity & Law Life Assurance Co., Law Fire Assurance Co., London & India Docks Co., Bank of New Zealand, Oxford University (from 1881),[93] Clarendon Press, Oxford (1881),[94] University College, London, and the Dean and Chapter of Westminster Abbey.[95] Other prestigious audit clients acquired during the period of his senior partnership were: Lloyds Bank (1888),[96] Orient Steamship Co., Westinghouse Brake Co., Westinghouse Electric Co., Horrockses, Crewdson & Co., the estates of the Duke of Bedford (1890),[97] Huntley & Palmers (1898) and J. J. Colman of Norwich (1898).[98]

Edwin Waterhouse was also called upon to undertake a number of investigations by companies, institutions and government bodies. Amongst the first were: in 1870 an examination of the profits of Fox, Head & Co. to determine the position payable in the form of a bonus to the men;[99] the devising of a sliding scale for the Consett Iron Co. in 1877, by which wages would be related to the selling price of iron;[100] an inquiry into the accounts of the Metropolitan Railway (1872);[101] a report on the way that funds collected through an appeal for 'social work' had been expended by the Salvation Army (1892);[102] and a reorganization of the finances of the Underground Electric Railway of London (1908).[103] In 1889 Edwin Waterhouse assisted Lancashire County Council in allocating receipts and expenditure between boroughs and urban districts under the new Local Government Act,[104] and in 1896 at the invitation of the London County Council conducted an investigation into the account keeping of their Works Department.[105]

In 1887–88, together with Frederick Whinney (1829–1916), another eminent city accountant,[106] Waterhouse produced a report on the accounting organization of the Woolwich Arsenal for a Parliamentary Committee chaired by Lord Randolph Churchill.[107] He was subsequently asked to conduct similar investigations into the Admiralty's dockyards (1888–89)[108] and the Royal Ordnance factories (1901).[109] A member of the 1894–95 Davey Departmental Committee on Joint Stock Companies, Edwin was responsible for representing the profession's views, as the Institute of Chartered Accountants made no formal submissions.[110] The committee's report formed the basis for the 1900 Companies Act, which introduced the important requirement for an external audit of the balance sheet and its presentation to the shareholders.[111] When further change was considered, Edwin Waterhouse was invited to serve on the 1905–6 (Loreburn) Committee.[112] *The Accountant* approved greatly of the choice: 'no one will be disposed to find fault with the selection of Mr Edwin Waterhouse, whose experience in company matters is unique'.[113] The 1907 Companies Act, which followed, required that an audited balance sheet be filed with the Registrar of Companies.[114]

Having become a member of the Institute of Chartered Accountants in England and Wales on its formation in 1880 and obtained a position of standing within the profession, it was natural that Edwin Waterhouse would not only succeed S. L. Price to the senior partnership of Price, Waterhouse & Co. when the latter died in 1887,[115] but also occupy his seat on the Council of the Institute.[116] He had already been elected a member of its Examination Committee and subsequently became a president of both the London and Birmingham Chartered Accountants' Students Societies.[117] In 1892, without having held the customary post of vice-president, Edwin Waterhouse was elected president, an appointment he held until 1894.[118] In his address to the ICAEW in 1893 he took the opportunity to express his belief in the need for clear statements to represent a company's true financial situation: 'each balance sheet is, indeed, a portrait, and should exhibit ugly and weak points, if there be any, as well as the more pleasant features; otherwise it is deceptive, and no index to the financial character of the undertaking it is supposed to describe'.[119] Not all his efforts were successful; in particular, his struggle to obtain a professional monopoly, as exercised by medical and legal practitioners, did not meet with government approval.[120] His presidency corresponded with the opening in 1893 of the ICAEW's purpose-built Hall in Moorgate, which was celebrated by a dinner for 260 guests.[121] In June 1915 Edwin resigned the presidency of the Chartered Accountants' Benevolent Association, a post he had held for 17 years, and a month later retired from the Council of the ICAEW.[122]

Aside from being the senior partner of what has become an international accountancy firm, one of the so-called 'Big Eight',[123] how can Edwin Waterhouse's professional achievements be summarised? Although not as intellectually gifted as his brother Theodore, his results at University College London suggested that he was not without academic qualities. Hard working, intelligent and possessing considerable professional integrity, Edwin was responsible for initiating improvements in the accounting methods adopted by the London & North Western Railway, a company which, through its predecessor, the London & Birmingham Railway, had been among the first of its kind to adopt the double-account system.[124] Convinced of the importance of separating capital and revenue expenditures (a differentiation often ignored by railway managers because it denied them much scope for increasing profits to a level where it was believed they would maintain shareholder confidence and stock prices), Edwin insisted that L.N.W.R. make such a distinction[125] and resisted any pressure to return to former practice.[126] He introduced a similar policy at both the London, Brighton & South Coast Railway and South Eastern Railway Companies, and it has been suggested that the similarity between the form of accounts prescribed by the 1868 Railway Act and those published by the L.N.W.R. implies that he may have been consulted by the Board of Trade when framing the new legislation. His work for the accountancy department at Euston facilitated the compilation of operating statistics which were used, in turn, to assess performance and the allocation of resources.[127]

Despite these achievements it would be wrong to view Edwin Waterhouse as one of the outstanding original thinkers in the accountancy profession, ranking alongside men such as Professor L. R. Dicksee (1864–1932),[128] John Manger Fells (1858–1925),[129] F. R. M. de Paula (1882–1954),[130] Sir Gilbert Garnsey (1883–1932)[131] or G. O. May (1875–1961).[132] His abilities lay not so much with the introduction of radical ideas but in the practical organization and running of a major City partnership; he had the skills to acquire new clients, maintain established connections and to ensure that work was performed fairly and efficiently. In this respect a parallel may be drawn with the career of his brother Alfred.

One of the most prolific and best-known Victorian architects, noted for the Natural History Museum (1869–80) and the Prudential Building, Holborn (1877–86), the secret of Alfred Waterhouse's success offers an insight to the personality of Edwin. A major achievement in 1867 was to win the competition to design the new Manchester Town Hall. After the entrants had been reduced from 123 to eight, the judges, Professor Thomas Donaldson (1795–1885) and G. E. Street (1824–81), ranked Alfred fourth on artistic merit but first in his planning, cost effectiveness and the facility with which the project could be executed.[133] His obituary in *The Manchester Guardian* emphasized the point:

> His style then was a free rendering of old medieval detail. It cannot be said that he ever thoroughly caught the spirit of the old work, as other men have done, but his buildings always have a distinct character of their own. The detail was old, but the setting was always modern. . . . His *forte* was planning. It is to this great gift which he undoubtedly possessed that his success was mainly due. It was also owing to his delightful and charming personality. Few men were so personally popular.[134]

It was often said that his smile was worth £40,000 a year to him in client relations, a bonus which was supported by one of the most efficient architectural offices of the day.[135] A further obituary in *The Manchester Evening News* acknowledged not only 'his genius for design and construction' but also 'an amazing record of industry'.[136] The qualities which lay at the root of Alfred's success (his indefatigability, great powers of organization, mastery of business and skill in committee)[137] also found expression in Edwin Waterhouse.

The capacity for sheer hard work and application, which Edwin exhibited, should not be forgotten in an assessment of his commercial success. On occasion, as his mother recorded, his exertions affected his health. In April 1879 she wrote,

> dear Edwin returned from the north [Middlesbrough] about four o'clock yesterday morning, very weary with his night's journey and exceedingly busy after he came home. I fear my precious sons are often too busy for their *bodies'* good.[138]

In his recollections of 57 years in practice, Ernest Cooper (1848–1926)[139] wrote of Edwin Waterhouse of whom he 'had at least one encounter ... he always showed me rather more courtesy than I deserved'.[140] Nicholas Waterhouse, his eldest son, observed that 'he never suffered a fool gladly but he had a wonderful insight into character, and those who really knew him held him in the highest respect and affection'.[141] An inability to tolerate any behaviour which might pass as slackness and his ingrained Quaker mores led to a prohibition of smoking. If Edwin 'found a pipe or pouch lying around in the office or in the audit room of a client, he thought nothing of throwing them on the fire but, then relenting, would compensate the offender with the price of a new outfit'.[142]

Similar characteristics had, in fact, been observed by Edwin of his elder brother Alfred, of whom he wrote: 'I am reminded of one or two incidents of my boyhood, in which he may have shown some heat of temper – but he soon learnt so to rule himself as to set us all an example of his calm judgement and humility.'[143]

Edwin Waterhouse appears to have been subject, on occasion, to bouts of melancholy. In 1881, he recalled, 'in the midst of all my blessings, I seem to have given way to some manner of depression at times'.[144] In a letter, written to Georgie, his wife, Edwin noted,

> I hope I shall get out of my glumness soon. I feel it is very wrong of me, but as it is not more than 14 hours growth I hope it will soon pass off.[145]

His mother, Mary Waterhouse 'passed through times of great spiritual depression alleviated but seldom by the joyousness which had been hers at an earlier date. ... Constant weakness and ill-health combined to bring about many times [of] lowness and grief of spirit'.[146] In May 1840 she herself had written 'in the last two years passed the cloud has seemed very much to rest on my tabernacle, whether in judgements for omissions, or in the right ordering of the Lord, it is not easy to say'.[147] Helen, Edwin's second wife, also 'suffered much from neuralgia, and nervous depression which continued for a long time'.[148] His devotion to Christianity and thorough application to work may well have served, in part, as defences against the depression that Edwin himself periodically experienced, and which he had seen virtually take over his mother's life.

Marriage, Religion and Politics

Although Edwin Waterhouse had been brought up as a Quaker by committed parents, in May 1864 he, along with his brothers William and Theodore and sisters Maria (1834–1905) and Kitty (1836–98), decided to enter the Church of England.[149] The baptism at Penge Church was performed by the Revd Stevens, a friend of his uncle, William Bevan, the City solicitor for whom Theodore had worked,[150] a step which had caused their mother 'many, many thoughts'.[151] In 1893 the Society of Friends challenged Edwin by letter as to whether he was merely a 'nominal' member of the Christian community.[152] The lengthy defence, in which he argued that there was no doctrinal differences of any substance between the two sects, satisfied his inquisitors.[153] Such religious disputes as Edwin subsequently engaged upon concerned the nature of the services held at St Mary's, where the rector, the Revd A. C. Hayes, had introduced elaborate rituals.[154] Accustomed to Quaker simplicity, Edwin conducted a lengthy and sometimes bitter dispute with the Revd Hayes, which ultimately resulted in his resignation as a churchwarden,[155] and as a trustee and chairman of the Holmbury St Mary Village Association (p. 176).[156]

On 3 April 1869 at Brixton church Edwin Waterhouse married Georgina Thöl (1848–96). He had met the Thöl family through his friend, John Wigham Richardson, who had married Georgina's elder sister Marian Henrietta.[157] Her father, Nicholas Thöl, the son of a Lubeck merchant, had emigrated to London where he became a glue and drug merchant. His wife, Agnes Propert, was the daughter of a Jewish banker of Hamburg. The fact that Georgina was not a Quaker rendered Edwin liable to expulsion from their body. After interviewing the couple Joseph Bevan Braithwaite and Richard Dell decided that he could remain within the Society of Friends.[158] They had four daughters, Agnes (1870–83), Theresa (1872–1948), Ellen (1880–1944) and Gertrude (1884–1947), known as Valentine, and two sons, William (1874–1900) and Nicholas (1877–1964). Georgina Waterhouse suffered from what appears to have been cancer and died in some discomfort, aged 48.[159] On 11 April 1898 Edwin re-married. His bride was Helen Caroline née Weber (1855–1941), the daughter of a German doctor, resident in Green Street, near Hyde Park.[160] They had one child, Theodore (1904–1976), who worked for a while at Price, Waterhouse & Co.

As a result of his birth, education and career, rather than religion, Edwin Waterhouse won ready acceptance within various socially exclusive bodies; he was, for example, elected a member of the City of London Club in July 1866,[161] and in January 1890 joined the Garrick Club.[162]

Introduction

As might be expected of a Quaker merchant based in Liverpool, Alfred Waterhouse Senior would most probably have supported the Whig party. Whether Edwin initially followed his father's politics was not clear. Just as he changed religions, he may also have switched political allegiances. The latter parts of *His Story* reveal him to have been a staunch supporter of the Conservative Unionists:[163] he was opposed to all the leading radical movements of the period, voicing his disapproval of Home Rule, disestablishment of the Church of England in Wales, reform of the House of Lords, and the extension of the franchise to women.[164]

Holmbury St Mary and 'Feldemore'

By the mid-1870s Edwin Waterhouse had become an established and comparatively wealthy professional figure in the City, and in common with his peers sought a country residence to which he could retreat at weekends and during the summer. His brother Alfred introduced him to G. E. Street (1821–81), the eminent Victorian architect, who[165] had recently designed a house, 'Holmdale' (1874–76), for himself, in the small Surrey village of Holmbury St Mary.[166] Street had not been the first Victorian to select the valley between Holmbury Hill and Pasture Wood as a site for a mansion, for in 1872 the Hon. Frederick Leveson Gower (1819–1907) purchased 'Holmbury', a house originally built around 1860.[167] In his memoirs, *Bygone Years* (1905), he revealed his motives for moving to the district:

> It had long been my wish to possess a home in the country, and in 1870 I was advised to buy Holmbury, in the Surrey hills, where I at present reside. My ambition had always been to live in some spot which commanded an extensive view, and at Holmbury I found one of surpassing beauty.[168]

Next to arrive was Henry Tanworth Wells (1828–1903), who built his house, 'The Aldermoor', around 1874;[169] he was a friend of Street who followed him to Holmbury shortly afterwards and, in turn, encouraged Waterhouse to settle in the village. Why, then, did the area prove so popular with a select circle of monied Victorians? The completion of the Reading and Tonbridge branch of the South Eastern Railway in 1849 with a station at Gomshall, about three miles to the north west of Holmbury, brought accessibility to the City of London.[170] Nevertheless, the principal attraction was the scenery. The ridge formed by

Holmbury Hill which continues eastward to Leith Hill provided panoramic views south to the Downs and English Channel. The steep slopes covered with evergreen fir trees bore a resemblance, in miniature, to the Alps of the Continent and English Lake District which Edwin Waterhouse and his fellow middle-class tourists often visited. The Surrey heathland, scorned in the eighteenth century, now won approval, perhaps because of its convenient resemblance to the Scottish Highlands.[171]

During October 1877 Edwin Waterhouse purchased a small estate, known as Great Inholme, which included Cooper's Copse, Bullmoor Farm and a brick and tile works, from a local landowner, Lee Steere.[172] He then consulted his brother-in-law, George Tunstall Redmayne (1840–1912), a Manchester architect. It was surprising that Edwin should have chosen Redmayne as the designer in preference to his neighbour Street and elder brother, Alfred. Redmayne had, however, been articled to Alfred and worked as his assistant for some years and the latter would, therefore, have exercised an indirect influence on the shaping of 'Feldemore'. Work began early in 1879.[173] Local building materials were used in the construction of the house; in particular bricks, sand and stone.[174] On 25 November 1880 Edwin Waterhouse spent his first night at Feldemore.[175] The first structure was not particularly commodious and as his professional career flourished Edwin employed Redmayne to design various extensions which enlarged the house considerably: between 1889–90 the hall, library and drawing room with bedrooms above were completed,[176] and in 1896–97 a new wing, containing a billiard room, lit by electric light, was added.[177] As an invalid in January 1891 Theodore Waterhouse with his sister, Maria, visited Edwin there and wrote,

> it is so nice to be here, and we never tire of admiring George's [Redmayne] beautiful work. I think the library, in which I am now sitting, is one of the most perfectly delightful rooms I ever saw.[178]

Extensive works were carried out to the grounds of Feldemore, and the landscape gardener, H. E. Milner, was consulted in 1878 and 1890.[179] Theodore Waterhouse also exhibited a 'love of nature, and especially of trees and gardening', which, according to Edward Fry, he had inherited from his father.[180] Edwin had a great interest in horticulture and in 1900, having purchased land in Pasture Wood, laid a splendid curving drive entered by Tralee Lodge and flanked on one side by magnificent Himalayan rhododendron bushes.[181] In 1883 a terrace and tennis lawn were laid down, a swimming pool was completed in 1885 and during 1895 a terrace walk with low walls capped in terracotta was built. Further projects followed which brought the gardens and woods surrounding Feldemore to a high standard of presentation.

Edwin Waterhouse also took a paternalistic interest in the affairs of the village of Holmbury St Mary. Employing so many staff at Feldemore (11 gardeners, two laundry maids, two parlour maids, three housemaids, a cook and a scullery maid),[182] it became necessary to build additional accommodation for them. In 1881 Edwin purchased 'some miserable cottages and hovels from Edser' on a site opposite his own entrance gates, and replaced them with an elaborately gabled butcher's and grocer's store. He then proceeded to build new houses and alter existing ones, using Redmayne as a consultant.[183] Edwin introduced the idea of 'village tidies', which were small enclosures where everyone was encouraged to deposit their refuse for collection by his men. It was said that on Friday evenings the Feldemore gardeners were sent through the village to pick up any litter before Edwin arrived from the City to undertake a tour of inspection, to make sure that the village was smart for the weekend when visitors could be expected.[184]

Along with G. E. Street, who had been responsible for merging the hamlets of Felday and Pitland Street to form the parish of Holmbury St Mary (named in part after his wife) and who built the church of St Mary's, Edwin Waterhouse was one of the creators of the unified village. He was instrumental in providing a system of running water and sewerage and was a founder of the 'Hollybush Tavern', a temperance coffee room and working men's club.[185]

Given his wealth and active role within the local community, Edwin Waterhouse became, in effect, the squire of Holmbury St Mary. Yet, as has been seen (p. 35), the village was favoured by other rich Victorians; Sir William Bowman (1816–92), an oculist, lived at 'Joldwynds', Sir Frederick Mirrielees (d.1914), head of the merchant bank, Currie & Co., owned 'Pasture Wood House' and the Hon. Frederick Leveson Gower, a relative of the Duke of Sutherland,[186] resided at 'Holmbury'. Although the last mentioned devoted a chapter of his *Bygone Years* (1905) to Holmbury,[187] he made no reference to Edwin. As the latter's *His Story* revealed, they were very well acquainted for some 30 years and had established a friendly relationship.[188] The explanation for the omission may have been snobbery; Leveson Gower, a member of an aristocratic family who included Gladstone among his regular visitors, could well have considered Edwin Waterhouse, the son of a prosperous Quaker broker of Liverpool, and a member of the youngest of

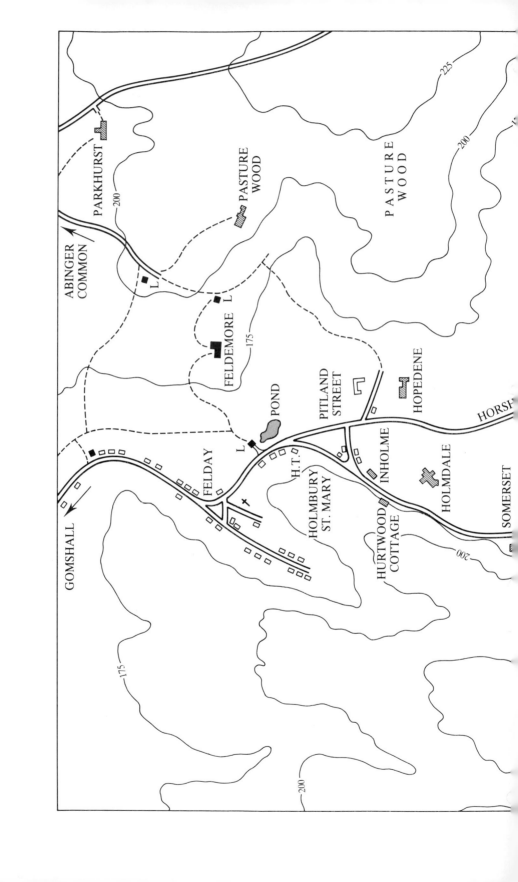

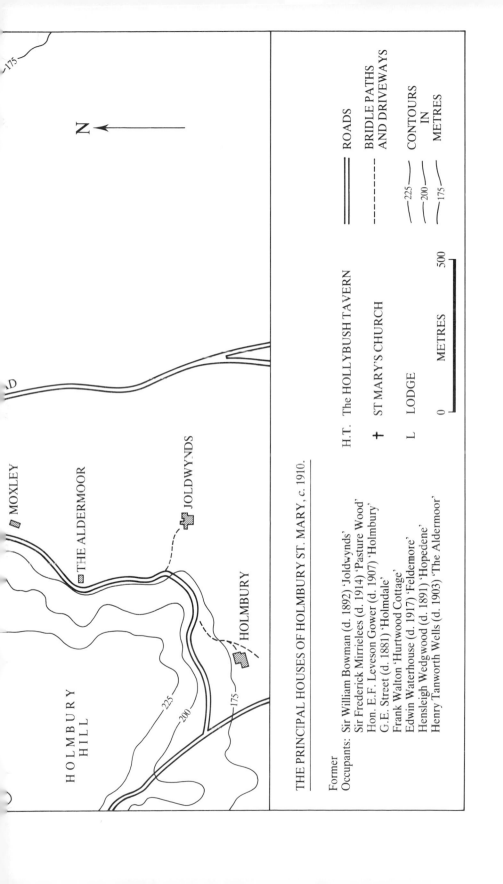

N

HOLMBURY
HILL

225
200
175

MOXLEY

THE ALDERMOOR

JOLDWYNDS

HOLMBURY

THE PRINCIPAL HOUSES OF HOLMBURY ST. MARY, c. 1910.

Former
Occupants: Sir William Bowman (d. 1892) 'Joldwynds'
Sir Frederick Mirrielees (d. 1914) 'Pasture Wood'
Hon. E.F. Leveson Gower (d. 1907) 'Holmbury'
G.E. Street (d. 1881) 'Holmdale'
Frank Walton 'Hurtwood Cottage'
Edwin Waterhouse (d. 1917) 'Feldemore'
Hensleigh Wedgwood (d. 1891) 'Hopedene'
Henry Tanworth Wells (d. 1903) 'The Aldermoor'

H.T.   The HOLLYBUSH TAVERN

✝   ST MARY'S CHURCH

L   LODGE

0   METRES   500

═══ ROADS

------- BRIDLE PATHS
AND DRIVEWAYS

—225— CONTOURS
—200— IN
—175— METRES

professions, slightly *infra dignitatem* when considering whom to include in his memoirs. The judgement of history has shown that Leveson Gower's discriminatory skills were on occasion flawed.

Given his contribution to the village and love of 'Feldemore' and its gardens, it was fitting that Edwin should have been buried with a simple headstone in the graveyard of St Mary's, Holmbury. There, too, was Georgina's grave, and his second wife, Helen, together with Nicholas and most of his children were also to be buried there.

'His Story': Motives and Methods

In was in 1907, at the age of 66, that Edwin Waterhouse sat down to write a narrative of his life and family, which he entitled *His Story*. According to his own account, he wished to put matters on record 'for the benefit of my own dear children', before they were forgotten or lost.[189] The keeping of a diary was a well established pastime amongst the Waterhouses. His mother had kept a journal from her girlhood,[190] and his brother Theodore had from the age of ten written up a daily account of his life.[191] It was not surprising, therefore, that Alfred Waterhouse, his father, in 1855, just before he began University College School, encouraged Edwin to keep a journal.[192] This he wrote up until 1868 when, under the pressure of rising professional commitments, he discontinued the task.[193] The idea of compiling a history of his own life and that of his family seems to have been triggered in 1905 by the inheritance of his mother's journals, which until then had been in the possession of his elder brother, Alfred.[194] For whilst reading them through in December 1906, it occurred to him to put 'down some recollections of my own life, and he contacted Bessie, Alfred's bereaved wife, to see whether there were any accounts among the latter's papers which might illustrate the Waterhouse dynasty'.[195] Starting work on *His Story*, in 1907 it took Edwin some four years to bring the early narrative to 1896,[196] and he continued to write the text until the summer of 1912 when having completed a summary, he ended his project.[197] Yet, in September 1914, stimulated by the outbreak of war, Edwin decided to produce an appendix which would bring his memoirs up to date.[198] This he continued to write until his death, the last entry being on 15 June 1917.[199]

Whilst most authors probably keep diaries for the benefit of them-

selves or immediate families, it is possible that Edwin Waterhouse
hoped that *His Story* might some day be published. For in December
1906, having embarked on his autobiography, he read through his
mother's journals, and 'formed the idea of printing extracts from them
for the benefit of a few'.[200] They were published by him in 1907,
having ordered a hundred copies from the printers R. Clay & Son, for
private circulation.[201] Under the editorship of Edward Fry, extracts
from the diaries and correspondence of Theodore Waterhouse had
been published in 1894,[202] and Lucy Fowler, Edwin's aunt, had written
an account of Nicholas Waterhouse, her father, in 1863.[203] In 1910
Edwin himself published *A List of the Descendants of Nicholas Waterhouse
of Everton*, a detailed genealogical list of his immediate relatives. It
would, therefore, be dangerous to assume that *His Story* is an uninhibited account, compiled for the author's own enjoyment. Given that it
was prepared for his relatives' edification, and that his family were
accustomed to publishing such documents, it seems safe to assume that
both factual information and interpretations have been subject to a
process of benign censorship.[205]

This impression is confirmed by an examination of the source
material employed by Edwin when compiling *His Story*. For the early
period (up to 1868), he had his own diaries (from which extensive
quotations were made) to consult together with those of his mother.
After 1868 business diaries and office correspondence were important
records.[204] In addition, a quantity of family papers were at his disposal,
and a selection of these he pasted into the blank leaves of *His Story*.
However, he showed a scant lack of historical awareness for the
remainder of the family archive:

> One good has resulted from my work is the destruction of a large
> amount of correspondence, which might, from the mere fact of its
> continued existence, have caused some trouble in the future.[206]

Whilst this act was probably not made merely with the intention of
concealing information, it has made it difficult to confirm or expand
upon some of the incidents recorded in *His Story*.

However, research into the professional papers of Price, Waterhouse
& Co. and into the Waterhouse family in Liverpool, Bristol, London
and Holmbury St Mary has substantiated much of the documentary
evidence presented by Edwin. Although *His Story* lacks the immediacy
and uninhibited frankness of a daily journal kept solely for the author's
needs, it remains a detailed and valuable record of an eminent
Victorian, his upbringing and beliefs, professional career, friends and

relatives, and the business and recreational environments which he occupied. It is in some respects a real *Forsyte Saga*,[207] a narrative of the rise and achievements of a successful, upper-middle-class family, revealing their motives, abilities, prejudices and preoccupations. To date, *His Story* is the only complete autobiography of a leading accountant, whose firm has become one of the eight largest in the world.

Notes to the Introduction

1 Nicholas E. Waterhouse, *Reminiscences 1899–1960* (typescript, 1961), preface.

2 *The Accountant*, Vol. CLII, No. 4,798, 2 January 1965, p. 27.

3 Edwin Waterhouse, *His Story*, pp. 3–4.

4 Lucy Fowler, *Sketch and Recollections of Nicholas Waterhouse* London (1863), pp. 5–6.

5 *Ibid.* p. 7.

6 *Ibid.* p. 9.

7 Thomas Ellison, *The Cotton Trade of Great Britain*, London (1886), p. 195.

8 Edwin Waterhouse, *A List of the Descendants of Nicholas Waterhouse of Everton* (1910), p. 2.

9 *Gore's Directory of Liverpool and its Environs* (1813), p. 258.

10 *Gore's Directory of Liverpool and its Environs* (1841), p. 475.

11 Fowler, *Nicholas Waterhouse, op. cit.*, p. 11.

12 *The Liverpool Mercury*, No. 651, 21 November 1823, p. 167.

13 Fowler, *Nicholas Waterhouse, op. cit.*, p. 16.

14 *Ibid.*, p. 13.

15 Ellison, *op. cit.*, p. 196.

16 Edwin Waterhouse (Editor), *Extracts from the Journals of Mary Waterhouse 1825–1880*, Privately Printed, London (1907), 13 May 1843, pp. 57–8.

17 *His Story, op. cit.*, p. 16.

18 *Journals of Mary Waterhouse, op. cit.*, p. 57.

19 *His Story, op. cit.*, p. 12.

20 *Ibid.*, p. 25.

21 *Ibid.*, p. 21.

22 *Ibid.*, p. 45.

23 Nicholas Waterhouse, 'Reminiscences' *op. cit.*, p. 1.

24 *Ibid.*, p. 5.

25 *Ibid.*, p. 3.

26 *Ibid.*, p. 2.

27 *His Story, op. cit.*, p. 21.

28 *Ibid.*, p. 45.

29 *Ibid.*, p. 58.

30 [Edward Fry, Editor], *Theodore Waterhouse 1838–1891, Notes of His Life and Extracts from His Letters and Papers*, Privately Printed, London (1907), p. 32.

31 *Ibid.*, p. 30.

32 *Ibid.*, p. 43.

33 *Waterhouse & Co. 1865–1965*: on 13 July 1865 Theodore Waterhouse 'took an office, the second floor of Lincoln's Inn Fields, engaged a small boy and painted up my name'.

34 *Theodore Waterhouse, Notes of His Life, op. cit.*, p. 57.

35 *Ibid.*, p. 85.

36 Waterhouse & Co., solicitors, 4 St Paul's Churchyard, London EC4.

37 *His Story, op. cit.*, p. 102.

38 *Ibid.*, p. 57.

39 *Ibid.*, p. 61.

40 *Ibid.*, p. 77.

41 Edwin Waterhouse's [Business] Diary 1864, 24 February to 7 March.

42 *Ibid.*, 26, 27 and 29 February, 1, 2 and 3 March 1864.

43 *DBB*, Vol. 3 (1985), R. P. T. Daven-

port-Hines, 'Sir J. S. Harmood-Banner', p. 43.

44 Edwin Waterhouse's Letter Book March 1864–August 1871, 2 April 1864, p. 4.

45 *Ibid.*, 3 May 1864, p. 8.

46 Diary 1864, *op. cit.*, 26 June 1864.

47 *Ibid.*, 27 April–2 May 1864, 26 June 1864.

48 Letter Book 1864–71, *op. cit.*, 4 May 1864, p. 10.

49 *Ibid.*, p. 17 June 1864, p. 16.

50 R.I.B.A. Library: Letter from J. Willey to Edwin Waterhouse, describing the use of Draughtsmen's Registers, a journal recording charges to clients and proposing a Day Book, 22 February 1865, quoted from Sally Maltby *et. al.*, *Alfred Waterhouse 1830–1905*, London (1983), p. 16.

51 Letter Book 1864–71, op. cit., 28 June 1864, pp. 20–22.

52 *Ibid.*, 8 August 1864, p. 43; 7 February 1865, pp. 173–4.

53 *Ibid.*, 19 July 1864, p. 35.

54 *Ibid.*, 25 August 1864, pp. 53–4.

55 *His Story, op. cit.*, p. 86.

56 Diary 1864, *op. cit.*, 15 April 1864.

57 *His Story, op. cit.*, p. 86.

58 *Ibid.*, p. 90.

59 *Ibid.*, p. 91.

60 *Mathews' Annual Bristol Directory* (1838), p. 157.

61 *Mathews' Annual Bristol Directory* (1833), p. 47.

62 *Mathews' Annual Bristol Directory* (1828), p. 63.

63 Information from private ledgers supplied by Tribe, Clarke & Co. of Bristol, 30 July 1964.

64 *Mathews' Annual Bristol Directory* (1848), p. 77; *ibid.* (1849), p. 239.

65 *London Post Office Directory* (1849), p. 963; *The Accountant*, Vol XII, No. 527, 10 January 1885, p. 15.

66 *London Post Office Directory Trade* (1859), S. L. Price, 5 Gresham Street, p. 1462.

67 *London Post Office Directory Commercial* (1851), p. 957.

68 *London Post Office Directory Commercial* (1856); they had also acquired premises at 13 Friday Street, Cheapside, and 1 Liverpool Street, Bishopsgate, and were described as 'warehousemen and outfitters', p. 1330.

69 *London Post Office Directory Commercial* (1858), p. 1086.

70 Price Waterhouse Archive File 10/25.

71 For summaries of Edwin Waterhouse's professional career see, *DBB*, Vol. 5 (1986), J. R. Edwards, 'Edwin Waterhouse', pp. 674–79; *The Accountant*, Vol. LVII, No. 2,234 29 September, 1917, p. 242; R. H. Parker, *British Accountants, A Biographical Sourcebook*, New York (1980).

72 An opinion by W. E. Edwards on the retirement of W. H. Holyland, 18 March 1871.

73 G. E. Richards, 'History of the Firm, The First Fifty Years 1850–1900'. (typescript, 1950), p. 5.

74 Price, Waterhouse & Co., Private Ledgers, fee income 1866–92; 1898–1902.

75 Price, Waterhouse & Co., Profit and Loss Accounts, Three Years to 30 June 1899.

76 Price, Waterhouse & Co., List of Clients 1891–2.

77 *His Story, op. cit.*, p. 72.

78 *Ibid.*, p. 99; Formal Notice printed by L.N.W.R., 9 Jan 1867.

79 PRO, Rail 410/13, L.N.W.R. Proprietors' Audit Committee Minute Book 1852–1922, Printed Note, 7 January 1867.

80 *Ibid.*, 21 January 1876.

81 *Ibid.*, 16 January 1874.

82 *Ibid.*, 16 February 1882.

83 *Ibid.*, 29 January 1913.

84 PRO, Rail 410/42, L.N.W.R. Board Minutes 1911–1914, 12 February 1913, item 25179.

85 Notebook 'London & North Western Railway, Edwin Waterhouse, 13 Gresham Street, E.C., 1870', pp. 1–25.

86 *His Story, op. cit.*, p. 961.

87 Price, Waterhouse & Co, Estimates of fees, 30 June 1898.

88 *His Story, op. cit.*, pp. 131–2, 346, 508 respectively.

89 *Inauguration of the Hall [ICAEW], London, May 10 and 11 1893*, Address of Mr Edwin Waterhouse, President, pp. 11–12.

90 *His Story, op. cit.*, pp. 209–10.

91 *Ibid.*, p. 210.

92 *Ibid.*

93 *Ibid.*, p. 256.

94 *Ibid.*

95 Price Waterhouse Archives, 'Personal Audits of Edwin Waterhouse at 1 January 1906'.

96 *His Story, op. cit.*, p. 398.

97 *Ibid.*, pp. 400–01.

98 *Ibid.*, p. 635.

99 *Ibid.*, pp. 132–3.

100 *Ibid.*, p. 135.

101 *Ibid.*, p. 141.

102 *Ibid.*, p. 458.

103 *Ibid.*, p. 848.

104 *Ibid.*, p. 379.

105 *Ibid.*, p. 586.

106 *DBB*, Vol. 5 (1986), Edgar Jones, 'Frederick Whinney', p. 767.

107 *His Story, op. cit.*, pp. 343–5.

108 *Ibid.*, p. 346.

109 *Ibid.*, p. 679.

110 *Ibid.*, p. 513.

111 J. R. Edwards, *Company Legislation and Changing Patterns of Disclosure in British Company Accounts 1900–1940*, ICAEW London (1981), p. 3.

112 *His Story, op. cit.*, p. 758.

113 *The Accountant*, Vol. XXXII, No. 1,576, 18 February 1905, p. 186.

114 Edwards, *Company Legislation, op. cit.*, p. 4.

115 *His Story, op. cit.*, p. 342.

116 *Ibid.*, p. 344.

117 *Ibid.*, p. 345, 449.

118 *Ibid.*, p. 448.

119 Edwin Waterhouse 'Presidential Address'; reprinted in *The Accountant*, Vol. xix, No. 962, 13 May 1893, p. 450.

120 *DBB*, Vol. 5 (1986), *op. cit.*, p. 677.

121 *His Story, op. cit.*, p. 640.

122 *Ibid.*, p. 990.

123 Leon Hopkins, *The Hundredth Year*, Plymouth (1980), pp. 47–64.

124 *Abacus* Vol. 21, March 1985, J. R. Edwards, 'The Origins and Evolution of the Double Account System', pp. 34, 41.

125 *Abacus*, Vol. 21, *op. cit.*, pp. 19–43, *DBB*, Vol. 5 (1986), *op. cit.*, pp. 675–6.

126 *His Story, op. cit.* In November 1905 a proposal was made which to Edwin Waterhouse seemed 'to mix up capital and reserve', he vehemently opposed the suggestion and had it defeated, p. 779.

127 *DBB*, Vol. 5 *op. cit.*, p. 675.

128 *British Accountants, op. cit.*

129 *DBB*, Vol. 2 (1984), R. H. Parker, 'J M Fells', pp. 335–7.

130 *Ibid.*, J. Kitchen, 'F. R. M. de Paula', pp. 71–77; *The Accountant*, Vol. CXXXI, No. 4,174, 18 December 1954, pp. 669–70.

131 *DBB*, Vol. 2 (1984), J. R. Edwards, 'Sir Gilbert Garnsey', pp. 487–90; *The Accountant*, Vol. LXXXVII, No. 3,004, 2 July 1932, pp. 9–10.

132 *The Accountant*, Vol. CXLIV, No. 4,511, 3 June 1961, pp. 707–08.

133 *Transactions of the Lancashire and Cheshire Antiquarian Society*, Vol. 81 (1982), J. H. G. Archer, 'A Civic Achievement; The Building of Manchester Town Hall Part One; The Commissioning', pp. 17, 20–24.

134 *The Manchester Guardian*, No. 18,421, 23 August 1905, p. 3.

135 Maltby *et. al.*, *Alfred Waterhouse, op. cit.*, p. 16.

136 *The Manchester Evening News*, No. 11,368, 22 August 1905, p. 6.

137 *The Manchester Guardian* No. 18,421, *op. cit.*, p. 3.

138 *Journals of Mary Waterhouse, op. cit.*, 30 April 1879, p. 325; 2 August 1879, pp. 328–9.

139 *DBB*, Vol. 1 (1984), Edgar Jones, 'Ernest Cooper', pp. 778–80.

140 *ICAEW Proceedings of the Autumnal Meeting ... October 1921*, London (1921), E. Cooper, 'Fifty-seven years in an accountant's office', p. 49.

141 Nicholas Waterhouse, 'Reminiscences', *op. cit.*, p. 3.

142 *Ibid.*, p. 102.

143 *His Story, op. cit.*, p. 773.

144 *Ibid.*, p. 243.

145 *Ibid.*

146 *Ibid.*, p. 13.

147 *Journals of Mary Waterhouse, op. cit.*, p. 51.

148 *His Story, op. cit.*, p. 673.

149 *Ibid.*, p. 82.

150 *London Post Office Directory, Trade* (1860), William Bevan, Solicitor, 6 Old Jewry E. C., home 27 Westbourne Park, Paddington, p. 1996.

151 *Journals of Mary Waterhouse, op. cit.*, 1 June 1864, p. 188.

152 *His Story, op. cit.*, p. 473.

153 *Ibid.*, p. 475.

154 *Ibid.*, p. 639–41, 704–05.

155 *Ibid.*, pp. 852, 932.

156 *Ibid.*, pp. 750.

157 *Ibid.*, p. 122.

158 *Ibid.*, p. 128.

159 *Ibid.*, p. 566.

160 *Ibid.*, p. 615.

161 *Ibid.*, p. 99.

162 *Ibid.*, p. 381.

163 *Ibid.*, pp. 905–06.

164 *Ibid.*, pp. 921, 967–8.

165 *Ibid.*, p. 192.

166 Nicola Westbury, 'The Country Houses of Holmbury St Mary' (B. Arch. Thesis, University of Liverpool, 1987), pp. 19–23.

167 *Ibid.*, p. 7.

168 The Hon. F. Leveson Gower, *Bygone Years, Recollections*, London (1905), p. 283.

169 Westbury, 'Country Houses', *op. cit.*, p. 14.

170 *Ibid.*, p. 2.

171 *Ibid.*, p. 3.

172 *Ibid.*, p. 44.

173 *His Story, op. cit.*, p. 199.

174 Westbury, 'Country Houses', *op. cit.*, p. 45.

175 *His Story, op. cit.*, p. 221.

176 *Ibid.*, pp. 365, 380, 388.

177 *Ibid.*, pp. 559, 594.

178 *Theodore Waterhouse, Notes of His Life, op. cit.*, p. 177.

179 *His Story, op. cit.*, pp. 187, 388.

180 *Theodore Waterhouse, Notes of His Life, op. cit.*, p. 1.

181 Westbury, 'Country Houses', *op. cit.*, p. 47.

182 Margaret Bird, *Holmbury St. Mary, One Hundred Years*, Bromley (1979), p. 13.

183 *Ibid.*, pp. 19–20.

184 *Ibid.*, pp. 21.

185 *Ibid.*, p. 24.

186 *Burke's Peerage.*

187 Leveson Gower, *Bygone Years, op. cit.*, pp. 283 ff.

188 *His Story, op. cit.*, pp. 233, 808.

189 *Ibid.*, p. 1.

190 *Ibid.*, p. 10a.

191 *Theodore Waterhouse, Notes of His Life, op. cit.*, p. 2.

192 *His Story, op. cit.*, p. 46.

193 *Ibid.*, p. 121.

194 *Ibid.*, p. 774.

195 *Ibid.*, p. 800.

196 *Ibid.*, p. 576.

197 *Ibid.*, p. 904.

198 *Ibid.*, p. 937.

199 *Ibid.*, p. 1006.

200 *Ibid.*, p. 800.

201 *Ibid.*, p. 826; Edwin Waterhouse (Editor), *Extracts from the Journals of Mary Waterhouse 1825–1880*, London (1907).

Notes to the Introduction

202 [Edward Fry, Editor], *Theodore Waterhouse 1838–1891 Notes of His Life and Extracts from His Letters and Papers*, London (1894).

203 Lucy Fowler, *Sketch and Recollections of Nicholas Waterhouse*, London (1863).

204 *His Story, op. cit.*, p. 121.

205 *Ibid.*, p. 931.

206 *Ibid.*, p. 576.

207 John Galsworthy, *The Man of Property*, London (1906).

Note: the page references above to *His Story* relate to the original manuscript volumes and not to the text which follows.

CHAPTER I

MY PARENTS

At the age of sixty-six I am taking pen and paper with the view of writing the story of my life. Why should I do this? It cannot be called an eventful life, it has been a commonplace one for I have possessed no qualities which would make it otherwise. I have gone in and out my fellow men as one of the crowd. But I feel that what I may be able to record may be of interest to those who now surround and love me, if not now when I am gone from them. I feel myself how interesting some short story of my dear father's earlier years would be, preserving those particulars of his boyhood and youth with which he would occasionally interest and amuse his children. All of these children have now passed away but myself and the particulars of his early life, other than the little that I, his youngest child, can retain in a failing memory, have passed away with them. Such a story would give a key to the character of the dear man whom I loved with all the love I trust of a dutiful and affectionate son.

But there is another feeling which leads me to begin this story. I should hardly like to pass away without putting on record for the benefit of my dear children, how much any little desire for good that is in me is due to the example and prayers of my dear parents and especially to the constant teachings of my saintly mother. And I wish to put down for their benefit also some memorials of the wisdom and love, which flowing from their own sweet mother, have directed their lives.

The present seems a fitting time for undertaking this little work, for within the last few months, after the death of my last surviving sister, Maria, there have come into my hands letters and journals, which with many other like papers already in my possession, left by my precious Georgie, should now be destroyed, and before this step is taken I desire to preserve some extracts . . .

I am now the last survivor of the seven brothers and sisters who from my birth in 1841, until my brother William was taken from us in 1869, preserved an unbroken record. I cannot well imagine a family circle in which the members could have been more to one another than was the case with our dear parents and ourselves.

I was born on the 4 June 1841 at Oakfield, Aigburth, near Liverpool, the fourth son and seventh child of Alfred Waterhouse and Mary his wife. [They were members of the Society of Friends as were also their progenitors.]

The family of which I thus became a member consisted of the following:–

Alfred Waterhouse   —   Born 15 June 1798
Mary Waterhouse   —   Born 25 October 1805

THEIR CHILDREN

Alfred   —   Born 19 July 1830
Ellen   —   Born 14 March 1832
Maria   —   Born 21 February 1834
Katherine   —   Born 20 April 1836
Theodore   —   Born 12 April 1838
William   —   Born 25 October 1839
Edwin   —   Born 4 June 1841

My father was the son of Nicholas Waterhouse, cotton broker, of Liverpool, who was the only son of Ellythorp and Sarah Waterhouse of the same town, being born on the 7th March 1768. Sarah Waterhouse, whose maiden name was Clough, was early left a widow, with her son Nicholas and three daughters to provide for on slender means. She continued her late husband's business at a shop in Pool Lane, Liverpool; while Nicholas was as a boy sent to learn the manufacture of fustians in Bolton. Thence he went into a cotton warehouse in Manchester, where he boarded with some friends named Richard and Martha Routh, near neighbours of Daniel and Mary Rogers, the parents of Ann Rogers his future wife. He subsequently started in business on his own account in Liverpool, being one of the first, if not the first, to do cotton broking in that city. The business prospered, and having the means, he secured for his residence a house which he had long wished to possess, having beautiful grounds and large and well kept gardens, at Everton, then a suburb of Liverpool.

My grandfather seems to have been a man of great integrity of character, keen business ability and strong religious faith. He had been brought up as and remained a strict Quaker; and as such set his face against the 'slave running' and privateering which were by no means unusual avocations of the Liverpool gentlemen of the day. Some descriptions of the house at Everton and my grandfather's manner of life are given in a short account of him written by my Aunt Lucy Fowler and printed in 1865. She speaks of him as 'humble, lowly and devout, upright and guileless as a child'. A sketch was made of the house by my brother Alfred in 1848.

My father used to tell us a story about its being difficult to prevent the lads of Liverpool from committing depredations on my grandfather's orchards, and he was advised to put up the usual notice about man traps and spring guns being set on the premises. He had one objection to doing this, as in reality no guns or traps were laid, and accordingly got over the difficulty by the notice: 'If the boy who left his foot in a trap on these grounds on Friday will apply at the hall door, it will be returned to him.' A very short exhibition of this notice is said to have cured the evil.

My grandfather died on the 19th November 1823 at the age of 55. His widow survived him by fourteen years, dying in 1837.

It may be well to record the names of their numerous sons and daughters, adding the dates of the birth and death of each:

Mary	—	Born 14 January 1791	Died 19 February 1874
Sarah	—	Born 9 May 1792	Died 18 April 1853
Margaret	—	Born 14 December 1793	Died 9 March 1852
Nicholas	—	Born 25 May 1795	Died 24 June 1828
Daniel	—	Born 10 September 1796	Died 16 April 1861
Alfred	—	Born 15 June 1798	Died 27 December 1873
Ann	—	Born 15 November 1799	Died 9 March 1804
Eliza (Merrick)	—	Born 13 January 1801	Died 25 April 1882
Benjamin	—	Born 7 February 1802	Died 21 October 1848
Lucy (Fowler)	—	Born 23 March 1803	Died 21 January 1869
Henry	—	Born 26 April 1804	Died 30 June 1884
Theodore	—	Born 15 July 1805	Died 13 March 1835
Rogers	—	Born 4 February 1807	Died 1 January 1868
Octavius	—	Born 22 April 1810	Died 7 October 1847

The three eldest sons, Nicholas, Daniel and Alfred, were taken quite young into their father's business, after having had some schooling with Josiah Foster at Southgate in Middlesex. My grandfather had left school and taken to work when he was fourteen, and he brought up his sons to do much the same. The style of the firm became 'Nicholas Waterhouse and Sons'; and their offices with sample rooms for cotton, sugar, molasses, rum, palm oil, ivory etc. were from a very early date established at No. 1 Old Hall Street, a corner house opposite the entrance to the Exchange. This was not far from the river, and I have heard my father say that he and his brothers used frequently to run down and have a bathe at the spot where the big Cunarders now draw up to the landing stage in the centre of miles of locks and warehouses. The style and business of the firm thus established by my grandfather still continue, but no Waterhouse remains in it . . .

The business of Liverpool, as carried on by my father and uncles was a very different thing to the business of later years. . . . The local business was transacted mainly 'on change', where brokers and merchants met; and exchanging civilities with their snuff boxes, discussed events of the day and the state of the markets. The uncertainty attending the arrival of the mails from abroad, and the press of business when they came to hand were a cause of trouble to the juniors as well as their employees.

On the 16th July 1829, my father married Mary Bevan, the only daughter of Paul and Rebecca Bevan of Tottenham.

My mother must have been a singularly beautiful girl. Unhappily there were no photographs in those days, and no sketch or painting of her as a young woman exists. She was of good height and graceful in figure, with perfect features and beautiful profile. A cast in one eye was a slight blemish in an otherwise perfect face, and this was soon forgotten by those who learnt the loveliness of her character.

She kept a journal from her girlhood which shows that from an early age she thought much on religious subjects, and was fully convinced of the truth of the doctrines of the Quakerism in which she was brought up. The journal as existing commences in 1825 [and is] . . . mainly a record of religious feelings, and the meetings she attended . . . she complains constantly of her own sinfulness, and the bitterness of soul which she experiences when, as was the case, sometimes a cloud came between her heart and the light of God's love.

As her brothers grew up one can imagine that the household at Tottenham was not altogether a very happy one, especially for the tender hearted sister. My grandfather's bringing up had not endowed him with much softness of character, and the narrowness of Friends' views did not help to bring him into sympathy with others. . . . After my mother married, and there was no longer her sweet influence in the house, it was but natural that the sons, all very clever, bright and handsome, quick to form companionship with their tastes, literary, artistic and musical, similar to [our] own, felt the constraints of their Quaker home more and more, and notwithstanding the kindness of their stepmother, troubles arose which are referred to in my mother's journal ...

The volumes of my mother's journal covering the period from April 1828 to 18th June 1830 appear to have been destroyed. Her marriage took place on the 16th July 1829, and my father and she went to reside at Stone Hill, near Liverpool. The journal shows that after her marriage my mother passed through times of great spiritual depression alleviated but seldom by the joyousness which had been hers at an earlier date. ... Constant weakness and ill-health combined to bring about many times [of] lowness and grief of spirit ...

Only two entries occur in the journal in 1838 (one recording the birth of my brother Theodore on the 12th April) and one in 1839, in which dear William was born on the 26th October. She again takes up her narrative in 1840, and describes her first utterances in [a] meeting on the evening of the 10th May, which she says were followed by a feeling of nearness to Christ. ... After this my dear mother's journals are full of descriptions of meetings, and of the part she occasionally felt compelled to take in them

CHAPTER II

CHILDHOOD

My mother's journal enables me to give particulars of my family life. ... I came into the world on the 4th June 1841.

The early part of 1842 is described as a very low time in my father's business, disagreements with America which threatened war affecting trade. The state of affairs in the Society, and specially in [the] Liverpool Meeting was trying. My father and Friends Robert Benson and his sister resigned their membership and my Aunt Daniel thought fit to be baptized. In October my mother to her great comfort was recorded a minister, a certain proof that her ministry, so far conducted in much fear and trembling, met with acceptance.

In 1843 my mother notes with satisfaction that my father has arranged to leave business. She was unable to go, as she had the previous year, to the yearly meeting in May but describes with pleasure a journey in price and folly to Lancaster and the Lakes, and to see her Aunts Mounsey.

In 1845 my brother Alfred began his school life at Givre House, Tottenham, a school which the sons of most Friends went to.

In 1847 my father began to look out for some residence in the South of England, the state of my mother's health seeming to require change to a softer climate and Aigburth not proving any desirable place for my father, now his connection with Liverpool was at an end. In June 1847 therefore we moved into a furnished house in Dorking [Stapyton House] in the expectation that a home would be found in the neighbourhood.

From Dorking we moved to Sandgate in August, where we stayed in a little house under the Folkestone West Cliff between the road and the sea, with a garden, abounding in lizards, running down to the shore. In October we went to a Friend's [Richard Marsh] house at Folkestone, and afterwards to a house at Reigate which my father had taken for the winter. This house, then known as 'The Retreat', was the one still standing just opposite the steps leading up to the west door of Reigate

54

church. ... The proximity of the churchyard tempted a worthless groom in my father's employ to act as a ghost among the graves on a moonlight night, causing much alarm to those who caught sight of him, until, threatened by stones and pitchforks, the apparition was forced to seek ignominious refuge in a stable yard.

My brother Alfred went early in the year 1848 to Manchester where he was articled for five years to Mr Richard Lane, architect.[1] He was very able with his pencil and his brush and desired to be an artist; but though my father was fond of drawing himself, and desired that all of us should be able to draw and sketch, he was unwilling that Alfred should devote his life to art. Indeed such a course would not have been altogether in unison with the views of Friends.

With the exception of Alfred we all returned to Aigburth at the end of March 1848. Soon after my mother was taken seriously ill and as soon as she could be moved, we all went to Southport where we remained until the end of the year. This place then consisted of its one street with only a few houses and shops in close proximity to the sand hills, which teemed with rabbits. There was no pier and but little of anything of an esplanade. I remember the very long drives we had to take in most primitive bathing machines to reach the sea at any state of the tide but high water.

Early in 1849 we were back again at Aigburth, but only for a short time for an opportunity of letting 'Oakfield' arose, and my father determined to leave. ... My recollections of the Aigburth house in which I was born are not very clear but it was a pleasant and commodious one. ... An old account book of my father's shows that the land, originally about twelve acres, cost him in 1824 and 1832 about £6000, the house, the gardens and lodge etc. after 1832 about £3000, and the extension in 1838 about £2000. In 1847 he sold off portions of land, about one acre each to Edgar Jarston, Emanuel Switchenbart and Ralph Dawson, realizing £4400. James Starkey became the tenant of Oakfield in 1849 at £400 a year; and my father subsequently in 1853 sold it to Benson Rathbone for £10,000.

At the time of our leaving Liverpool my parents were total abstainers and also homeopathists. While in charge of her father's house and since her marriage, my mother's journal frequently speaks of trouble with the servants owing to intemperance. On one occasion the cook was brought home in a wheelbarrow by a sympathizing friend. Total abstinence seemed the only cure and the example had to be set by those in authority. My father no longer offered wine to his friends, and the stock of port, to prevent it doing harm, was poured into the fishpond at Oakfield. Some evil disposed persons were afterwards heard to say that the fish suffered, but of this there was no distinct evidence.

Homeopathy was esteemed as a happy alternative to the horrible physic, bleeding and leeches which were the popular remedies of the day. My parents were converted to its principles soon after their marriage, and many were the occasions on which my mother rejoiced the apparent efficacy of the simple remedies which the homeopathic doctor prescribed. The recoveries were no doubt largely helped by her effectual prayers, and might have resulted even if the medicine had been dispensed with. But she never ceased to give thanks for the benefits believed to be conferred by the tiny globules, a little store of which she soon learnt to dispense herself.

[In the Spring of 1849 they moved to 'Redland Hall' in Bristol.]

My mother in describing in her journal the members of the household on our moving to Redland Hall, records the finding of an excellent new nurse in the place of our old friend and servant, 'Mercer', who had been a more faithful servant and kind nurse to at any rate all the younger ones of the seven children. Sarah Ann Burlingham, also mentioned, was our then governess. She had succeeded Catherine Stringer, who was I think my first teacher, and by no means a favourite one. She did not love my brother William and myself the more from hearing us rejoice in her supposed death. While moving a heavy wardrobe one day at Aigburth . . . it fell on her and she was pinned to the ground with its weight. The noise brought her two young pupils in from the adjoining nursery, who seeing the position of matters coolly remarked 'Iassermes [sic] dead now', and calmly looked on until the bright idea seized one of them; 'Run, tell Mercer.'

Redland Hall, just at the entrance of Burdham Down by the road from the northern part of Bristol, proved pleasant quarters. My mother's health, however, continued very indifferent. . . . [My father] soon made the acquaintance of the Bristol Friends, including William Tanner, Dr Edward Ash, Robert Charleton and other able ministers in the Society.

But my father was looking for a more permanent resting place, to which the furniture from Aigburth, what was then warehoused, might be transferred. He was soon tempted by 'Snead' or 'Sneyd Park' the old house beyond 'Cooks Folly' at the further side of the Burdham Down. . . . It had many comfortable rooms and a most delightful garden, sloping with its fields, south to the River Avon on the other (or

Childhood

Somersetshire) side of which rose the beautiful Leigh Woods. Though the stream, even at high tide, could hardly be seen from the house, every ship or steamer that came up to or down from Bristol passed in front of the woods as a pageant across a stage. Sometimes the sound of a band on an excursion steamer, the noises of command, or the songs of a ship's company, would float in for a few moments through the open windows. Banksea roses covered the south of the house, thick yew hedges and old walls clothed with figs and apricots made the garden famous, while overgrown thickets of laurels and other shrubs incited my father to the exercise of his landscape gardening tastes.

Here were spent the happy days of my boyhood from 23 April 1850 to 1855, when I was nine to fourteen years of age. In 1850 my brother, 'Fred', aged twenty, was in Mr R[ichard] Lane's office in Manchester as a student of architecture; my three sisters, Ellen, Maria and Kitty, aged eighteen, sixteen and fourteen, were bright, healthy, happy girls, with no little pretensions to good looks. Ellen, much her mother's daughter, taking a share in household duties, and doing something towards the education of her little brothers, until a tutor was found for them. Maria and Kitty also domestic in their tastes, the latter especially fond of the poultry yard – while 'Theo' and 'Billy', aged twelve and ten, were constant companions of their younger brother [Edwin], all three rejoicing in considerable liberty, and in the escapations and pleasures which a country house with their own gardens, carpenters shop and a pony could afford.

My sisters had had four governesses, but of music and the lighter side of literature, they knew nothing. These were up to the Sneyd Park days forbidden subjects. But the voices were not to be restrained, and before very long with the help of an excellent German gentleman, who was secured as a tutor to us boys. ... We learnt to sing little catches, part songs and hymns, which were a pleasure to the innate musical taste of my father. ... A piano was however not allowed an entrance into our house until some years afterwards.

The friendships which were soon formed by my sisters among Bristol Friends were a source of the greatest pleasure and profit to them. The children of Joseph Fry of Charlotte Street, Clifton, and of Francis Fry, his brother, of the Tower House, Cosham, were constant visitors to Sneyd Park, while the Charlotte Street house was always open to those of us who went into Clifton or Bristol for evening lectures or other purposes. Edward Fry, subsequently so kind a friend to my brother Theodore, and to all of us, was then studying law in London, and we did not see much of him; but his younger sisters, 'Sally' and 'Jenny'

57

were among my sisters' most intimate friends, and some of the merriest times that I can recollect at Sneyd were those where these friends with their brothers Lewis, David and Albert, came over to join in characters or other pastimes with my sisters and Theodore. Among others of my sisters friends at this time I recollect Jenny Lister, subsequently Mrs Smith Harrison, Mary Jane Fowler, at whose wedding to Edward Leatham at Melksham in 1852 my father and mother were present, and 'Bessie' Gibson of Saffron Walden, afterwards Mrs Lewis Fry.

In April 1851 my mother visited Friends in Devon and Cornwall, under a certificate, my father accompanying her but her health was not sufficiently strong to allow her to undertake the journey to London for the yearly meeting in May, as she had done the previous year. My father however went up being a 'representative' from Bristol, and he took my brother Theodore with him that he might see the wonderful exhibition in Hyde Park.[2] In July my three sisters were taken to London for the same object by my father and mother, the latter being always ready to pay a visit to her parents at Tottenham.

In the summer [of 1852] my mother took my brother Theodore to Malvern, and I was allowed to go with him as a companion. He had long been suffering from headaches and had become extremely stout. At Malvern he was, by baths and rubbings, reduced in a few weeks to a condition of comparative slimness, and after that he grew rapidly in height. But he was never strong, at this time of his life – the headaches continued, lessons or studies of any kind were prohibited, and several years, which might have been very productive, were passed in comparative idleness.

At the end of 1852 it was arranged that Mr Heinrich Just of Stuttgart should come to us daily as our tutor. He was on the point of being married to a German lady, and his duties were to begin as soon as he had brought his wife over to this country. He taught us Latin, German, Arithmetic and most things except French in which Mlle [Louise Aimée] Sudre [their French governess in 1850–51, and subsequently 'a great friend and favourite'] instructed us. In the midday interval between lessons he was a capital playmate, in the garden, and we soon learnt to respect and esteem him. He was a man of similarly strong and Christian faith.

In May [1853], my brother Alfred, whose five years with Mr Lane had expired, set out for a lengthened stay in France and Italy as part of his architectural education, having as his companion for part of the time, Thomas, the son of my mother's old and dear friend, John Hodgkin of Tottenham – a barrister of some note, and also a very acceptable preacher in the Society of Friends. I believe that in my mother's early years he taught her Latin, and that his love for her and her children continued till his death. My brother's journey was in every way successful, and the letters which he sent home describing his travels were looked forward to and received by all with great interest. He did not come back until February of the following year [1854], bringing home with him a very large number of beautiful watercolour drawings and many architectural studies.

In July my father and mother took my brother William and me for a few days sight seeing in London, as we had missed a visit to the Great Exhibition two years before.

The winter of 1853–54 was a severe one – my mother refers [in her journal] to the suffering among the poor. We enjoyed skating on the ponds of the Zoological Gardens at Clifton – the nearest available water for this purpose.

In June 1854 we made as a family the first of a series of visits to the English Lake Country,[3] which as years went on grew increasingly dear to us. The house we then stayed at was known as 'Fisherbeck', on the then new, now the old, road between Ambleside and Waterhead. I remember the delighted surprise with which in a walk with my father before breakfast on the first morning after our arrival, I saw Windermere in perfect calm. Alfred, who was then commencing in business in Manchester, came over to us, and our Aunt Flounders also joined us. We saw something of our cousins, the George Crewdsons of Windermere, and I remember a joint excursion to Patterdale, eight from each family, in which all we could do, owing to the pelting rain, was to drive to the hotel to rest our horses and eat the provisions for our picnic in a parlour.

The year 1854 was rendered memorable by the engagement of my sister Ellen to Wilson Crewdson Junior of Manchester.

After five years at Sneyd Park my father determined to leave it, and gave notice expiring at Lady Day 1855. He had always wished to possess a place which could be more his own . . .

A move having to be made, my father took for a few months, a furnished house in Clifton, known as Mortimer House, adjoining the footway passage leading to Victoria Square.

To us boys the days at Sneyd Park were, or ought to have been, very happy ones. Our father gave much of his time to us, and took great interest in our carpentering and other pursuits. He was fond of riding and liked us to go out with him in turn on one pony. I remember a lovely white half Arab pony which he bought for us, by name 'Fairy'.

Childhood

In carriages my father had his particular taste. A large roomy vehicle for station and monthly meeting use was designed for him by Bristol carriage builders. . . . When we were about to leave Sneyd Park, we made the acquaintance of Frank Firth, the photographer of Egyptian temples and scenery, and photography being then in its infancy, he was struck with this carriage, as being just the thing he required in his travels as a place in which to 'develop' his photographs. It accordingly became his property, and was fitted with yellow glass windows, and shelves etc. for the apparatus needed.

The birds at Sneyd Park were a constant source of interest. We were not allowed a gun, nor did my father possess one, but he managed with the assistance of the gardener and usher to make a collection of all the British singing birds which were to be found there, and these were admirably arranged in a case, matching a case of stuffed humming birds which he had made at the same time. While at Aigburth he had made a very large collection of foreign stuffed birds which he thought fit on leaving Liverpool to present to the City Museum. . . . Though I had no gun at Sneyd Park, I did my best with a crossbow of my own manufacture, and one day managed, more by accident than precision of marksmanship, to bring down a poor nuthatch.

Early in 1855, and before we left Sneyd Park, my brother Theodore, whose health had somewhat improved went to London, to spend a short time in his Uncle William's office in the Old Jewry (No. 6, now pulled down), and see whether the profession of a solicitor would be likely to suit his tastes. . . . Theodore came back home with a touch of the air possessed by some of those who being resident in the Capital, look down upon the provincialisms of others. This fault soon discovered by our neighbour and true friend, Mr Burges, was speedily and kindly aired by one or two of his laughing, but deeply convincing remarks, which could not fail to produce the result intended. I remember one day at the breakfast table in his own house, I, as a shy and ill mannerly boy, stooped, with my head down, over my plate. 'Edwin, I know you'll be a good man because your father (pronounced feather) and mother are good, but you'll never be an upright man, if you hold your head so; I can't tell how the food goes down.'

We moved to Mortimer House on the 12th March 1855. It was a large and commodious house, and though quite near to the heart of Clifton it had a pleasant garden at the back and a paddock adjoining. . . . Our lessons with Herr Just were also kept up, Theodore being strong enough to have his own hours of instruction. The enforced idleness of the last three years did not appear to have in any way impaired his mental abilities. . . . He became a great reader, and picking up a fair knowledge of English literature, he in a few months to a large extent, made good the arrears on the education of his boyhood.

The stay at Mortimer House came to an end in August 1855. It had been arranged that Theodore should go back to his uncle's office; that William should study at University College London, and that I should go to the junior school of the same institution. My parents desired to make a home for us three boys . . . and therefore contemplated taking a home in London as soon as term commenced at the end of September. In the meantime we stayed at Dover . . .

While we were at Dover, on the 10th September [1855], news came of the taking of Sebastopol, and the consequent possibility of the dreadful war [the Crimean] with Russia being brought to an end [which] made the heart of England glad.

CHAPTER III

SCHOOL AND COLLEGE

A furnished house, 29 York Terrace in the Regent's Park was taken in September [1855]. On the 25th my father entered me at University College School in Gower Street and I began my daily walks for morning and afternoon lessons on the 26th.[4] It was peg top time and I immediately bought my first top at a shop in Paddington Street close to us, with which I succeeded in making sundry holes in the oil cloth of the hall at No. 29.

University College being open to all, without any regard to religious faith, was patronised by Friends. Dissenters of all schools, Jews, Unitarians and others. I was therefore cautioned not to make friends hastily, if at all; and to confine my attention within the walls of the school to my lessons. This was a difficult task. Before long a dear little Unitarian schoolfellow, Guy Paget, lodging at 'The Hall' close by the school, asked me to join his birthday party at tea. I was so shocked at having allowed our intimacy to grow to such a height as to render such an invitation possible, that I nearly fainted; and I gave him an unintelligibly rude refusal. But we continued to be good friends and I do not think I ever suffered from the religious views of my schoolfellows. Later on, at the college, one learnt to admire much of the results, consequent on religious belief, found in the character of many Jews, Parsees and others, while among the Baptists and Unitarians were some of my brother's, Theodore's, and my most intimate and valued friends.

My brother William, for whom a calling in life had not yet been fixed, took up some of the classes at the College, devoting himself mainly to mechanics, for which he thought to have a taste. He and I had from our earliest days been inseparable companions. All our lessons and pleasures had been in common. We fed together, slept together, indeed at one time we had a common purse. To be separated in our studies was a great grief to both of us. In November 1855 we moved to a more pleasant house, also in Regent's Park, 11 Cumberland Terrace, which my father took furnished for a year. My walk to and from school was by Albany Street, across Cumberland Haymarket to the Hampstead Road and George Street, which took me straight to the school.

The year 1856 was spent by myself mainly in my daily visits to University College School. I had in 1855 commenced, at the express wish of my father, to keep a diary, and the simple facts there related enabled me to supplement the records of my mother's journal!

The meeting that we went to was that known as 'Westminster Meeting', located in comfortable quarters up a passage on the west side of St Martin's Lane ... we used usually to go to Westminster Meeting in the morning ... but very often in the evening some of us went to Regent's Park Chapel ... where Mr Landells, a Baptist Minister, officiated. At Westminster Joseph Bevan Braithwaite, a barrister of Lincoln's Inn, and a well known minister, invariably addressed the meeting; but his excellent and learned sermons lost in their effect by the slowness of his delivery and painful stammer. The 28th May was observed as a general holiday and day of thanksgiving in respect of the peace just concluded with Russia. There were to be great displays of fireworks in various parts of London, and the roof of our house was supposed to command a good view of those on Primrose Hill. Accordingly a large party met to witness them, and I find there were present with us Philip and Anna Tuckett of Frenchay with their sons, Phillip, James and Bessie Tuke, Alexander Peckover and his son, William Berris Smith, Richard Fry, Edward Fry,[5] and Elizabeth Pease, Alfred and Theodore Fox, Edward and Howard Lloyd, Bessie and Frank Gibson, Jane Lister, our cousins Robert and Charlotte Fowler, our Aunts Backhouse, Mounsey and Harris, Dr Thomas Hodgkin and John Hodgkin and our grandfather and grandmother. The fact of its being yearly Meeting time may account for so many worthies of the Society being in London at the date.

On the 1st August there was the school distribution of prizes – I had the first prize in the 3rd Class French, 2nd prize in Geometry and perspective, and mentions in Greek, Latin, Algebra, natural philosophy, chemistry, political economy, drawing and German.

Our holiday in 1856 was spent for the second time in the Lakes. [Staying at Nab Cottage, Rydal Water]. ... The greater part of August and September was spent by us in this delightful spot, then comparatively quiet as compared with what it is fifty years later. The few coaches and carriages then passing along what is now a very dusty and much frequented road, were no more than sufficient to enliven the place. Our stay was made intensely enjoyable by the presence of friends, Edward and Lewis Fry,[6] who stayed at a neighbouring cottage ['Week End'], and Farmer Bell and his sister Eliza. ... On the 8th September many of us were photographed by William D. Crewdson at his house 'Fieldfoot' under Loughrigg.

A few weeks after school re-opened for me, my brother, Willy, left London to spend some time in Alfred's office in Manchester, until some other occupation should present itself to him. The parting was sad for all of us, and especially for me; and would have been severely felt had not my separate schooling to some extent made me less dependent on him than I had been 'all through my boyhood'.

On the 12 January 1857 my dear brother Theodore[7] entered at University College. My mother gives the reasons for his so doing in her journal, but she does not state that her very kind friend Edward Fry had advised him to obtain his father's permission to take the step. By taking a bachelor's degree he would reduce the period of his articles in a solicitor's office by two years, and three years at college would secure him the degree. To my great pleasure therefore he and I were working under the same roof and his being at college was a great incentive to me to qualify myself for the education which I trusted my father would permit also in my case. My diary records that at the distribution of prizes in July I took first prize in the third class of Latin, second prize in the fifth mathematics, second mention in the fourth French, and sixth Greek, first prize in chemistry, second in natural philosophy and 'mentions' in German and writing. The year (1857) was made famous by a journey made by the whole family, except Wilson and Ellen, to the Rhine, Switzerland. None of us, except Alfred and Theodore, and excepting my parents, had ever before crossed the Channel. ...

I may mention that we left London from what is now known as the Low Level Station at London Bridge – then, I believe, the only departure platform for the continent in London. Railways were generally available on our route. At Olten, between Basle and Lucerne, we had to take carriages for a while, a tunnel now being complete, and we drove by road from Interlaken to Veray, via Berne, Freiburg and Balle. We had to drive also on the way home from Geneva to Seqsect, the railway not being completed. My father had engaged a courier, Prospère de Keuster, who was no doubt a help, but who was doubtfully honest, as he managed to do not a little smuggling of tobacco on the absolutely false ground that the old gentleman and his sons were great smokers.

From Paris my brother William hastened back to Liverpool, as an opening was offered him in my father's old office of which he was glad to avail himself. He took up his quarters with our very kind aunt, Mary Flounders, in the Prince's Park.

On the 14th October [1857] I began lectures at University College, joining my brother Theodore there. The classes I took up were the higher junior mathematics (under Professor Augustus De Morgan), the junior Greek (Henry Malden), the junior Latin (Francis Newman) and the junior English (David Masson).

Theodore took the same mathematics and English, and the senior Greek, Latin and German.

The year 1858 was spent diligently at University College, but my brother's health was not all that he could have desired at examination times – notwithstanding this he showed great progress in his studies, and was generally first in his examinations. Thorny How, Grasmere, was taken for our summer holiday, where we were a large party – William from Liverpool and the Manchester members of the family all coming for part of September.

My father continued to look out for a house in the country, and in August agreed to purchase an estate at Rusper in Sussex. The title however, examined by Edward Fry, proved defective and the purchase fell through. He soon after saw some land near to Reading, part of the estate known as Whiteknights, and including gardens laid out, 60 or 70 years previously, by a Marquis of Blandford, which greatly pleased him. There was no house, but the lessee, Mr Charles Easton, a solicitor of Reading, was about to build one in order to make the place more marketable. In the result my father agreed to take a lease on the completion of this building, and Mr Easton offered his own house, 'Redlands', in the immediate neighbourhood, as a temporary residence. It was arranged therefore for Theodore and me to go into lodging in London, and for our parents and two sisters to remove to 'Redlands' shortly before Christmas.

The lodgings which were chosen for us were near to the canal in Camden Town – their chief recommendation being that they were let by some Friends of whom our parents knew something. They proved however unfit and we moved after a few weeks to Chalcot Villas, Haverstock Hill, close to Chalk Farm Station. My first visit to Reading was for the Christmas holidays and the attractions of the place were naturally great. Mr Easton's house was a large and comfortable one. ... My father's lease covered about a fourth of the 400 acres or so of which the estate consisted, and which had passed from the Marlborough family into that of the Goldsmiths, from whom Mr Easton held it. .... Theodore and I managed to spend our Sundays almost without exception at our Reading home, sometimes taking Saturdays as well. The change of surroundings and occupation was so great and the interest of both of home and college so absorbing that I seemed to be living two lives.

The change from London to Reading was naturally in some respects unpalatable to my sisters, who missed the pleasant interests of their London life, and the society which residence in London secured to them. The Meeting appeared dull and the possibilities of companionship small. After a few months, a better acquaintance with their surroundings, and the interests of the home life, including some work among their poorer neighbours made matters wear a much pleasanter aspect.

[They finally occupied the new house at Whiteknights on 28 November 1859.]

One of the pleasant events of the spring of 1859 was the success of my brother Alfred in the competition of architects for the design and building of the Assize Courts at Manchester; another one, in the autumn, was his engagement to Elizabeth Hodgkin, whose visit to us while we were in the small house at Redlands, as our sister elect, remains . . . as a specially memorable and happy occasion.

The winter was a severe one, and the big pond, [at Whiteknights] was frozen over. A young friend, named Bernard Messer, venturing early one morning on the ice, before its strength was tested, was drowned; the event casting a gloom over our Christmas gathering.

On the 8 March 1860 my brother Alfred was married at the Meeting House at Lewes. There was a large gathering of the two families at Barcombe House, near Lewes, where John Hodgkin then resided.

1 April [1860] I resumed a short diary of events which I had discontinued since February 1858. . . . From it I find that we had at Whiteknights at Easter 1860, the company of our old friends, the Burges children, Janet, Isabel and Dora. . . . Sonning church about three miles off was a favourite walk on Sunday, where one generally came in for an excellent sermon from the good rector, the Revd Hugh Pearson, in the beautiful old building.

Theodore and I changed our lodgings early in the spring for others at 2 Harley Road, Adelaide Road, not far from our friends Professor De Morgan and his family. I annex some extracts from my diary: –

April 19, Thursday. Had our first singing class at the De Morgans. The class is composed of 'Dr William', George, Miss Dotty, Miss

Chrisy, Miss Mary, Theo and myself.

May 9, Wednesday. Conferring of degrees. Went there with Jan, Isie and Dora, Julian Goldsmid,[8] Ralli E. Baines, Pye-Smith and others took their degrees.

July 3, Tuesday. Papa, Maria, Kitty, Theo and myself went up to town to attend the distribution of prizes at University College. Lord Stanley gave them away. I was first in Extra Greek and took the prize; took a second prize in senior English; 3rd certificate in comparative grammar; and other certificates in senior Latin and logic. Theo had the first prize in moral philosophy and the history of philosophy; took first prize in comparative grammar, and a high certificate in senior Latin; he also bore off the prizes for the English and Latin essays – there were however unhappily no competitors. . . . My success was greater than I expected.

July 11, Wednesday. Went with sisters and Theo to the Royal Academy, and to see [William] Holman Hunt's [1827–1910] great picture of the 'Finding of the Saviours in the Temple' – most beautiful and will bear an hour's study.

Theodore and I were to go up for our degree examinations in the University of London in October. The intermediate months were spent largely at Whiteknights, where Willy came from Liverpool for his holidays. . . . The final examinations for our degrees took place from the 22nd to the 25th October. I wrote in my diary: –

October 26th, Friday. I came home early in the morning not feeling in the humour for more work. Theo stayed as there was a meeting of the committee of the Reading Room which he had to attend. The new committee had been selected on Wednesday: the members being Cozens-Hardy, Peto, Bruce and Theo, who was made president. The committee last session consisted of Julian Goldsmid, president, Stepburn secretary, Farrer Herschell treasurer, Bompas and myself, who acted for Herschell, who was not much at college.

October 29th – Monday. Went [on] a walk in the morning with De [Morgan] and then got back to town with Theo in time to hear the result of the B.A. examination. Of the 50, or thereby, second B.A.s, 20 are plucked, and only 10 of the remainder are put into a first division. Jardine, Carpenter, Hyatt and Theodore were among the ten. Albert Goldsmid, Tom Jevons, Fox and myself were among those in the second division. Poor Charlie Martin, one of the cleverest fellows, was plucked. We all felt for him extremely – Hepburn, Japp and others of our friends passed at the same time the whole B.A. We heard afterwards that there were only three in the first division at first, and that the examiners had been induced to add on seven out of the huge second division of twenty seven. I am glad to say that Theo was one of the three.

It was high time to make up my mind what line of life I was to follow, for with all the interests and excitements of college, I had allowed this important matter to be in abeyance. I knew nothing of business, and felt a dislike of the 'city' and to the pale and anxious faces which I saw on my infrequent visits there. A doctor's career might have suited me, but I had no special bent that way, and I feared a failure. My dear mother also feared the interruptions of a quiet home life which necessarily attended success. The consideration of the subject gave me many painful hours, and I know was the cause of anxiety, to my parents. Matters were arranged for me in a simple but unexpected way. Among our neighbours at Whiteknights were three ladies, sisters of William Turquand,[9] the 'accountant', to whom my parents thus became introduced. My father considered a training in an accountant's office, giving me an insight into City and commercial life, just what was wanted for me. I acquiesced and it was soon arranged that after a holiday, I should go to the office of Coleman, Turquand, Youngs & Co. of Tokenhouse Yard, E.C. and learn something about business generally from the point of view of the public accountant.

I had enjoyed my three years at college immensely. It was a quiet time compared with what a similar period at Oxford or Cambridge might have been; for, as a rule, we met our College friends in the classrooms and library only. I had the advantage of the constant companionship of a wise and loving brother, whose example and precept helped to keep my feet from falling, and led my attention to my studies. Perhaps I was a little too anxious to follow him, and leaned too much upon him, for we were seldom apart out of classroom hours, and those of whom I saw most were his, rather than my, friends. I failed therefore to get into a separate circle in which my conversational powers might have been developed better than in the constant company of those to whom it satisfied and behoved me to act as a listener. Among them were the names above mentioned. Henry Selfe Page Winterbotham and Herbert Hardy Cozens-Hardy[10] had already left college, but were lodging in the neighbourhood and kept touch with their old college friends. The former soon after he had been called to the Bar entered Parliament as a member for his native place, Stroud in Gloucestershire, where he soon attracted Mr Gladstone's attention, who made him Under-Secretary for the Home Department. He died in Rome in 1873, to the inexpressible grief of his friends. The latter, after a distinguished career at the Bar and on the bench, latterly as one of the Lords Justices of Appeal, is now (1907) Master of the Rolls. Both of these were among my brother's best friends, and they kindly extended their friendship to me. Henry Peto, Sir Morton Peto's[11] eldest son, Edward Winterbotham, Henry's younger brother Thomas, Henry Hepbourn, whose sister Cozens-Hardy afterwards married, were like Henry Winterbotham and Cozens-Hardy all old boys of Amersham School, which was removed by its proprietor, Mr West, a Baptist, to Caversham in 1860. The last three were among my contemporaries and best friends at college. Julian Goldsmid, the nephew of Sir Francis Goldsmid, and heir to the Goldsmid estates was my brother's [Theo] companion in many of his classes, and a friendship grew up between them which lasted all their lives. I was a class mate with the two younger brothers, Walter, a poor invalid, and Albert, both of whom died shortly after leaving college. Farrer Herschell[12] . . . was one of my brother's set, and a very kind friend to me. We little looked upon him then as a future Lord Chancellor, though his great talents and powers of debate would have justified our so doing. Henry Mason Bompas, now his Honour Judge Bompas, was senior to both of us, and with the help of his sister kept a boarding house for University College students, acting as their tutor. He was a great favourite with us all. Our friends Alfred and Philip Ashworth came under his charge after we had left college. Edward Baines Pye Smith of Sheffield and Thomas Jevons of Liverpool were also amongst those of whom I saw much while at University College. Jevons's elder brother, William Stanley Jevons,[13] was also with us, having returned to college after his work at the Sydney Mint. I find a reference to my brother in a letter from him to his brother Herbert, 25 July 1860, quoted by his wife in the 'Letters and Journal of W. S. Jevons' published by her in 1886, p. 154. It is as follows: –

> In the college examinations I only went in for the mental philosophy and political economy. In the first the result came out, equal prizes and certificates – Theodore Waterhouse and W. S. Jevons. This is, on the whole, a satisfactory result since T.

> Waterhouse is certainly the first student of the college during the session, and has carried all other prizes before him. I had hopes of beating him, but am satisfied, considering that he has attended, better to the lectures than myself, to be equal.

The professors at University College who mostly tutored us were dear old Henry Malden, Professor of Greek, who had taught me also at the junior school in a class where his son Charles Edward and I generally held the two highest places, Augustus De Morgan,[14] whose lectures in mathematics were always a delight, Francis Newman, the brother of the Archbishop, who taught us Latin, and David Masson, who occupied the chair of English Literature. With the family of Professor De Morgan, to whom we were introduced by the sons who were at college with us, and the two younger at school with me, we became intimate and experienced great kindness from them while living near their house in Adelaide Road.

At the house of Professor De Morgan we met many interesting people. John and Mary Howitt of Highgate were friends of his house and their daughters Margaret, with Miss Malock, who was afterwards to charm the world with her novels, and two young ladies, sisters, named Philott, one of whom afterwards married Professor Iseley. . . . I remember also meeting Robert Chambers of Edinburgh, and a Mr Owen, the author of 'Footfalls on the Boundary of another Life', a gentleman whose stories of the spirit world made him an acceptable visitor at a house where 'spiritualism' was not just put aside as an idle talk. Professor De Morgan was a great lover of music and played the flute well.

The autumn of 1860 was spent chiefly at home where I enjoyed long rides. In December I went with Theodore on a visit to Alfred and Ellen and Willy in the North, coming back with Willy for Christmas at home. The season was intensely cold, and we had excellent skating on the lake, making further acquaintance with my future master, Mr Turquand, who was a great skater.

CHAPTER IV

APPRENTICESHIP

On the 7th January 1861, when in my twentieth year, I began work in the City. I called at Mr Turquand's wish at his private house in Mansfield Street where I found him busy on some important railway work which had taken one of his partners to America, and he gave me a note of introduction to one of his partners, who on my arrival at Tokenhouse Yard, took me under his care, and gave me some simple work to test my abilities in copying figures. Theodore began his office life on the same day, being articled to Messrs Clayton, Cookson & Wainwright of 6 New Square, Lincoln's Inn, next door to the house where he had spent so many fruitful hours with his kind friend Edward Fry.

I soon began to take up work with a principal clerk as his assistant, and before very long to carry through small matters without assistance under the instructions of the partner, Mr Weise, who to a certain extent looked after me, and who gave me a seat at a table in his room, when I was not occupied away from the office. My diary shows that almost without exception my Sundays were spent at home at White-knights, and that I was able to get down on the Saturday generally in time for a longish ride with Theodore or one of my sisters, or one of the Burgeses. . . . On the 10th September I left with Alfred, who had asked me to accompany him, for the Rhine stopping at Namur, Treves, Speyer and Heidelburg (where we found Theodore and his companions and stayed with them a day or two) then to Mainz, Bacharach, St Goar, Coblentz, Laach, Cologne, Neuss, Aachen, Ostend and home. It was Alfred's desire to study some specimens of round-arched Gothic architecture and I was interested in what I saw under his guidance. At Bacharach we got locked up in the church, and forgotten by the 'knoter' and might have been long detained if I had not found a broken pane of glass through which I put my head and astonished some people in the street below. The beautiful old abbey at Laach, practically a ruin, situated in a valley surrounded by most magnificent beech woods, and by the side of a large and lovely lake, struck one as well worth a visit. We walked there from Andernach, through Wassenacht, about six miles, largely across fields which were suffering from a plague of field mice – and came back a much prettier way along the valley of the Brohl to the village of that name.

My diary subsequently relates: –

> October 26, Saturday. Alfred and Philip Ashworth came down to Reading with us. ... The Ashworths were the two youngest members of the family of Edmund Ashworth of Egerton near Bolton.[15] He and his brothers, Henry and Thomas (the former a well known Free Trader and friend to Richard Cobden), were among my father's oldest friends, and we naturally formed acquaintanceship with Alfred and Philip when they took up quarters with H. M. Bompas, and entered University College. So also with Robert Barclay, the eldest son of Joseph Gurney Barclay of Knotts Green, Essex, and Lombard Street, who with his and our distant cousin J. H. Blackhouse of Darlington, was being tutored during the short time they were at college by W. S. Lean.

> November 18, Monday. Busy moving our books etc. from Harley Road to 14 Woburn Place, where we have found rooms after a long search in the neighbourhood of Russell Square.

> December 25, Christmas Day. Alfred, Maria, Kitty, Theo, Willy and myself all went to hear C[harles] Kingsley[16] at Eversley, a most beautiful day. We came home by Bramshill and Heckfield common. Some walked, and some including dear W[illiam] drove in the phaeton.

My diary refers frequently to Mr Thomas Porter, an old business connection of my father, as the owner of sugar estates in the West Indies. He had, at my father's introduction, secured another portion of the Whiteknights estate, and had asked Alfred to design a house for his erection there. He and his wife continued our most kind and valued friends until their deaths many years after.

In August [1862] I took my holiday – going on the 4th to Manchester, where I visited the Assize Courts then in course of building under Alfred's supervision, thence to Egerton to see my friends the Ashworths, and to Liverpool where I joined Willy, and we steamed to Llandudno, where our parents were staying with Kitty and Theodore.

I find in my diary frequent mention of the pleasure given by the

Apprenticeship

oratories which I attended at Exeter Hall, often with one of my sisters.
. . . Our touch with our old friends of University College was also kept
up by our connection with the Reading Room of which I find I was
president for the session 1862–63. I also attended the lectures on
political economy, which were held after my office hours.

I extract the following from my own diary: –

> December 3rd, Wednesday. Theo went up for the Joseph Hume
> Scholarship examination at University College. He had two
> competitors. He has been suffering much from cold and headache
> lately and hardly stood a fair chance.

> December 7th, Sunday. Heard by a letter from Hardy the
> moderators at College that the Council had awarded the scholar-
> ship to Theo.

> December 20th, Saturday. I went up for the matriculation
> examination of the Institute of Actuaries.

The Christmas of 1862 was spent in Willy's company at Manchester,
where Maria was also staying. We visited Alfred and Ellen and our
various Uncles and Aunts.

I had now [1863] been two years at the offices of Coleman & Co.,
my father having paid a premium of £270 without any definite period
of pupildom being fixed. Three years were supposed to be long enough
to educate a young man sufficiently to be in a position to take up
business for himself – but there did not exist at that time any society or
institute for the examination of which a student of accountancy had to
qualify himself under articles. The firm therefore at the end of two
years kindly considered my position with them, and I find the
following in my diary: –

> January 18, Sunday. I earned my first penny last week, Mr Weise
> giving me a present of £2.6.5, as a reward for my services, with
> the promise of a salary during the year.

> February 23, Monday. In a meeting of the Institute of Actuaries
> in the evening, when I was formally admitted as an Associate,
> having passed the examination . . .

> March 19, Thursday. Heard W. S. Jevons' paper on the 'Fall of
> the value of gold' at University College.

> July 1st, Wednesday. Distribution day at College. Maud and
> 'Willy' came. Theo was first in 'English Law', jurisprudence and

also took the 'Lawrence Counsel' prize of £10. I was second in political economy.

November 23rd, Monday. Father advised me strongly on Saturday to leave Colemans at the end of the year, and set up for myself in the City. I am in doubts as to my own capabilities, but think it may prove best for me.

Theodore's evenings were frequently spent with his friends the Frys at Highgate. Edward Fry after his marriage with Mariabella Hodgkin went to live near to the life of West Hill, and the pleasant hours of study spent by Theodore in Edward's chambers in Lincoln's Inn were to some extent made up for by frequent visits to Highgate.

On the 31st December I was at work again and told Mr Turquand of my intention of leaving the office. They kindly offered to keep me for a time that I might gain more experience, but I adhered to the advice given me by my father, who was strongly supported by my brother Alfred, and said 'goodbye' to Tokenhouse Yard on the 7th January 1864.

My three years at Coleman, Turquand, Youngs and Co. were on the whole very interesting to me, giving me considerable variety of experience. At first I was able to do only the simplest casting or calling over, and found the work very dull, and the meaning of the book entries was often unintelligible to me. Before long, however, I was given little matters of audit or investigation to carry through myself, and the work then soon became of interest. I remember an examination into the accounts of the manager of a Union Workhouse, on which I made a long report while yet a novice at my work. For many weeks I was engaged in assisting a principal clerk in putting in order the accounts of some Army agents in Westminster, work which was interesting to me owing to the methods adopted for ensuring accuracy in our results and the satisfaction which followed. The head of the firm, whose acquaintance I thus made, was one of my kind business friends afterwards. I was occasionally sent to the offices of the London & North Western Railway to assist in Mr Coleman's[17] work as public accountant in the service of the auditors. Mr Coleman was connected also with the London, Chatham & Dover Railway, then carrying out its metropolitan extensions, and I gained not a little experience in examining into the trade claims for loss of busines on change of premises, and in sometimes giving evidence in the court of arbitration. John Horatio Lloyd, who had made his name a household word as the inventor of 'Lloyds Bonds', and Henry Hawkins, afterwards Mr Justice

Hawkins and subsequently Lord Brompton, were generally pitted against one another in these trade compensation cases. Henry James, afterwards Lord James of Hereford, was also frequently employed.[18] I remember that once when I was in the box, James, in cross examination somewhat unkindly endeavoured to make me more nervous than I was by suggesting that I should have time given me to complete what I was engaged in doing – viz. stroking my moustache, or rather that portion of my lip where I hoped a moustache might sometime be – an unconscious action on my part from which I am glad to think his remark did not lead me immediately to desist. But he softened as the years went by. Lloyd was too old and kind a man then to do such a thing; and Hawkins though awfully quick, was not I think to be feared in the box. The business of a public accountant concerns itself with all manner of trades, and the resulting constant change of thought and occupation is one of its great advantages. One of my last pieces of work was in connection with the accounts of some collieries which were about to be converted into a joint stock company through the instrumentality of Mr David Chadwick of Manchester.[19] This gentleman had at the time a great reputation in this line and it was interesting to me to be thus brought across him. I think Bolckow, Vaughan & Co. Ltd and Palmers Shipbuilding & Iron Co. Ltd amongst many other limited companies owed their existence to him and his Manchester friends. But he was not universally successful and little was heard of this class of business by him after the troubles of 1866.[20]

CHAPTER V

START IN BUSINESS

My brother Theodore having entered Cookson & Wainwright's office, for three years at the same time as I went to Coleman & Co., his years of service were over at the same time as my own. He thought of reading law for a while in the chambers of Edward Fry; it was my intention to put up a brass plate for myself. I soon found two small and suitable rooms in an upper floor at No. 11 Old Jewry Chambers. But before settling down to try to make a business for myself, I took some holidays at home. . . . After this, Alfred being somewhat over worked (he had just taken London offices in New Street, Charing Cross), I joined him in a little trip to the Riviera – Theodore being unable to accompany him as was intended, having a bad cold.

I put my name at 11 Old Jewry Chambers on the 24th February 1864; my first work was to send out business cards to my friends.

> February 28, Sunday. Had a most kind letter from Mr Glyn, who had sent one of my cards to Mr Murray (solicitor of Glyn, Mills & Co.).

> March 5, Saturday. Have been at my office daily from 10 to 5, working at annuities &c. for the second Actuaries examination in December, and a little bankruptcy law &c. Had very encouraging letters from some of those to whom I sent my cards.

Among these letters was a characteristic one from Mr William Topping, a director of the North Western Railway, and an old friend of my father for whom Alfred had done a good deal, or was then doing a good deal, at his beautiful house and village of Brasted, Kent.

> March 18th, Friday. In the House of Commons from five till half past eight. The debate on Gladstone's Amnesty Bill, and the Mazzini and Stansfeld Question were very exciting. . . . Had a letter from Mr Glyn giving me my first job.

But no work came in for some weeks and I began to think I might have made a mistake. Mr Ball[21] of the firm of Quilter, Ball & Co., the only other firm among accountants of that date of equal standing with Coleman & Co., who was a friend of my uncle William, kindly sent for me and after putting some questions to me to test my abilities, which I think I was too nervous to answer very properly, told me that some further practice with Coleman & Co. would have been good for me. But I remembered what my brother Alfred told me after his own experience, that one little matter carried through by myself and for myself would teach me more than a month of clerkship – and I waited. My father had given me £2000 to start on, which with my small savings made a sum of £2078.18.5, and I made calculations and estimates as to how long, with compound interest, I could subsist on this sum at my current rate of expenditure.

> April 2. Rejoiced to get a letter from Mr Banner of Liverpool, which seems as if it might lead to my first piece of work.
>
> My brother Willy suffered much in his health about this time, so much so that the doctors advised him to give up his work in Liverpool, where he had laboured hard for seven years in the hope of partnership. He came home to Whiteknights however for a few weeks, and soon recovered his usual good health. It was a great pleasure to me to have him so near.
>
> April 27th. Received Alfred's books from Manchester. My first job.
>
> April 29th. Prospect of more work, this time through Uncle Willy.
>
> May 10th, Tuesday. Convocation of the London University at 5 p.m. Theodore and I went there to vote for the chairman &c., meeting many that we knew. Then to Brixton to the Thöls. Mr and Mrs Richardson [Mr J. W. Richardson had married the eldest daughter of the Thöl family] had come back from their wedding tour, and were staying in London. So Theo was asked to see them, and he kindly took me. We had a very pleasant evening. Mr and Mrs Elk were there, and one Fraulein Thöl, Georgina, the others being away from home.

Little did I then guess how this sweet girl, then 15 years of age, was to enter my life!

> May 28th, Saturday. Willy having some months ago sent in his resignation to the Friends at Liverpool has been thinking for some time past to be baptised. Most of us also have for long desired to

take the Communion, and for this purpose, sisters especially have been anxious to join the Church of England. As Uncle and Aunt Willy had kindly offered to 'stand' for us, we agreed to meet at Sydenham, with Willy, and there be baptised together by Mr Stevens, a friend of uncle and aunts, who said he could procure Penge church for the purpose. ... At noon we went to Penge, where Mr Stevens very impressively read the service for Maria, Kitty, Theo, Willy and myself. Uncle and Aunt and Ellen were the only others present. I feel to some extent I have been led to take this step now by the example of my brothers and sisters, but I believe that I have taken it in the earnest desire to fulfil Christ's commands. ... We all returned to Reading in the afternoon. Alfred joined us later on – so we were a large party all of us together.

June 3, Friday. To Eliza Barclay's to an evening party. Met Edward Leatham and his wife; John Bright, Gurney Barclay, Henry Fowler, John Hodgkin with their wives, Miss Eliza Bell, Mr Bunsen, Dr Hodgkin, Dr Sterne, George Head and his wife, Edward Fry and his wife, William and Miss Ford Barclay, and many others whom it was a pleasure to see.

Edward Leatham,[22] the radical Member of Parliament, had married Mary Jane Fowler, the only daughter of John Fowler of Melksham, and an old friend of my sisters. Samuel Gurney (the younger) was a member of the firm of Overend, Gurney & Co., which came to such sad grief in 1866. He had little to do with the business and gave his time to philanthropic pursuits, and was very liberal with his purse. He kindly encouraged me in my business, by asking me to look into the affairs of a little charity with which he was connected in his village of Carshalton. This brought me into contact with his friend John Lee, the secretary of the Drinking Fountains Association, and led to my joining the committee of that institution. Mrs Ernest Bunsen of Abbey Lodge was Samuel Gurney's sister. Joseph Gurney Barclay was the head of the banking family of that name. He lived at Knotts Green, Leyton in Essex, where he had a magnificent garden. His son Robert was at University College and I saw a good deal of him and his brother William, their mother being a Leatham. ... Henry Fowler, the eldest son of John Fowler of Melksham, had married a sister of Gurney Barclay. He had a large family and two of his sons, if not three, subsequently came into my office, one of them becoming my partner. Dr Thomas Hodgkin was the brother of my mother's kind friend John

Hodgkin, and distinguished as a philanthropist as well as a physician. He was much interested in the Jews and went out to the Holy Land on some mission with his friend Sir Moses Montefiore.[23] I think he was also connected with that gentleman on the board of the insurance company which took the name of the 'Alliance', owing to the directors and clientele being composed largely of Jews and Quakers.

Miss Bell, of Alton, was the sister of Jacob Bell, the chemist and collector of pictures, and of James Bell, subsequently of Fawe Park, Keswick.

> June 11th, Saturday. On Thursday Willy came to town from Reading. The Liverpool doctor had told him he must take a three months holiday to cure his bronchial tubes which have thickened owing to repeated colds. He came up to consult doctors Chapman and Williams. . . . He will go shortly to Switzerland.

> July 31st, Sunday. I have Woburn Place to myself last week, but was not lonely being busy at work in the City and at Barking for Mr Hallet, a new nice piece of work. The Manchester Assize Courts were opened on the 26th. . . . I wished much to have been present at the opening, but was prevented from going by my new work.

I was also much away from London owing to business in Leeds, where John Fowler[24] had entrusted me with a heavy piece of work in planning a system of cost accounts for his steam ploughs, which seemed likely to prove a great financial success, orders having come in from the Khedive of Egypt and others for a large number of sets. My Sundays in the north were generally spent at Manchester or at Liverpool with Willy. Another heavy piece of work reached me through our friend Smith Harrison, who had married my sister's friend Mary Jane Lister, in connection with the parish of West Ham – an examination into the accounts of the Great Eastern Railway, and those of the Gas and Water Companies within the parish, with a view to an increase in their assessments. In my work at the railway offices I was much assisted by the advice of my kind friends in the accountants office of the L. & N.W. Railway at Euston, who knew at any rate how anyone examining traffic accounts on behalf of a parish could be put off the scent. They told me that persons coming to their offices for the purposes had in earlier days been put under the charge of a young man named Edward Watkin, who brought out every kind of book except the one that would give the required information. The railway company in my own case soon admitted their liability for a much larger sum than they were assessed at, and a satisfactory arrangement was quickly come to.

My first clerk other than an office boy was W. H. Hardy, previously the Under Secretary of University College, whose acquaintance I had made when at college, and who was seeking a wide field for his business capacities. He was a man of ability and very gentlemanly presence, and was very helpful to me.

It was there [Leeds] that I learnt that my kind friend and employer, John Fowler, had broken his arm in hunting the previous Saturday, the 12th November [1864]. This accident proved fatal. . . . I had conceived such an admiration for John Fowler's character that his sudden death greatly affected me.

During the year 1865, Alfred who already had a London office in Spring Gardens, Trafalgar Square, purchased the lease of No. 8 (subsequently No. 20), New Cavendish Street, Portland Place, into which house they moved from Manchester early in 1865. One of the reasons which induced my brother to leave Manchester was the trouble he had had in consequence of a Trade Union dispute over the work at the Assize Courts – threatening something like a boycott of work on buildings designed by him, and rendering it desirable that he should make London rather than a provincial city his headquarters. He wrote a pamphlet, 'A Chapter in the History of Strikes', describing what had taken place at the Assize Courts. No. 8 Cavendish Street soon became a great resort for Theodore and myself, the various works in which Alfred became engaged being of great interest to us, especially Theodore. We had other interests there as well, e.g. Italian classes were started there in 1865, Professor de Tivoli of University College teaching Alfred, Bessie, Theodore and myself.

My brother William was admitted a partner in the Old Hall Street business in Liverpool on January 1st 1865. . . . I was able frequently to pay him a visit from Leeds where my work still required my frequent attention at the Steam Plough Works.

CHAPTER VI

PARTNERSHIP

During my frequent stays at the [Queens] Hotel in Leeds, I saw a little of Mr Holyland,[25] a principal clerk of Mr Turquand's, who was engaged in winding up the Leeds Banking Company, which had come to grief. He told me he was about to join his friend Mr S. L. Price,[26] an accountant of Gresham Street, in partnership, and suggested that I should make a third in the arrangement. I had been doing very well for myself during the last few months, but the offer seemed to open out chances of quickly attaining a wider experience, whilst ensuring a more steady practice and affording me the advantages of assistance should I need it. After consulting my father and some business friends, I accepted the terms offered [to] me, and we arranged to put up our names as a firm on the 1st May 1865.

> March 14th, Tuesday. To Leeds in the evening, travelling down with Turquand, whom Holyland had told of our intended partnership.

Mr Eddison, a partner in the Steam Plough Works, and his wife were very kind to me, and I was often at their house at Headingley for the night.

> March 16th. Sat up late composing with R. W. Eddison a short life of John Fowler for the journal of Mechanical Engineers.

We started the firm of 'Price, Holyland & Waterhouse' at 13 (afterwards 44) Gresham Street, the south eastern corner of the junction of Gresham Street with King Street, with offices on the first, second and third floors. By a lucky foresight I prevented the carrying out of an order for a brass plate on our swing doors, which had the doors been ajar, would have resulted in 'Price, Holy Water' being seen on one, door, and 'Land and House' on the other.

On the 1st September [1865], Maria, Kitty, Theo, Willy and myself met at Thorny How, Grasmere, where in the absence of father and mother who remained in the south, dear Aunt Flounders acted as hostess and chaperone [plates 15, 16]. Janet, Isie and Dora Burges joined our party. The weather for the whole of September was perfect and we had many excursions and picnics ... and our evenings were spent in charades, singing &c. ... I write in my journal: –

> In the afternoon to Rydal Mount with Miss Cookson, then tea with Mrs and the three Misses Cookson, old but very charming people, and a late row by lantern light in the glassy lake. ... The Monday we devoted almost entirely to Mr Baldry, the photographer, who took various groups and views of Thorny How.

On November 8th, I write: –

> We are all excited about Alfred's chance of being appointed architect to the Commission for building the great new London Law Courts. The Commission have already made him their adviser and he is instructed to prepare ground plans. He is very busy.
>
> My first six months with Price & Holyland expired on the 31st October. I feel it a great blessing to have come across such men as my partners. Price's character I greatly admire, and I believe him to be a large-hearted Christian man. Both his and Holyland's behaviour to me is all I could desire. Financially too our partnership seems to have answered. I have this afternoon made up the Profit and Loss account for the six months, and find my own share of profit will more than cover the premium which I paid on joining Mr Price.

The first two months of 1866 were spent by my father and mother at Alfred's house, at 8 New Cavendish Street, my father having put himself under the charge of Mr (afterwards Sir Henry) Thompson, who after repeated operations, endured by my father without the assistance of any anaesthetic, removed what had been affecting his health for some years, and added probably ten years to his life. Mr Thompson's assistant was a very clever young man, John Foster, an old schoolfellow of mine at University College School, and brother of the distinguished physician, Michael Foster, who subsequently represented the London University in parliament. John died early in life.

> 10th [May] early in the morning to the Royal Academy where we met the Misses Ashworth. Intense excitement in the City in the afternoon. Overend [& Gurney] having failed.

May 11th 'Black Friday'. A run on the banks. Bank Act suspended.

The financial crisis did not at the moment throw any heavy work upon the firm, but the troubles in the Indian cotton trade which followed a month or two later led to our having to take charge of the affairs of Dadabhai Naoriji, a very interesting and virtuous Parsee merchant who failed for a large sum, of those of Jamsetzee Musserwanjee Tata, and the winding up of the Commercial Bank of India, a very heavy matter of business which occupied Mr Holyland for some years, entrusted to us by Messrs Freshfields as representing the Bank of England.

> July 11th. William Gladstone gave a concert, and invited some of our singing class to perform. The Duke of Argyll, the Duchess of Buccleuch, the Maharajah of Jahore, and a great number of swells among the audience.

In July 1866 I was elected a member of the City of London Club, George Grenfell Glyn having kindly proposed me for membership. In October, Theodore and I managed to move our London quarters from 14 Woburn Place to No. 60 (late 34) Park Street, Grosvenor Square; a tiny house just able to hold us with a spare room for a guest, a servants room upstairs and a box for a man in the basement. It was soon called the 'Bachelors' Bijou'. We were able to move to it in January [1867].

On the 16th November I had the pleasure of accepting, in the name of the firm, the appointment of public accountant to the auditors of the London & North Western Railway, being sent for to Euston by Henry Crosfield for the purpose: my old master, Mr J. E. Coleman, who had held the appointment, resigning.

Early in 1867 the plans of the competing architects for the new Law Courts were exhibited in Lincoln's Inn.

> January 16th. Much is said about Alfred's great designs. Most people speak in his favour, and he has more admirers certainly than any other competitor.

In business I was very fully occupied. In May [1867] our connection with the London & North Western Railway led us to be chosen to assist a committee of investigation into the affairs of the London, Brighton & South Coast Railway. Mr (subsequently Sir Philip) Rose[27] instructed us on behalf of the committee, the chairman of the committee being Sir

Charles Jackson, a man of great honesty of purpose and experience as, I think, an engineer on Indian Railways; but Mr Samuel Laing,[28] late Finance Minister for India, and some of his financial friends were behind the scenes, and when, with the committee's help the board of the Brighton Railway had to resign, Mr Laing was appointed Chairman. The finances of the Company had certainly been terribly mismanaged, dividends paid out of capital, and much money wasted, and the laxity of account keeping which was then brought to light was one of the main causes of the legislation with regard to railway accounts which followed in 1868. Our work was undertaken mainly by Mr Holyland, for my experience in those days was but slight. Mr Price also lent his aid but I fear that after all we made but a bungle of our report, and I often wished years later that I had the investigation to do over again. Sir Charles Jackson was, however, a most agreeable man to have anything to do with. I remember his laying his hand on my young shoulders, and encouraging me with the words, 'Mr Waterhouse, you will some day be a very eminent man in your profession'.

My next heavy piece of work was an examination into the affairs of the Cambrian Railway, on behalf of the London & North Western board. I spent some time at Oswestry and Shrewsbury and drew up a report which I remember provoked some harsh remarks from Mr William Quilter,[29] one of the most leading men in our profession, largely interested in Welsh railways, and whose views on some matters differed from my own. I believe I was of material assistance to my employers, who, in the presence of Mr Bancroft, one of the deputy Chairmen of the L. & N.W.R., gave their views to the Cambrian Shareholders at a meeting held at Crewe on the 20th August, which I was invited to attend. My diary at this time was written up irregularly, months elapsing without an entry, but I find the following:

> August 1st . . . Theo told me with a very heavy heart that the committee of judges for the new Law Courts designs had recommended Barry and Street as the architects – I went to see Alfred who had just got in from the North when I arrived, and had been told by Bessie. The way he bore the news was exemplary.

The year 1868 was an eventful one, full of sorrow and full of blessing. . . . In January I was gratified at being sent for by George Grenfell Glyn, and by being nominated by him and by one of the partners of William Deacons & Co., debenture auditor of the South Eastern Railway. The position of the money market and wide spreading distress made it difficult for railways to renew their terminable debentures, and Sir Edward Watkin[30] Chairman of the South Eastern, determined to convert the whole of that company's floating debt into debenture stock, the issue of which stock was to be watched by Mr Glyn and his colleagues, as trustees, assisted by an auditor of their own choosing. The conversion was satisfactorily accomplished at the expense of saddling the company with four per cent interest on the bulk of its debentures in perpetuity, but the auditorship continues, and it was only this morning, after an interval of more than 40 years, that I paid my fortnightly visit to the office for the purpose of countersigning the debenture stock certificates.

Mr and Mrs Thöl kept open house on Tuesday evenings to such of their friends who like to look in after dinner – and often had some good music. I accepted this hospitality occasionally and once took Maria with me. ... Though both German, they had lived [here] for many years and educated their children mainly in England.

I generally managed to get a ride on Saturday when at Reading. But the doctor recommending more frequent exercise, I arranged with my kind friend Mr Withers, an old acquaintance of Mr Edward Burges, to supply me with a horse before breakfast in London. The rides in the park in the spring were very pleasant, and I soon picked up an acquaintance among the professional men who used 'the Row' at the same morning hour. William and Edwin Freshfield were often riding together, and I sometimes joined company with Mr Henry Hawkins Q.C. on his favourite chestnut.

> February 13th. Henry Crosfield sent for me during the day to Euston and expressed, as did also Mr Bancroft and a body of directors, their surprise and disgust at what had been done in the Caledonian matter. This greatly grieved me though I do not see what *we* have done, which is either blameable or impolitic.
>
> February 14th. Spent a very pleasant half hour with Bessie in the evening. Alfred away in the North – he has just completed his great and beautiful designs for the Manchester Town Hall.
>
> March 17th. Tuesday. James Thöl's wedding day. Took a cab out to the church at Streatham, arriving just in time. There were six bridesmaids, Fletchers, Thöls and Schroeders. Miss Georgie Thöl was put under my care, by far the most lovely of the six.

Ever since the 10 May 1864, when the shy maiden of 15 sat in a corner of the drawing room at Bedford Cottages, had the sweetness of her face remained in my memory, and I admit having, when in the Tyrol in

1867, bought several photographs of the young bethrothed Queen of Bavaria, as reminding me of it. The matter referred to above as bringing upon my firm the wrath of Henry Crosfield and some members of the London & North Western Railway board was a letter reflecting upon the financial methods of the Caledonian Railway as disclosed by their published statements of account, addressed to a client, who without our knowledge made use of the same to the possible damage of the market value of the Company's stock, publishing it as written by the 'auditors of the London & North Western Railway'. The matter worried me much at the time as the relations between the two companies were of a most friendly character, and we were accused of going out of our way in an endeavour to make them otherwise. So far as I was concerned the matter soon blew over, and I retained the confidence of my friends at Euston; but I learnt a lesson from the episode, and am glad to think I never after was concerned in a similar *faux pas*.

Another business trouble which gave me thought at this time was the introduction into our firm of a fourth horse to our coach in the person of Mr George Jay,[31] an elderly gentleman of considerable experience in accounting; but, as I thought, not likely to be of use to us to compensate for the share which he thought he should receive of our earnings. In this result I was right, and Mr Jay was the first to acknowledge the position, asking leave to retire after the experience of a few months.

> March 19th. Mr Jay called on our firm today and we arranged the details of our partnership. I hope this is a wise step. I have not acceded to it without much consideration for it has been brought about by the wish of my partners, rather than by any desire of my own. I shall have to sacrifice some of my present income for uncertain advantages; but I shall not regret this much I think for I feel that I have very much more now than I deserve – certainly very much more than I anticipated.

> June 25th. Barry has petitioned the House of Commons against Street's appointment as architect for the new Law Courts. This has induced Alfred also to petition the House on the subject. He has no chance I should say now, but he is in great spirits, finding all his work pleasant to him.

My autumn holiday [1868] was spent at Thorny How, Grasmere, which my brother Alfred and his wife had taken from the middle of

Partnership

August. ... The party ... consisted of Alfred and Bessie, our responsible hosts, their dear children, Paul, Monica, Florence and a baby boy, Kitty, Theo, Willy and Janet, Dora Burges and Georgina and Rosie Thöl [plate 18].

We had many very pleasant picnic excursions. ... Our party was much reduced before it finally broke up on the 27th. Kitty and I then went to Liverpool with Georgina Thöl, who was to be the guest of Willy and Janet for two nights. Kitty stayed at Aunt Flounders, and I at my Aunt Rebecca's in Lake Lane, but much of our time was spent at the little house at Allerton, where for me were my strong attractions. I rejoiced to see the strong affection and admiration for each other which had sprung up between my sweet sister-in-law and Georgina Thöl.

October 11th. Sunday. 'I had a stroll with father on Fox Hill, in the afternoon, and told him of my love for Georgie. His pleasure on hearing of it, and his hearty wishes for my success did my soul good!

October 12th. A day to be remembered – the birthday to a new life – the story of which should be written in letters of gold!

CHAPTER VII

1869–1873

The private diary which I had kept more or less regularly up to the year 1868 was then discontinued; the present was perhaps then felt to be more to me than the past could ever be. I have no further entries therefore to extract, and am dependent for any records upon my business diaries, showing the disposal of my office hours, and on such correspondence as may have survived.

Nicholas Johann Philipp Thöl [the father of Georgina, whom Edwin was to marry] was the son of a Lubeck merchant and was born in 1802. He had carried on business in his native town and also in Triesk, ultimately settling in London, as a dealer in glues and drugs. He had been married there, his first wife being a lady, Laibach, by whom he had a daughter, Gabriella. ... His second wife, whom he married in 1840, was Agnes Augusta Popert, the daughter of Samuel Meyer Popert, a banker of Hamburg and Emilia Oppenheim.

At the time of our marriage, Mr and Mrs Thöl were living at one of two semi-detached houses known as Bedford Cottages, in the Barrington Road, Brixton. ... Loughborough Road Station on the London, Chatham & Dover Railway made the place easy of access.

The family then consisted of: Marian Henrietta, who had married our friend John Wigham Richardson, to whom I owed my introduction to Georgie; Theresa Hannah, who had first married Elli Gilman; James Popert, who had just married Henrietta Groves; Georgina Emma Catherine, born 30 October 1849, at a house in Kennington, where her parents previously resided; Joanna Philippa ('Rosie'). Though Mrs Thöl was of pure Jewish descent, both she and her husband belonged to the German Protestant Church, and had thought fit to bring up their children as members of the Church of England. The children had been educated mainly in this country, but Georgie had spent some time abroad with her mother at Leip and other places; and, subsequently to my first making her acquaintance as a young girl in 1864, had stayed with a friend a considerable time in Stuttgart, studying music and other subjects.

We were married on Saturday 3rd April [1869] at Brixton Church by Mr Garland, the rector of the parish. It was the church the services of which Georgie and her sister usually attended, and at which J. Wigham Richardson[32] had been married in 1864. . . . Alfred Ashworth was 'best man'. . . . Our wedding trip, which began with Easter Sunday at Worthing, took the shape of a tour along the south coast to the Lands End, meeting the spring in Devon and Cornwall . . .

The little house [in London] had been vacated by my brother Theodore in my favour, he moving to 43 Weymouth Street. . . . Georgie had not seen it before I brought her into it as my wife and she was pleased with its brightness and with the prettiness of its decorations, due to the extravagance of a former occupier, and which went far to make up for the smallness of the house and its rooms. . . . Soon after our marriage Mr and Mrs Thöl with Rosie had left London, and taken up quarters at Berka-an-der-Ilm, a little Bad near Weimar; the business being handed over to James and his partner Mr Christy. Our autumn holiday was delayed, partly owing to my partner, Mr Price, having been appointed liquidator of the Albert Life Assurance Company, a heavy matter of business, involving great distress among the policy holders – and partly by the severe illness of my dear brother William . . .

Our journey home [from their Continental holiday] was hastened owing to the bad accounts of my dear brother. We came through Stuttgart and Paris; and I think that it was at the latter place that we learnt by telegram of his death on 1st October [1869], just one year after [that of] his dear wife. Leaving Georgie at Whiteknights, I went to the funeral at Liverpool, staying with my brother Alfred at Uncle Rogers' house at Mosley Bank. . . . His [William's] death removed a most loving brother, who up to then had been my chief friend and companion; and had it not been for the intense happiness of my new life, I should have felt stricken. The loss of dear Willy and Janet was a terrible reminder to Georgie and myself of the instability of all human happiness . . .

My marriage with one who was not of the Society of Friends rendered me open to expulsion from that body, and the fact that my wife was reported to be a German . . . made my case the more hopeless. But the good Westminster Friends did not wish to act hastily or harshly, and so deputed two of their number, Joseph Bevan Braithwaite . . . and Richard Dell, to call on us, and learn a little as to how matters stood.

[In the discussions Georgina] said she thought she might be at heart as good a Quaker as her husband, for she had recently been attending [the] Newcastle meeting with her sister Mrs Richardson, and had profited much from the sermons of Mr Thomas Hodgkin. Thus the two dear friends found matters much better than they had evidently expected and without laying any burden upon us, said they would report the result of their pleasant interview to the meeting, and hope that we should find it convenient and pleasant sometimes to join friends at Westminster at worship. A matter which occupied me at this time was the St Martin's Court Coffee Shop, which had been established early in 1868 for the benefit of the poor in the neighbourhood of Westminster meeting; Edward Fry and other Friends . . . contributing to the cost of acquiring and fitting up the premises. I was treasurer and looked after the general finances . . . and continued for some years to be connected with a kind of working men's club which met on the premises, by giving some lessons in writing, book keeping &c. . . . To this I gave up most of one evening in the week . . .

Dear Georgie had similar work in connection with Mrs Brougham, who soon became one of her greatest and most valued friends, and interested her in her endeavours to assist the shop girls of Westbourne Grove district to dispose of their evening hours to greater advantage than was then the case. She had opened a room or home for the girls in the Garway Road, and after she (Mrs Brougham) left the neighbourhood to reside at Carshalton, Georgie was generally there on the same evenings that I spent at St Martin's Court. Either owing to the example set by Mrs Brougham, or other circumstance, the chief shops in the district, including the large establishment of Whiteleys, some three or four years after Georgie joined in the work, provided very much improved accommodation for their assistants, with reading rooms and libraries, thus filling the requirements for which the Garway Road Room had been provided . . .

Sunday the 3rd April 1870, the anniversary of our wedding day was spent at Worthing.

On the 14th June, our sweet Agnes Mary was born, a new and strange delight. She was named after her two grandmothers . . .

After the dear baby came I began to think that the arrangement which I had made with my brother for continuing at the little 'bachelors' bijou', at the expense of his removal, was hardly a wise one. The place was now too small, and in the autumn [of 1870] I spent some time in trying to find another house. [In January 1877 they moved to 13 Hyde Park Street.]

My most interesting matter of business about this time was the winding up of the 'Royal Copper Mines of Cobre', an important matter put into my hands at the instance of Mr Pascoe Glyn of Lombard Street; Mr R. I. Palmer, a solicitor of Trafalgar Square, being appointed jointly with me as liquidator. The mines were in Cuba, of very old working and said to have been inaugurated by Las Casas early in the sixteenth century. They had paid magnificent dividends on 'bearer' shares which at one time were of great value. The output and returns had however fallen off and there was a possibility of the shares becoming valueless. Nearly all the holders had enrolled themselves under the limited liability acts to provide means for carrying on the mines with a moderate and definite liability on their shares. It was the liquidators' duty to make calls and discharge the floating indebtedness. One of the holders of the old shares to bearer had registered these in his son's (a minor's) name, evidently hoping, while sharing in any surplus, to escape liability in the event of a call. I had the pleasure of hearing his action most severely censured by the Vice-Chancellor – I think it was Lord Hatherley (then known as Sir William Page Wood) – and of putting him on the list. The mines were worked by what were practically slaves, and I had to continue the employment of these men under conditions which did not appear to me harsh, until I could get their indentures transferred to someone else. During the term that my colleague and I held the property, it was repeatedly the scene of more or less sanguinary contests during the Cuban insurrections. It was a long time before we were able to bring the liquidation to a close.

The work I had with Whitwells was in connection with their large ironworks at Stockton. Thomas Whitwell[33] was the inventor of the stoves which bore his name, and which were a great success in cheapening the production of iron. He was one of the best men I ever met, doing good to all he came in touch with. I had an interesting visit to Germany with him on business in 1874. But our friendship was of no long duration for a frightful accident in one of his own furnaces cut off a very promising career at a comparatively early age.

Early in 1870 I was employed by Fox, Head & Co. in assisting to determine the proportion of their profits, which under a profit sharing scheme was apportionable as a bonus on the wages paid [to] their men. The attempt thus made to avoid conflict between labour and capital promised well, but circumstances prevented the management being of long continuance. I made the acquaintance of Theodore Fox, staying with him and his wife at Pinchingthorpe when engaged on the matter, and also of Jeremiah Head,[34] both men continuing my kind friends through life. The year 1870, full of home interest to me, was that of the terrible Franco–German War, of which one's thoughts were always full. In September Henry Winterbotham[35] came straight to us after being an eye-witness of the crushing defeat and capitulation of the French at Sedan.

Our friend Henry Winterbotham was early in 1871 appointed by Mr Gladstone under-secretary of state for the Home Department, an appointment which led him to give up the Bar and look forward to a political career. His chambers in New Square then became occupied by Cozens-Hardy.

Our holiday in 1871 was taken in connection with some business I had in the north of England relating to the iron trade of the district. This matter of business was of great interest to me for many years and, strange to say, I must accuse myself of having myself solicited it. I remember no other occasion on which I asked for a piece of work to be given me. There had been for years frequent disputes between the masters and men as to the wages in the iron mills for rolling rails, ship plates, bars &c. Happily, there was a joint committee of which our friend David Dale,[36] the Chairman of the Consett Iron Company, and who had recently been admitted a partner in the coal and ironstone business of the Peases of Darlington, was chairman, which met and settled not a few questions arising between the employers and the employed; but not infrequently, when demand arose on either side for a general alteration in wages, found it necessary to make use of the services of an arbitrator. Mr Rupert Kettle had arranged matters for them sometimes, and Mr Thomas Hughes, Q.C. on other occasions. In 1871 a serious conflict of opinion arose on a question of an alteration of wages. Mr Hughes sat as arbitrator; and, as on former occasions, had particulars of the recent changes in selling values brought before him, to assist him in aiming at his decision. He gave his award, but at the same time intimated that, as his duties so largely consisted of a rule of three sum by which he fixed the rise or fall in wages, future disputes of a similar character might be settled by a correct ascertainment of the variation in selling prices. Indeed, he proposed that an independent accountant might ascertain average selling values, and that the wages of the men should rise or fall in accordance therewith under a sliding scale to be agreed upon beforehand. This suggestion of Mr Hughes appeared in the morning paper; and my partner, learning that I was not altogether a stranger to Mr Hughes, urged me to take a cab at once to his chambers and put myself forward as the 'independent account-ant'. I consented, but my heart almost failed me when in the big man's presence, and I beat about the bush. 'Oh', he said, 'I see, you think you are the man. Is that it?' 'Well', I said, 'I suppose it is.' 'I think so too', he added most kindly, and said he would propose me should the occasion arise. Shortly after the 31st July he sent for me, and gave me instructions for a preliminary investigation and report to himself. So I spent the August Bank Holiday in perusing the papers given me and finished the round of some 23 iron manufacturing concerns in the north in the course of a month, examining into the accuracy of the returns put before Mr Hughes in his arbitration. The master's secretary was a Mr Jones, the men's a Mr Kane, both excellent in their respective positions.

A letter of Sunday, 17th November [1871] to my mother in Manchester describes some of our doings: –

... we had a big concert for the St Martin's Club on Thursday, got up by Willy Winterbotham. ... I believe my song was the most applauded chiefly for the reason that it was much more acceptable than the book-keeping that I had been giving to members the night before. Fifteen joined my class, and I have my work before me if they are all to become accountants ...

The Christmas holidays were spent at Whiteknights, where we were a large family party – 'twelve here and six at Fox Hill' as dear mother writes in her journal.

Early in 1872 I had much business in Middlesbrough in connection with the estate of the late Joseph Pease, and the revaluation of the properties of the Middlesbrough owners. The valuation was made by Philip Debell Tuckett, who had married Rachel, the eldest sister of Mr Joseph Whitwell Pease, and the widow of Samuel Fox of Tottenham.

Our holiday [1872] was cut short by some business in connection with the Metropolitan Railway, undertaken at the request of Sir Edward Watkin, whose friends, Mr Pochin and Mr Whitworth, had attacked the policy of the board, and obtained the appointment of a committee to investigate the Company's affairs. I was asked to make the investigation as secretary to the committee, the chairman being Mr Joseph Shuttleworth of Lincoln, a very large shareholder in the line. We returned therefore to London on the 3rd September, and I went immediately to work. The committee issued their report early in October, and soon afterwards a new board was appointed, Sir Edward Watkin subsequently being elected chairman. After that I had a very heavy piece of work, which took me many months in unravelling the capital accounts of the company, which had been kept without any regard to principle or arrangement, and needed dissection to show the cost to the innumerable properties and interests purchased. I discovered certain forgotten and unrecorded deposits which more than covered the cost of my work. On the 15th October 1872 our second child was born.

We went down to Reading for Saturday the 30th November, where the little one was christened 'Theresa' at Sonning Church by dear Canon Pearson. Our business in Darlington, Stockton, Middlesbrough and Newcastle had now considerably increased. The connection with the iron trade, which necessitated periodical visits to most of the larger places, was a great introduction; and either the firm or myself became professionally connected with the Skerne Iron Works Co., the Darlington Iron Co. and other concerns at the time of their formation – our connection with them lasting through good times and bad, even to the winding up of the affairs of some of them in liquidation.

On the 6th December [1872] I was called in by the directors in London of a company holding a very large timber estate in Norway to make an investigation. Their secretary, who bore the appropriate name of Grabham, had made off with all he could lay his hands on, after discounting a considerable amount of drafts which an over trusting chairman had put his signature to without ascertaining that they were in order. The company was forced to suspend payment, my partner, Mr Price, being appointed liquidator under the court. The estate carried some 1,250,000 acres of mountain, lake and forest, the company's business having consisted mainly in the cutting and export of timber. The creditors determined not to place the estate in an auctioneer's hands but to realize the timber of which a large quantity was available, and await the issue. A lengthy matter of business thus arose for Mr Price: and what I learnt of the beauty of the estate and the excellence of the trout fishing led me to look forward to some interesting and pleasant holidays.

My frequent absences in the North of England continued during 1873, Georgie often staying with the two children at Whiteknights. Jonathan B. Hodgkin, a half brother to my sister-in-law [who married Mary Anna, the younger daughter of John Pease] as also both Harry and Gurney Fox, had each filled up some months of the last few years in studying account keeping in our office, as a preliminary to engaging in commercial life.

Much of my business time in the summer [1873] was occupied in connection with the 'Serle Street and Cooks Court Improvement Company', for the formation of which my brother [Theodore] was responsible. Being under the impression that the area bounded by Portugal Street, Carey Street and Serle Street was likely to increase in value after the building of the Law Courts between Carey Street and the Strand, he acquired under the name of the 'Metropolitan Estate Company Ltd', with money contributed privately by my father, some of my father's old Liverpool friends and others, a large proportion of the property by private treaty; and then, on the ground that a distinct public improvement would result, obtained an Act of Parliament for the Serle Street & Company, enabling that company to purchase the remainder by compulsory powers. It fell to my lot to examine into and report upon a number of claims made for loss of business by enforced removal.

When the whole area was bought and cleared, the large block of chambers and offices known as 'New Court, Lincoln's Inn' was designed by my brother Alfred and built: the total capital required for the land and buildings being about £320,000, of which about half was raised on mortgage. Julian Goldsmid, who was a client of my brother, had an interest in the company, and was its chairman for some years. Financially and from the dividend point of view, the company was only moderately a success.

In May 1873 I was instructed by Lord Erne and the directors of the Irish North Western Railway to make a report of their line, a matter which took me to Dundalk, Londonderry and Belfast, where I stayed with old Mr Macrory, the solicitor to the line. The report had reference to arrangements with the London & North Western Railway and brought me somewhat into contact with the authorities at Euston. This may have been one of the circumstances which led to my being associated with Mr Henry Crosfield, as one of the shareholders' auditors, on the sudden death of his colleague, Mr Hand – an appointment which it was desired I should hold temporarily until a contemplated amalgamation with the Lancashire & Yorkshire [Railway], for which there was a Bill before Parliament, took place, when one of the Lancashire & Yorkshire auditors was to take my place: my firm continuing as public accountants to assist the auditors throughout. I accordingly had the instructive pleasure of going over all the manufacturing and engineering departments of the railway at Crewe,

Stafford, Wolverton &c., after the close of the half year in company with Mr Crosfield, and learning the admirable system whereby he made himself cognisant of all that was going on in the great spending departments of the line. Mr Crosfield was an intimate and valued friend of Mr Richard Moon,[37] chairman of the company for so many years, and [who] took a great interest in its affairs. He was looked to as a great authority on questions of its finance, and occupied a position of far greater influence than that of an auditor generally. Though he devoted a very great proportion of his time to the Company, he received only £100 a year as his fee, thinking it an honour to be connected with so 'respectable an undertaking'. I continued my nominal position as auditor and his colleague for a few half years only. The Bill did not pass, and the amalgamation did not take place, and when the time came round for my retirement, it was arranged that I should not seek re-election, and Mr (afterwards Sir) Edwin Lawrence[38] was recommended for the post. As an intimate friend of Mr Crosfield, he was a persona grata to him: and I knew him slightly as the husband of a sister of my dear brother-in-law George T. Redmayne.[39] The audit fee was then increased to £500 a year for each auditor.

It was also in the Spring of 1873 that I received from David Dale, who had just been taken into the business of Joseph Pease & Partners, a request to put the accounts of their large colliery and ironstone departments on a good footing, and to audit them in future half yearly. The matter was a difficult one, for the methods of book-keeping were antiquated, and the staff, to a large extent Quakers of mature years, averse to change. I succeeded, however, in time, and to Mr Dale's satisfaction, being largely assisted by Reginald Ryley, then on our staff in Gresham Street, who had a link with the firm, having married a sister of Mrs Arthur Pease. For our autumn holiday I had planned a trip to Norway to see the timber estate which Mr Price had in hand. We took berths on the S.S. 'Tasso' of the Wilson Line from Hull to Trondheim . . .

In the autumn of 1873, I had a great business trial: – the secretary of a company the accounts of which I had audited and passed, proving a deceiver and a clever thief of a large amount of the company's monies. The Company was engaged in North Sea Fisheries, the chairman being a gentleman whom I greatly esteemed, Mr J. A. Hallett, the army agent of Westminster, whose acquaintance I had made while with Coleman, Turquand & Co. The board were not very careful in looking after their secretary, and allowed him considerable drawing powers in

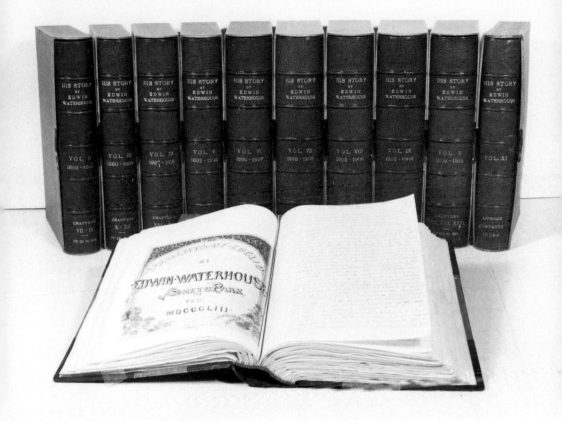

1 The eleven volumes of *His Story* by Edwin Waterhouse

2 Mary Waterhouse (1805-80), mother of Edwin, photographed *c.* 1863

3 Alfred Waterhouse Senior (1798-1873), father of Edwin, photographed
 c. 1863

4 'Oakfield', Aigburth, near Liverpool, where Edwin Waterhouse was born.
A copy of a sketch drawn by Ellen Waterhouse in 1855

5 Edwin Waterhouse aged about 18

6 Theodore Waterhouse as sketched by his elder brother, Alfred, in June 1851

7 Ellen, Maria and Katherine (Kitty) Waterhouse, Edwin's elder sisters. A coloured pencil sketch by Alfred Junior in September 1852 while they were living at 'Sneyd Park', Bristol

8 'Sneyd Park', near Bristol. A pencil sketch from the east by Alfred Waterhouse Junior, 10 June 1850

10 Alfred Waterhouse, *c.* 1860, eldest of the four brothers. He would at that
time have been in private practice as an architect in Manchester, moving to
London in 1865

9 *top left* Left to right: William, Theodore and Edwin Waterhouse, *c.* 1860

11 *bottom left* 'Whiteknights', from the west, the home of Alfred and Mary
Waterhouse near Reading from 1859

12 Left to right: Alfred Waterhouse Senior and his daughter, Maria, with
   Willy Crewdson, in the gardens at 'Whiteknights'

13 William Turquand, with whom Edwin received his accountancy training

14 Edwin Waterhouse, c. 1864, the year that he set up his own practice at No. 11 Old Jewry, in the City of London

17 In their formal walking attire for the Lake District fells, William (left) and
    Edwin Waterhouse, September 1865

15 *top left* The Waterhouse family on holiday in the Lake District in September
    1865, photographed in front of 'Thorny How' near Grasmere. Left to right:
    (back row) Aunt Flounders, Dora Burges, Edwin and Maria Waterhouse,
    Isabel Burges; (seated) Janet Burges, Katherine and Theodore Waterhouse;
    (standing) William Waterhouse

16 *bottom left* Grouped at the rear of 'Thorny How' at the entrance to Easedale
    with Helm Crag behind in September 1865 are, left to right: (rear row)
    Katherine Waterhouse, William Waterhouse, Janet Burges, Theodore
    Waterhouse, Maria Waterhouse, Isabel Burges; (seated) Dora Burges and
    Edwin Waterhouse

18 On another Lake District holiday (in September 1868) the four
Waterhouse brothers dressed to tackle the fells: standing left to right,
Alfred and Theodore; seated left to right, Edwin and William. Alfred
appears to be holding a sketchbook

19 A slightly flattering photograph of
Georgina E.C. Thöl (1848-96)
while in her teens

20 Georgina Thöl in 1868 at
the time of her marriage
to Edwin

21 Alfred and
   Mary Waterhouse,
   Edwin's parents,
   photographed not long
   before the former's deat
   in 1873

22 George Edmund Street (1824-81),
   who was a close neighbour of Edwin

23 Edwin Waterhouse in middle age

24 'Feldemore', Edwin Waterhouse's country home at Holmbury St Mary. This view early in 1896, from the north east shows the main entrance after the library had been added but before the construction of the billiard wing

my first ideas of my requirements.

George Redmayne's improvement.

25 Two preliminary sketches of 'Feldemore': above, Edwin Waterhouse's initial impression of how the house might appear; below, the revised design produced by George Redmayne

26 *top right* The sitting room at 'Feldemore' in 1881, which later became the dining room

27 *bottom right* The west front showing the bay window to the library with bedrooms above, *c.* 1896

28 An unidentified interior of 'Feldemore', April 1894

29 The vegetable garden at Bullmoor Farm, part of the 'Feldemore' estate,
April 1894

30 The rear of 'Feldemore' after the completion of the new wall for the rose walk, *c*. 1901

31 The north front of 'Feldemore' after the construction of the billiard wing (left), *c*. 1902

32 The Hollybush Tavern, a temperance working men's club at Holmbury
St Mary

33 The clubroom in the Hollybush Tavern. Portraits of Gladstone, Queen
Victoria and G.E. Street have been hung, while the female portrait over the
fireplace may be of Street's wife, Mary

34 On holiday in August 1894 staying at Garramor. From left to right:
Miss Sandbach, Miss Sandbach, Georgina Waterhouse, Colonel Lloyd,
Mr Sandbach, Mrs Sandbach, Miss Sandbach, Edwin Waterhouse, Theresa
Waterhouse, Nicholas Waterhouse, Mrs Lloyd, Miss Sandbach, Ellen and
Valentine Waterhouse

35 Another group portrait taken while at Garramor in 1894. Seated at the front
left to right: Georgina Waterhouse, Mrs Lloyd, Edwin Waterhouse, Colonel
Lloyd; behind, left to right: William MacEachan, Mrs Sandbach, Miss
Sandbach, Theresa Waterhouse, Valentine Waterhouse, Ellen Waterhouse
(holding the dog), Nicholas Waterhouse, Miss Sandbach, Miss Sandbach,
Miss Sandbach (No. 4) and Mr Sandbach

37 A bronze relief of Edwin Waterhouse by Joseph Kopf. The likeness was
originally sculpted in marble in Kopf's Rome studio in 1898. Edwin
Waterhouse subsequently had a bronze copy made which he presented to
the Institute of Chartered Accountants in England and Wales

36 *left* A late Victorian photograph of Frederick's Place, off Old Jewry, in the
City of London. Price, Waterhouse & Co. occupied No. 3, where they had
moved from No. 44 Gresham Street in 1899

38 Helen Caroline née Weber (1855-1941), Edwin Waterhouse's second wife

39 Alfred Waterhouse in later life

40 A group of visitors to 'Feldemore', *c.* 1898. Standing left to right: William
Waterhouse, Ruth Merriman, Miss Strode, Vicary Gibbs, Valentine
Waterhouse holding 'Laddie', Theresa Waterhouse, Martin Redmayne
holding 'Rob'; seated: Miss Frood, Edwin and Helen Waterhouse, Mrs
Richards and Miss L. Hewri; seated on the grass: Margaret Merriman and
E. Richardson

41 At 'Feldemore' *c.* 1898. Standing left to right: William Waterhouse, a lodge
visitor, Ellen Waterhouse, a lodge visitor, Mr Matthews (the organist),
Theresa Waterhouse; seated: May, Valentine Waterhouse with 'Laddie',
Helen and Edwin Waterhouse, Mrs Aikinson with 'Rob', and a lodge visitor

42 At 'Feldemore' *c.* 1898. Standing left to right: S.C.R.B., William Waterhouse,
    B.A., Theresa Waterhouse, Gertrude Valentine Waterhouse; seated
    May Waterhouse, R. Lawrence, Helen and Edwin Waterhouse,
    Sir Edward Lawrence

43 A group of family, friends and servants, in front of the semi-circular
    pergola, built at 'Feldemore' in 1902. In the centre are Nicholas Waterhouse
    and his fiancée, Audrey Lewin; Edwin Waterhouse stands on the extreme
    right, while the Revd. J. Forrest and Theresa are on the left. The
    photograph was taken on 15 August 1903, a week before the wedding of
    Nicholas and Audrey Waterhouse

44 Nicholas Waterhouse (1877-1964) and his bride Audrey Lewin, on their
    wedding day, 22 August 1903. They were married at Abinger Church by
    the Revd. J. Forrest

45 Edwin Waterhouse *c.* 1907 in his mid-sixties

46 Edwin, Theodore and Helen Waterhouse while staying at the Pump House Hotel in Llandrindod Wells in the spring of 1911. The photograph was taken by Miss Foxwell, governess to Theodore

a banking account kept in his sole name. The audit too may not have been as methodical as such an audit would be at the present time. My representative had gone through the accounts under my supervision, and they had been passed by me subject with production of a certificate from the bankers confirming the balance stated to be in their hands. A day or two's delay arose in this coming to hand; my clerk had passed to other work, when the certificate was brought to me personally with some reasonable excuse for the delay. It seemed in order. But it ultimately turned out to be false, concealing a heavy overdraft on the account in the secretary's name. The man had decamped. The matter caused me much distress and some sleepless nights. After much negotiation a compromise was effected with the bankers, whose clerk had evidently been outwitted by the thief and who took a considerable part of the loss upon themselves, and I continued to hold the confidence of Mr Hallett and his friends.

Another fraud came before me soon after. I had to draw up a balance sheet for some solicitor friends of ours at Haverfordwest. One of the partners had died and they wished to know how their respective capital amounts stood. I was to take the books, as posted up by their old cashier in whom they had the greatest confidence, as the basis of my account. My work was soon done and I returned home the day after my arrival. Not long after this, one of the partners appeared in Gresham Street with the sad news that the old cashier had bolted, having appropriated on its receipt much of the money that still appeared on the books as due from clients. He had represented that an aunt had died, and left him money which he had to invest. Indeed he made use of his employers' services in conveying property to himself purchased out of his misappropriations of their own monies.

At the close of the year I was busily engaged in an investigation of the affairs of the Great Western Railway Company of Canada so far as disclosed by the books in London, involving a visit to Canada by one of our principal clerks.

[Edwin Waterhouse mentions the death of his father, apparently caused by a heart attack after a fall while walking in his gardens at Whitcknights.]

CHAPTER VIII

1874–1877

In February 1874 I went to Dusseldorf to examine in conjunction with Thomas Whitwell into the affairs of a concern in which friends of ours, including Henry Bewley of Dublin, who came with us, were interested. As the place was on the way to Weimar, Georgie came with the party, bringing Mary with her . . .

On Sunday the 6th December 1874, our precious William was born at 13 Hyde Park Street.

In December, on one of my journeys north, I stayed for a Sunday with Dr & Mrs Merz, 12 Regent Terrace, Gateshead, thus getting to know a little of that very interesting and very able man, who had been for long among dear Georgie's friends. He had married Alice Richardson, J. Wigham Richardson's sister, and was greatly esteemed by his brother-in-law. He had asked me to audit the accounts of the Blaydon Chemical Company of which he was the Chairman, being a very great chemist, although perhaps his chief delight was in the study of philosophy and metaphysics. . . . Among other business appointments he was a director of the Tharsis Sulphur & Copper Company, a concern which claims to work the large mines of Tharsis, [and] which proved so remunerative in the days of Solomon. He [Dr Merz] of course visited the mines, which are in Spain, and was fully acquainted with the ancient as well as the modern workings.

There is a good story of his having sat up late one night with Wigham Richardson discussing the present methods of separating the sulphur from the copper ore. . . . Richardson, not being so keen a chemist as his brother-in-law, was a little wearied by the talk, and with his head full of analyses of ore and chemical formulae went off to bed. In the morning he described an interesting dream. He was in Piccadilly on a bright May afternoon when there was much coming and going. A magnificent carriage passed him going west, which everybody turned to look at. He saw at once that it must be the Queen of Sheba on her way to King Solomon at Buckingham Palace. He immediately went up to the carriage, which was moving at a royal walking pace; 'Oh, Queen, may I go with you? I do so want to ask Solomon a question.' The answer was a gracious one, 'Do get in Mr Richardson; I shall be delighted.' The Palace was reached and all the Queen's questions satisfactorily answered. 'Now, Mr Richardson what can I do for you?' The inquiry with regard to the Tharsis processes was put, and a ready answer given but it was so technical in its phraseology that Richardson could not digest its meaning and he awoke. But he was able in the morning to give enough of the answer to Dr Merz as to lead that gentleman to exclaim, with a delighted look 'of course, that would do it! I shall try it at once'. But the anticipated rise in the value of the Tharsis Company's shares did not at the moment come.

Business in the north took me away from home from 13th to 26th February [1875], and after two nights in London I was off again on the night of Sunday 1st March for three or four days in Paris to investigate the accounts of a banking house which was about to be absorbed by a London firm. I took with me Mr Lancaster Rose, then learning account keeping in our office, who was a very pleasant companion both on the journey and at my work.

The Easter of 1875 was spent with the children at Whiteknights and my holidays were occupied by the perusal of papers relating to the issue of loans by the agents of the Honduras and other foreign governments, the subject of a parliamentary enquiry brought about by the exertions of Sir Henry James. It was indeed high time that the public should be made aware of the methods adopted in such matters, and of the waste and plunder which found its way into the pockets of those who were supposed to be acting in the interests of the governments concerned. Sir Henry James's friend, Mr Snagge, a barrister of high repute, was assisting him in the matter and as someone was required to disclose, as a witness before the select committee of the House of Commons, the facts ascertained as to the issue of the bonds and the disposal of the proceeds; they, I think rather at the suggestion of my friend William Fowler, then one of the members for Cambridge, chose me for the purpose. The matter was intensely interesting. I had various and many interviews with Sir Henry James, who instructed me as to the line which my examination would take, and I was assisted in the preparation of the accounts I handed in by Reginald Riley, then in our office. I gave evidence before the Committee on the 12th April, and also on the 14th June. Sir Henry James wrote me afterwards a letter thanking me for the services I had rendered, and the manner in which I had given my evidence. I wondered if he recollected as well as I did his reference to my behaviour in the witness box on a previous occasion.

The facts made public were a nine-days wonder, and the disclosures were no doubt in themselves a lesson. But no further action was taken, and the parties mainly responsible were not called to account. Mr Bischoffsheim however left London, finding Paris a pleasanter place of residence . . .

[Reference to the Committee may be found in Sir Henry Drummond Wolf, *Rambling Recollections*, Macmillan (1908), Vol. II, p. 54.]

Entries in my business diaries remind me that I had to do with the audit of the Neufchatel Asphalte Company about this time. That company, founded a few years before, had very successfully worked the deposits of asphalte near Neufchatel under a concession expiring in twenty years. To increase its output and profits, it had just bought quite a number of subsidiary companies to trade in the article in various countries and localities. After the shares of these companies had gone to a considerable premium, the undertakings were swallowed by their parent with the view to avoid friction and economise working expenses, the price, given in shares of the original company, being put at a very high figure to cover the premium. The result was a most inflated capital account, all of which, it appeared to me had to be redeemed out of the profits within the term of the concession; and I pointed out in our certificate that, under the circumstances of the capital account, no balance was apparently available for dividend for the year under review. The question thus raised opened out a conflict between the non-cumulative preference shareholders, and the ordinary, and there were some stormy meetings and exciting polls, Mr John William Maclure being the leader of one party. The litigation which resulted, bearing on the question of the writing off of wasting assets, was one of intense interest and importance to the accountants' profession.

On the 10th June [1875] Georgie had a little musical 'at home'. . . . On the evening . . . I remember that the Liebeslieder of Brahms was very well sung, and gave great satisfaction. [The guests are listed] as indicating some of those persons whose friendship added so much to the happiness of our lives at the time: –

Mrs Robb . . . a widow lady, the sister of Mr Matthew Boulton of Great Tew, Oxfordshire . . . being a [grandchild] of Mr Boulton . . . the partner of James Watt.

Mr & Mrs Jenery Shee were musical neighbours in Bayswater; he being a barrister of some repute; as was also Mr W. Donaldson Rawlins. Mrs Wickham Flower, whose maiden name was Walton, was the wife of a solicitor of many interests . . .

Mr & Mrs Beavington Atkinson, an art critic of Quaker family . . .

Mr Charles Chadwyck Healey, the son of our friends at W . . . hurst, and his wife. He had chambers with Cozens-Hardy in New Square. His career at the bar was a distinguished one.

Mr Douglas was the husband of our old friend Rosie Burges, and came with his sister-in-law, Dora.

Mr & Mrs George Burges were the uncle and aunt of the 'Burgeses'.

Henry Lucas was an old college friend who married Miss Montefiore – and was a near neighbour – Arthur Lucas was his younger brother. They were members of a large Jewish family. Two other brothers were at University College – Horatio and Edward.

Sebastian Waterhouse was the eldest son of my uncle Daniel of Liverpool.

Professor Seely was by that time the admitted author of 'Ecce Homo'.

The Misses Goldsmid were sisters of Julian and two other Goldsmid brothers with whom we were at college.

Mr George Crosfield of Warrington, Lancashire, was a director of the London & North Western Railway, and a kind friend of mine there. He was a cousin of Mr Henry Crosfield, the auditor. His wife was a daughter of Henry Ashworth of the Oaks, Bolton, and was therefore a first cousin of my friend Alfred Ashworth.

John Francis Rolton, one of the 'Aristotle Club', and my brother Theodore's old friend . . .

Samuel Grubb was an old school fellow of mine at University College School; a Quaker by family and now a discount broker, Mrs William Bevan, my dear Aunt . . . [and] her sister Miss Mabel Read and her brother Tom.

Dr and Mrs Phillips were our kind doctor and his wife . . .

Mr and Miss Duffield were the son and daughter of a lady friend of Georgie's, who was an accomplished painter of flowers.

Mrs Phillips and her son and daughter were friends of Mr & Mrs Thöl, who had made their acquaintance in Weimar.

Mr & Mrs Fry.

Mr & Mrs Jarret Anderson ... the lady being the well known physician.

Dr and Mrs Julian Fox, whom we called cousins. Dr Fox was of a most charming personality, and was soon to attain eminence in his profession as one of the physicians to H.M. the Queen.

Mr Myles Fenton was the general manager of the Metropolitan Railway, and soon after occupied the same position on the South Eastern.

In June 1875 I was entrusted with the winding up of the affairs of a large mercantile and banking firm, some partners in which were personal friends of my own. The founder of the firm had died only some six months before, leaving it was supposed a considerable estate outside his business. This proved not nearly so large as was thought probable, but an impossible endeavour was made to separate the existing liabilities for which he was responsible from those which had arisen since his death, with a corresponding division of the assets into two portions, applicable respectively to the two classes of liabilities. The problem proved beyond my powers, and also puzzled the astute lawyers who represented the separate interests, and at last it was agreed to merge, as I had recommended, the supposed two estates into one. Even thus I found the matter a heavy piece of business. In the autumn I was asked to attend to another matter in connection with the labour question, being instructed, through Mr Samuel Morley and Mr Thomas Hughes, to examine the accounts of the National Agricultural Union in Leamington, which owed its existence to the exertions of Mr Joseph Arch.

I find a letter from my mother of the 10th August [1875] referring to the death of her cousin, John Pim, a somewhat eccentric old batchelor gentleman who lived with his aged sisters at Wandsworth. ... From him came my proprietary membership of the London Institution in Finsbury Square as I purchased his bronze medal from the estate.

On the 16th August [1875] Georgie and the three children accompanied me to Saltburn where they benefited from the sea air while I had business in the neighbourhood; also at Sheffield and Leamington. From the last place I got a peep at the Kenilworth ruins, and went to some business at the Dynevor Collieries at Neath.

In January 1876 I had an examination of the books of [the] colliery owners in South Wales at Cardiff, Newport and Aberdare, meeting accountant representatives of the men, for the purpose of a wages adjustment. This and work in the North of England kept me very busy and much away from home.

We went to Salisbury for Easter Sunday, and during Easter week had three or four days together in Paris, doing some business there with the assistance of Gurney Fowler of our office. The same business took me again to Paris in May.

In September [1876] I had to go to Berlin and Frankfort a.d. Oder on some business in connection with the waterworks at the latter place. Georgie came with me and from Berlin we went on to Jena.

Business in the early months of 1877 was much as before but the work in the North continued to increase. I find I was in Darlington for five days at the end of January, the Dales kindly making me welcome at West Lodge . . .

The affairs of Anthony Harris & Co., who suspended payment in Middlesbrough, took me away much to the north that month . . .

In April [1876], after being engaged in a very heavy arbitration for Lawes' Chemical Manure Company, which somewhat knocked me up, I was entrusted with an examination of the books of the Nottingham Lace Manufacturers by Mr Crompton and Mr Mundella. This and other work, chiefly in the North, kept me very busy during the spring.

We made one or two acquaintanceships among the persons living in the neighbourhood [of Dorking, Surrey], including Mr & Mrs Frank Walton . . . a schoolfellow of my cousin Crewdson Waterhouse, and an intimate friend of William De Morgan. On the last Sunday of this stay in Surrey . . . probably 18th July, Mr Walton showed us a piece of land at Felday, which he thought was in the market. I fell in love with it at first sight. . . . I wrote to my mother from Hyde Park Street on the 8th July: —

> I rather want Theo's advice about another piece of land. . . . It faces the South . . . and has a most lovely view of hills in the foreground and blue distance as far as Arundel beyond.

I went again to inspect the place on the 14th with Theodore . . . again on the 31st; and in August I had the pleasure of a day there with George Redmayne, who was himself moving into the country at

Alderley Edge from Manchester. Alfred also had a look at the place when he was staying a night with the Frys at Hopedene. . . . He was much pleased with the site, and advised me if I became the owner to cut down the oaks and give precedence to the beeches.

Dear Georgie was unable to visit the place again with me just then for on the 14th August Nicholas Edwin was born.

On the 13th September I went down to Manchester [from visiting Theodore at Upcroft] with Theodore (staying with Crewdson Waterhouse at Alderley Edge) to be present at an evening ceremony in connection with the opening of the new Town Hall. Alfred and Bessie, with Paul, also George and Kitty, were with us at the building early in the day, and Alfred showed us all over it. In the evening I was a little alarmed at the swaying of the tower when the bells were, for the first time, rung. But I was assured this was a sign of stability in the architecture. The movement was quite sufficient to make some persons feel sick.

I . . . made up my mind that I must have the little piece of land at Felday, and the contract was signed on the 4th October [1877].

[He had recorded in a letter to his mother that 'there are 64 acres, but the man wants £100 an acre, and will not I think divide it. It is close to Mr Street's, the architect, Miss Wedgwood's and several of our friends'.]

I went to the spot again repeatedly before the end of the year; on December 6th with George Redmayne, whom I desired to act for me as architect, and Mr Milner Senior, the landscape gardener.

A matter of business which occupied me much in June and July [1877] was the investigation into the affairs of the Artizans, Labourers & General Dwellings Company. This company was seeking to interest the public in an extension of its operations, when its methods were severely attacked, and a committee of a very influential character, consisting amongst others, of Mr Evelyn Ashley, Mr Thomas Brassey, Mr F. D. Mocatta, Mr Samuel Morley, Mr C. M. Palmer and Mr W. H. Stone, was appointed to enquire into all matters relating to its business. That committee appointed me its accountant, and I reported to them on the 19 July. During the investigation the manager and secretary, who bore the name of Mr Swindlehurst, resigned; and the Chairman, Dr Baxter Langley, placed his own seat and those of all the then members of the board at the disposal of the Committee. The Committee took steps to prevent Mr Swindlehurst leaving the country; his intentions to do so having come to my knowledge. In the result, it was discovered that both the Chairman and the Secretary had been intermediaries between the vendors of land and the company, appropriating large sums to the company's loss. Terms of imprisonment were meted out to both, and the Chairman did not again figure, as he had previously, in the political world.

CHAPTER IX

1878–1880

About half a mile to the south of the village [of Felday] Mr George Edmund Street R.A.,[40] the architect, had in 1872 bought some fields. He made the purchase with the intention of building a house there, and looked forward to spending much time with his wife. ... But Mrs Street died in 1874. Mr Street married again in 1876 but in eight weeks time was a second time widower, Mrs Street having contracted a malarial fever in Italy when on their wedding journey. The house, so far as Mr Street intended then to build it, was nearly finished in 1877. ... Having made his acquaintance through my brother Alfred, with whom he was on terms of sincere friendship, I wrote and asked him some particulars with regard to Felday as a place of residence ...

The year 1878 was full of business journeys as were its predecessors, and my frequent absences from home were matters of regret both to dear Georgie and myself. Early in the year I was engaged in an investigation of the accounts of the Lilleshall Company in Shropshire, Earl Granville, the Chairman, having instructed me in the matter. I was a little surprised during one of my visits to Felday to meet Lord Granville driving through the village, but he explained that he was on his way to his brother, the Hon. E. F. Leveson Gower, who had a country house just under the point of Holmbury Hill. The investigation and the report which followed it led to a long connection with the Lilleshall Company as auditor, and proved an introduction to Mr Leveson Gower, who was also a shareholder in the concern, and who proved for many years a most kind and courteous neighbour.

At Whitsuntide we went to Alderley to discuss plans with George Redmayne, who had kindly consented to be my architect.

In December 1878 I went for the first time to Messrs Hollins & Co. of Mearley, Nottinghamshire, on business, staying at The Vale House, then without its usual occupants, where I was most kindly received by Mr Ernest Hollins; and on the next day at Nottingham, where Mr Arthur Hollins showed me kind hospitality. This was the beginning of a business connection which was always a pleasure to me.

In the same month I received instructions in a sad matter affecting our kind doctor, Charles Phillips. He had some time before been shaken by the sudden drawing up of the engine of his train on the South Western Railway near Nine Elms. The extent of the injury was not apparent at the time, but by degrees severe damage to his nervous system was evidenced, and his condition became so painful that death would have been considered a release. His friends claimed compensation from the railway company on his behalf, and I was employed to ascertain the profits he had made in his profession. They were considerable – many eminent doctors gave evidence that he would not recover. The compensation claimed was therefore large. The jury gave him £4000. His advisors insisted on an application for a new trial, which took place the following year, when the damages were assessed at £16,000; perhaps the largest sum ever awarded as personal compensation for an accident, but far less than the loss of income he sustained. After this, he began gradually to regain his nervous and muscular power and before very long took up his practice again.

The building [of Edwin's house at Felday] was commenced early in the year [1879] and I found much to do in laying out the grounds, fencing the drive, and in the operations of the little farm.

In August we had two or three pleasant days with our friends the Crosfields at Warnley Abbey, which they had taken for a few months, and entertained their friends there. We met one or two colleagues of Mr Crosfield on the board of the L.N.W. Railway, and also John Bright, to whom as my father's son, I was known; and who charmed Georgie by his conversation on the education of children . . .

The year 1880 was spent, so far as it could be spared from business, mainly looking after the building operations at Felday, and in laying out the grounds. The farm house, as in 1879, was available for us, and many were the walks across the 'moor' and up the wood to see the progress of the work.

Many oak trees surrounded the house, most of which have been cut down. One stood just in front of the alfresco dining room, and somewhat shadowed it too much, but dear Georgie wished it to be retained. One day when I was looking after things, Mr Leveson Gower, who took an interest in the building, came around with his great friend Mr [W. E.] Gladstone. I put a question about cutting down this tree to the latter thinking I should certainly secure an ally. But he took dear Georgie's view of the matter, and for a while the tree remained.

During one of our visits to Berka, we met a Mrs Phillips, a widow with several sons and one daughter, who had been kind to Rosie in her illness. When she came to England, she resided at Epsom with her children; and as the boys grew up one went into my brother Alfred's office, another to Theodore's, and a third to mine, with the intention of taking up our several professions. But the result was that they all took to ranching in North America, and after that other pursuits.

Several of the large joint stock banks began to avail themselves about this time of the advantages afforded by the limited liability acts. On revising their constitution for this purpose they had to give consideration to be subject of audit, and were inclined to make use of the services of public accountants. I had the pleasure of being consulted by Mr Richard Blaney Wade, Chairman of the National Provincial Bank of England, a man of most singular qualities both as a gentleman and a man of business, with whom it was a great pleasure and advantage then to be brought into contact. He wished to know whether, if my appointment jointly with Mr Mackay, the chief representative of the firm of Robert Fletcher & Co., as one of the auditors of the bank, was acceptable to the shareholders, I should be willing to act. There was, of course, only one answer. About the same time I accepted a similar appointment in the London and Westminster Bank, jointly with Mr Turquand, my old master, then at the head of the firm of Turquand, Youngs & Co.

A letter to my brother Theodore on the 21st May [1880] gave him some account of what I was doing in business and refers to many other things [including] . . . Henry Eck, also known as 'Justus' [who] was one of the two sons of Georgie's half sister. He invested the little that came to him after his father's death in education at Oxford – and had taken up electricity in its various branches as his life's study and work. He was then in the employ of the telephone companies in London, their business being of great interest to my brother Theodore, who had formed the Edison Telephone Company, having taken up the then marvellous invitation of the young American scientist at the request of Colonel Gour and his representative in England, who had come to me in the first instance for assistance towards introducing the invention to the English public. But others were working in the same field of science as Edison, and an amalgamation of interests resulted. . . . The telephone invention was followed by Edison's filament electric lamp, with the bringing out of which in this country my brother had also much to do; and, oddly enough, very much the same results attended his efforts with regard to electric light as with regard to the telephone – an amalgamation of interests ultimately taking place with those who were developing a similar invention of Mr Swan of Newcastle.

The fraud at the offices of the Metropolitan Railway was indeed a grievous trouble to me. The man had manipulated the depositors' passbooks in every conceivable way, duplicating some, and stitching duplicate leaves into others with singular cleverness. There was great difficulty in ascertaining the full amount of his frauds. I wrote to Mr Crosfield, whom I considered the person most versed in railway auditing that I knew, and was to some extent comforted by the letter he kindly wrote to me. Sir Edward Watkin's energy in dealing with a matter of the kind, indeed with all he took in hand, was I think invigorating and helpful to me. But he did not exhibit the disinterested zeal and forgetfulness of self which distinguished such men as Richard Moon and R. B. Wade in their direction of the affairs of the concerns they had to do with, and I was always a little afraid of his account keeping – H. D. Pochin[41] was, I think, Deputy Chairman of the Metropolitan Railway at the time, a man with a great reputation for his scientific knowledge but without much sympathy, so I thought, in his nature. He usually wore even in the day time what one even then very rarely saw; large frills in an expansive shirt front. Watkin had the reputation of being a kind friend, and I always found him so myself, having, mainly on his introduction, to do with him on the Metropolitan, East London and South Eastern Railways.

[In September 1880 Edwin Waterhouse decided to call his new house 'Feldemore' because 'Mr Reginald Bray of Shere, the lord of the manor, who had died a few months before in 1879, had told me that the name or "Feldaymoor", had been the old name of the village of Felday'.]

My mother's health, which had for some time caused us much anxiety, seemed to be giving way in October. She was able to do little else than lie quietly in her bedroom, where the light was shaded so as to protect her eyes, which were often very painful. . . . She sunk peacefully away about 10 o'clock on Sunday the 7th [November], the funeral taking place on the 11th. My sister Maria and brother Theodore, the two home children, deeply felt my mother's death. Indeed I think they never got over the loss, especially dear Maria.

CHAPTER X

1880–1882

[In November 1880 Edwin spent his first night in their new home, 'Feldemore'.]

Some little distance beyond Joldwynds, just under the top point of Holmbury Hill, was the house of Mr E. F. Leveson Gower,[42] called 'Holmbury'. Our first introduction was one Sunday afternoon in 1878, soon after some trees had been cut down on the site we had chosen for our house, and he had strolled up with his little white dog to see what was going on. He had heard from his brother about my purchase, and asked me whether I thought Mr Waterhouse was going to cut down all the trees that interfered with the distant view. He proved a very kind neighbour and interested us and others by the company he entertained at Holmbury. He was a strong Liberal in politics, member for Bodmin, and from the circumstances of his birth and position, was in friendly touch with a very large number of distinguished men, politicians and others. Mr Gladstone[43] was one of his most intimate friends, and Holmbury was visited by him every year; and Mr Leveson Gower being an excellent host, his house was a pleasant resort for tired members of the Cabinet in Parliament for the weekend.

The first time I saw Mr Gladstone in the neighbourhood was an occasion, I think in 1878, when he got out of a train at Gomshall [station] at the same time as myself. It was very wet and his shoes, surmounted by white socks, looked anything but suitable for the muddy roads. He was evidently then somewhat of a stranger in the place, for old Baker, the stationmaster, did not know him. He asked Baker, as I passed the two, the best train from Gomshall to Tunbridge Wells, a question which, though the places appear to be on a direct line one to the other on the railway map, it would be hard even for a South Eastern Railway official to answer off hand. The reply evidently unsatisfactory, I asked Baker if he knew who had been speaking to him, and when he heard, he stroked his knees and doubled up with laughter at the thought. The rain was so heavy that I took the only conveyance at the station, a little wagonet for two . . . I soon overtook the great statesman and, finding out the direction in which he was going, begged him to allow me to give him a lift. He consented, remarking that the little carriage was more of a 'minibus' than an omnibus. After some pleasant conversation, the rain somewhat ceasing, he resumed his journey on foot.

As an illustration of Mr Gladstone's love of a perfectly quiet day on Holmbury Hill, Mr Street told us that on a lovely Sunday afternoon he made his way to a secluded dell among the fir trees on the common, known to [be] fancied to very few others beside himself, for a perfectly quiet half hour. But he found the exact spot occupied. Peeping over the gorse bushes he discovered that the man in possession, lying at length under a tree, was the 'grand old man'.

In the midst of all my blessings, I seem to have given way to some manner of depression at times [1881], for I find I wrote soon after from a L. & N.W.R. train, as I am going north on the 17th May: –

> I hope I shall get out of my glumness soon. I feel it is very wrong of me, but as it is not more than 14 hours growth I hope it will soon pass off . . .

In August I was on the point of taking up some work in America for some of my Darlington friends, and Georgie was prepared to go with me. Happily my friends went to the States themselves, and we were able to go to Dresden, where I was desirous on behalf of some friends of seeing Dr Frederick Siemens[44] with regards to his invention of toughened glass.

From Dresden we went to Karlsbad, as a place from which we might meet Dr and Mrs Siemens at his Ellenbogen Glass Works. Here I saw the manufacture of toughened glass, and was asked to test its quality by throwing a brick at an office window. It was the brick that suffered.

The close of the year [1881] was saddened by a great sorrow which fell on Holmbury St Mary – the death of our friend Mr Street. . . . He appeared to have a constitution of iron that could stand any work or worry, but it was evident that he had overtaxed his powers. His death was a great loss to the village, for he was greatly beloved and esteemed, and his strong personality made itself felt.

[Then occurred] the sudden death . . . of Mr Henry Crosfield of Liverpool, my friend and one of the auditors of the London & North Western Railway. He, poor man, had felt his mental powers failing him, and the future was more than he could face. . . . The question of the audit was a pressing one, as the half yearly accounts for the 31st

December were in course of preparation, and the meeting was to be held the following month. To prevent any break in the audit, an application was within a few days made to the Board of Trade for me to fill the vacant office pending the ascertainment of the wishes of the shareholders through the audit committee. I consequently acted as Mr Edward Lawrence's colleague in respect of the December accounts.

[Edwin Waterhouse refers to Joseph Chamberlain MP, later Colonial Secretary, who had attended University College School, 'preceding me by two or three years, his brother Arthur being my contemporary there'.]

My brother Theodore had at the same time [summer 1882] taken No. 4 Chester Place, close to us in Hyde Park Street, where he had made a home for Julian Crewdson when in London. Being near to Paddington, it was easy for him to visit Upcroft[45] from thence; and he frequently did, sometimes in the early morning, before going to his office in Lincoln's Inn.

The business records of the year [1881] were notable not only for my new position in relation to the London & North Western Railway audit, but for my appointment as auditor to the Clarendon Press and to ... Oxford University. I think the appointment came at the suggestion of the Revd Professor Bartholomew Price, who was the manager and secretary of the Press, and who may also have consulted Messrs Freshfields, the solicitors to the University, in the matter. Professor Price was a man of singular business ability, which he displayed in his conduct of the very large business of the Press, and other University matters. Rules under new statutes had been laid down as to the form and audit of the University accounts, and as to the contributions to be made by colleges for University purposes. An auditor of the University accounts, such as the Bodleian Library, the Galleries, the Museum &c., had to be appointed, and the choice of the Hebdominal Council fell upon me.

Early in November I spent a day in Newcastle going over the works of Sir W. G. Armstrong & Co. and looking into the accounts in the interests of two gentlemen, who had been, independently of each other, asked to join the board of a company which was about to take the place of the private firm. They had both, also independently, written to me for my advice in strict confidence, and I thought it best to bring them together, which I succeeded in doing; and received instructions to report to them jointly. Lord Armstrong received me by himself, and took me over the works, or such portion as I was able to visit, himself. I drafted my report in the train as I came back to London, and both the gentlemen accepted the suggestion which had been made to them. At the close of the year I became connected, at the instance of Mr E. L. Beckwith, with the New British Iron Company, near Birmingham, one of the oldest manufacturing companies in the Kingdom.

CHAPTER XI

THE DEATH OF OUR
FIRST BORN

The year of 1883 was a year of sorrow for us, for in it our precious Mary was taken from us to Heaven. The early months of the year were spent as usual in Hyde Park Street. I had many business trips, and often spent Saturday or Sunday at Feldemore. . . . On 7 March Mary fell ill with measles, and though she soon recovered from these, she was left an easy prey to pneumonia which followed. On the 19th she was alarmingly ill. Dr Murray and Dr Nelson Fox were unremitting in their care but the fever would not yield, and after a very hard fight for life, the dear child sank away on 10th April.

The building of the stables [at Holmbury St Mary], and of the shops opposite the entrance to take the place of the wretched hovels I had bought were matters of interest in 1883. The raising of funds for the building of the village Tavern and working men's club was another work, undertaken mainly at the instance of our good rector. . . . Mitchell, the builder of Thatford, was employed for the erection both of the shops and the Tavern.

My business continued much as before in its frequent visits to the north. In December fresh absences were occasioned by the investigation of the branches of the Yorkshire Union Bank. My North Western Railway work also took up much time, as I was desirous of preparing half-yearly books of statistics of the railway, even more comprehensive than those of which Mr Henry Crosfield had somewhat prided himself, and which he delighted should be of use to his friend the chairman. After the completion of the half-yearly statement of statistics, I handed it to Mr [Richard] Moon, and he kindly praised my endeavour to make myself conversant with the affairs of the railway, saying my work was 'worthy to stand alongside "Henry's"'. I took the opportunity to ask whether I had earnt a gold, in lieu of the leather, pass on the line, a mark of his favour which he had bestowed on Mr Crosfield – and he immediately granted me what I subsequently termed the 'order of the Moon', to wear on my watch chain. He generally after this took my

The Death of Our First Born

half-yearly volumes of account home with him, or on his holidays, to study, bringing back a number of queries to put to me for his further information.

[A letter from Edwin Waterhouse to his wife, from the Queen's Hotel, Leeds, 18 October 1883:]

> ... I came down by the Pullman train, and not having had time to eat anything in London, dined en route – a sumptuous dinner, all cooked on the train. The dining car was for the first time lighted by electric light, generated as we went along by batteries under the car – eight beautiful little incandescent lamps. The battery is a new discovery, the chemicals used being mainly a common substance, costing little or nothing so the engineer told me. If so, the problem of electric lighting is solved, and we shall have it at Feldemore within a year. The cost, I was told, of a lamp equal to six candles, was one penny for fourteen hours, i.e. 6d a night for a house using 20 lamps for 4 or 5 hours a night!

CHAPTER XII

1884–1886

On the 14 February, St Valentine's day, was born to us in Hyde Park Street another daughter. The day dictated her name, and Gertrude Valentine was christened during Easter week by Mr Shearme in Holmbury St Mary Church.

Feldemore appears to have been our headquarters after Easter. Little Valentine kept Georgie somewhat at home during the summer, but we had many visitors.

In April and May [1885], Georgie often joined me in London for social and musical pleasures, including the Richter concerts, then given in St James Hall, a very excellent concert hall between the Quadrant, Regent Street and Piccadilly. . . . On the 23 May we left London for a trip to Venice and the Tyrol, reaching Milan on the evening of the following day.

The later months of 1885 were spent much as usual between the two homes. . . . In August the swimming bath in the field below the hydraulic ram worked from the pond was completed, and became a great source of pleasure to the children, their cousins and friends. It was of oval form, 30 feet long, of brick sides and concrete bottom, 3 feet deep at one end and 6 feet at the other, with a little dressing shed; and the soil which was taken out formed a bank which when covered with evergreens gave the privacy required.

Henry Russell Greg, a director of the London and North Western Railway, spent a night at Feldemore in May [1885], a man of great sweetness of character. He remarked, I remember, on the beauty and healthiness of the trees and hedgerows as we drove up from Gomshall.

There was a good story told by Mrs Broadwood – Lucy B's mother – about the care taken by some of her friends not to allude in her company to the trade by which the family fortune had been made. On calling on an elderly lady one day, she noticed a little nervousness in her hostess, evidently arising from the fear she had that the conversation might turn on music or pianofortes. This increased until it was time to leave, when the good lady rang the bell, and when the servant appeared asked him to see 'whether Mrs Broadwood's piano was at the door'.

Business in 1885 had continued much as before. My visits to the North of England and absences each half year on London & North Western Railway work – although these latter were made so pleasant by my being able to stay with George & Kitty at Alderley Edge – were trying to dear Georgie. I had also additional work in the North in the audit of the accounts of the huge mills and warehouses of Horrockses, Miller & Co. at Preston and Manchester, a very interesting matter of business. The firms subsequently amalgamated with or absorbed some other businesses, under managements whereby Mr Frank Hollins, a brother of my friend Mr Ernest Hollins of Pleasley, and my cousin Crewdson Waterhouse, and Alfred Crewdson of Manchester became directors. I was also appointed arbitrator in a little dispute which had arisen between the East London and the London, Brighton & South Coast Railways. I was very hard worked, far more so than my partners, and when an opportunity arose for a review of the partnership arrangements with Mr Price, I asked for a larger share of the profits than he was to receive. To this he demurred, but the matter was arranged to my satisfaction by reference to others. Mr Holyland had retired from the firm so early as 1873, and Mr Price and I had taken in as junior partner Mr George Sneath, who had been a very competent assistant for many years.[46]

It may be worthwhile to record a singular fraud which was perpetrated soon after Mr Holyland left our firm. His attention had been given during the later years of his partnership very largely, if not almost exclusively, to the winding up of a large Indian Bank, and his work in connection with the liquidation had not quite come to an end in 1873. He accordingly continued the services of the clerk, a Mr Alabaster, who had been assisting him in the matter, and took some rooms at the top of the house, 44 Gresham Street (late No. 13), in which we had our offices, for the work which had still to be done. At first he attended frequently to see to things requiring his personal attention, after a while only once a week or at longer intervals. One morning a very well dressed young man called on Alabaster, and representing that he was Mr Holyland's nephew, said he brought a message from his uncle to the effect that, not being well, he intended to go to the seaside for a week or two and desired to know whether there was anything Alabaster wished to communicate: also that so soon as his uncle could give him his address at the seaside, he would write to him.

The youth then appeared to be about to leave, but turned around and said, 'Could you show me the way to the Bank of England? I have a cheque to cash for my uncle and do not know the City'. 'Oh, certainly,' was Alabaster's reply, 'I am going out for lunch and will show you the way.' When in the street the young man lit a cigar, and offered one to Alabaster, which was declined. They reached the door of the drawing office of the bank and Alabaster was about to take leave, when the young man exclaimed that he was afraid he could not go in with a lighted cigar, and asked Alabaster should further to oblige him by cashing his uncle's cheque at the counter, saying he had instructions to draw it 'short'. Alabaster saw no reason why he should decline, but was somewhat surprised to find the cheque was for £300, in lieu of the £10 or £20 cheque which he had been in the habit of encashing for his employer. But all seemed to him in order, as also to the cashier, who soon handed him three £100 notes. These he took out to the young man, who, after thanking him very politely, was lost to view somewhat more rapidly than would have been likely for an affectionate nephew of Mr Holyland's. The terrible fear then flashed upon Alabaster that he had been made use of as a tool in a mean and successful theft, and might be looked upon as an accomplice. He went back to the office thinking that the police might be already on his footsteps, and wrote to Mr Holyland at his home address, telling him there was nothing requiring his attention and referring to his nephew's call with whom he said he had gone to the bank and assisted in cashing Mr Holyland's cheque. Mr Holyland was naturally at the office first thing in the morning. The cheque was proved to be a very clever forgery and the bank had to bear the loss.

The good character which Alabaster bore prevented any suspicion attaching to him, but I do not think the culprit was ever found. The cunning employment of Alabaster, well known to the bank, to cash the cheque on his master's account proved him to have been adept in his work.

At the close of the year I had two interesting matters of business in Ireland. On the 1st November [1886] at the request of Sir James McGarel Hogg, then a director of the London & Westminster Bank, and better known as chairman of the Metropolitan Board of Works, I went to Magheramorne, about three miles from Larne in Antrim, to look into some matters of dispute between the worthy baronet as owner and worker of some very large limestone quarries, and the workmen in his employ. Sir James had come in for the beautiful property of Magheramorne ('The Hill of Beauty') from the McGarel family whose name he had added to his own, on the understanding that he would make it his chief home. But circumstances or inclination prevented this, and he apologised for not being able to receive me on the spot. He told me however that I should be well looked after by his housekeeper, and offered me the key of the wine cellar. But I thought that, having regard to the nature of my work, it would be well that I should not appear indebted to him even for hospitality, and I stayed at the Old Fleet Hotel, Larne, instead, a very comfortable place. Sir James's agent showed me the farms and something of the neighbourhood, and I was much struck with the beauty of the conifers and young plantations. Two or three days sufficed for my work. I received a deputation from the discontented workmen, and drew up a report with some suggestions which I believe met the circumstances.

Before the month of November was over, I again crossed to Larne by the pretty Stranraer route – this time in the interests of the Belfast and Northern Counties Railway. A question had arisen at the board as to whether some expenditure should be treated as capital or revenue outlay; and I was requested to examine into the accounts and report. I went down on the night of the 30th and was back in London on the 3rd December, staying the night of the 2nd at the house of the chairman of the company, the Rt Hon. John Young of Galgorm Castle, Ballymena, about one hour distant by rail from Belfast. I was much interested in the old house, adapted as a residence from one of the old castles of refuge of a more turbulent age.

Before I left I pointed out to Mr Stewart, the secretary, a weak point in the company's methods of account keeping; so also an apparent inaccuracy to which I thought the attention of the company's auditors ought to be called. Soon after my return, I learnt that the accountant and cashier had thought it fit to make themselves scarce, and that extensive frauds upon the company had been discovered. I was asked to suggest a new and reliable accountant and had the pleasure of recommending a Mr Bailey of the South Eastern [Railway] offices, a gentleman of whose abilities we had formed a high opinion. He became a very useful official of the Irish company. The accounts were carefully examined into and reported on by Price, Waterhouse & Co. and subsequently audited by them half yearly; and the business of the company under the chairmanship of Mr Young steadily improved. It was interesting to learn many years afterwards from Mr Pirrie of the firm of Harland & Wolff of Belfast that I owed a matter of business to him.[47] He was then on the board of the Belfast & Northern Counties Railway and was not satisfied that the accounts were being quite correctly dealt with. He accordingly asked his friend, Mr Ismay of the White Star Line of Steamers, and of the North Western board, who he thought would be a proper person to look into the matter. He gave my name, Mr Moon being also asked independently also named me, so the board of the Irish railway instructed their secretary to write to me.

CHAPTER XIII

1887–1888

I very frequently, while we were staying in London, went down myself to Feldemore for Saturday and Sunday. There was an early Sunday morning train from Victoria to Ockley, arriving soon after ten o'clock in time for me to reach the church for morning service. I went down by this train on Sunday, the 6th March [1887] with Mr Dahl, whom I have mentioned .... he being in this country, and I being desirous of showing him the scenery of Surrey. He met me at Victoria without having had any breakfast, and in order to save him from starving during our church service, I begged some biscuits from the station master at Ockley. We had a pleasant day together. He had come to this country in connection with the affairs of the North of Europe Land & Mining Company, of which Mr Price was liquidator. The estate had been largely denuded of trees since Mr Price's appointment [in 1873] but the creditors' claims had been paid out the proceeds, so that the estate was again the property of the shareholders solely. It was put up for sale at the auction mart in London but there was no bid. Two or three gentlemen however who knew something about it, including H. Evans Broad, the accountant, his friend, Richard B. Martin, the banker, and Jabez Balfour, all directors of the Assets Realization Company, considered that though the property should not be dealt with by their company, it might prove a pleasant investment for a few persons, having regard to the possibilities of sport and timber in the course of twenty years or more being again worth cutting. A small company was therefore formed, the North of Europe Land Co., and to it the property was sold with the sanction of the Court for, I think, £7000, something like 1⅓ pence per acre. I invested to the extent of two £500 shares in a capital of £14,000. The estate consisted of forest lands, mountains and lakes extending from near the Vessen Fjord to the frontier of Sweden, with the saw mills and the manager's house on the island of Halsoen on the Vessen Fjord, some outlying lands and a number of small farms. Mr Dahl had come to England in connection with this change in ownership. His services as manager were secured for the new company and he was instructed to build a Norwegian house or two for the accommodation of any one of us who liked to visit the estate. I think the first meeting of our new company, the statutory one, was held soon after at the Victoria Hotel, in the evening, when a little party was entertained at dinner by Mr Jabez Balfour, then member for Croydon, and a gentleman of high repute. His real character was disclosed not many months after, and he naturally ceased to be connected with us.

On the 19th May [1887] my partner, Mr Price, died, after an illness of some weeks.

Queen Victoria's jubilee day fell on the 21st June [1887]. There was much discussion as to whether we should go to London or not, and we resolved to join in the festivities in the village, which were to take place on the 20th and to share a quiet day on the 21st, when Willy was allowed an exeat from school, would be preferable, to the expected crush in London. Mr John Shearme [the first Rector of Holmbury] organized everything here to the satisfaction of everyone. A dinner and a tea on the village green, games on the common, and a procession through the pine woods at night to the top of Holmbury Hill, with a host of Chinese lanterns, were eminently successful, and the last extremely pretty.

In Holmbury was a huge and well laid bonfire, which with similar fires on all the hills of the southern Home Counties, was lit at a given signal. We could count 60 fires; ours was one of the best, and blazed magnificently. On the morrow I went early to London, and joined the North Western Directors at the parliamentary office of the company at the corner of Bridge Street and Parliament Street, Westminster. From here we saw the procession admirably as it came over Westminster Bridge and turned below us into Whitehall. I must say that I, in company with many others, had many misgivings about the day – the risks of accident to the beloved Queen, the possibilities of wrong doing, or of some fearful catastrophe, seemed great. But in every sense God seemed to shine on our dear Queen that day. The weather was perfect – the procession magnificently imperial, notwithstanding its simplicity in many ways.

After the completion of my half-year's work at Euston, we, i.e. Georgie and myself with Theresa, Willy and Nicholas, had a little excursion into Sussex in our wagonette from Tuesday the 23rd [of July 1887] to the following Saturday. Dear Georgie jotted down our doings in the little memorandum book . . . the only incident I remember which she failed to record related to a singular phenomenon which presented itself to most of us as we walked from the Dolphin Inn at Chichester to the station. The evening was very sultry, thunder clouds overhead, and the air charged with electricity. Suddenly there came into sight on the other side of the road to which we were walking, and about 20 feet above the ground, a transparent cloud of light in the shape of an irregular cigar, about 30 feet long. It moved slowly and disappeared as it had come. I was in front with Theresa and Nicholas, and we all saw it. Georgie was some way behind with Willy, and there was not time to draw their attention to the thing before it was gone. It appeared again however more faintly for a second or two.

Mr and Mrs Gamlen came to us for the Bank Holiday in August [1887] and the preceding Sunday; Mr Gamlen, as secretary to the curators of the University Chest in Oxford, had given me for some years past great assistance in my work on the audit. The accounts and administration of the University funds could not have been in abler hands, and my work was made still more pleasant by the kind hospitality shown me by Mr Gamlen and his wife during my visits to Oxford.

There was not very much work being done at Feldemore during the year. The kitchen garden wall was built to enclose what I thought was ample ground for our requirements; but as soon as this was up Hurst found reason for making almost as large a garden inside the wall, which had to be sheltered from the north by a plantation of trees. Plans for a lodge [were] also got out by kind George Redmayne.

In business the year [1887] was an eventful one. The death of Mr Price put me at the head of the firm. Joseph G. Fowler,[48] who had stayed with us after completing his articles, and had done good work for us, was made a partner; but we made no alteration in the style of 'Price, Waterhouse & Co.'.

The business was growing and an American connection was springing up which made it necessary for us to send Mr Sneath, or a principal clerk, frequently across the Atlantic. English capital was being attracted to American investments, and investigations on behalf of English investors were frequently required. This soon led to the establishment of the American office in New York, with men of proved abilities, L. D. Jones[49] and [W. J.] Caesar in charge. At the same time work was constantly turning up for us in Paris and various parts of the Continent.

In London for the latter part of the year, I was made very busy by an investigation into the accounts of the Woolwich Arsenal. I find that I wrote to dear Georgie on the 11th July: –

I am amused at being requested to call on Lord Randolph Churchill on Wednesday, as he thinks he can make use of me in his investigation into the accounts of the Woolwich Arsenal and other government departments. I thought some one of our class would be called in, and am pleased to find it is myself! He is chairman of the parliamentary committee.

The call took place, and on the following Saturday I met him at the house of Mr (afterwards Sir) Henry Burdett in Porchester Terrace, where a very informal but very interesting discussion took place as to the line of action to be adopted by the committee. I attended the committee, as one of the public, on one or two occasions, and may have been of assistance to the chairman in the hints I conveyed to him as to the nature of the questions on the accounts which he might put to the witnesses. I find that I wrote to Georgie on the 26th [July, 1887]: –

I stayed in London today to attend Lord Randolph's committee. At the end of their sitting today the committee determined to employ professional assistance if the House of Commons permit, and I fancy that Lord Randolph Churchill will ask the House tonight – so look in the papers tomorrow.

I much hoped that the Committee would ask for my appointment, but I learnt afterwards that Mr Stanhope, who was on the committee, had recognized me in the Committee Room as a somewhat too interested onlooker, and objected. The then president of the Institute of Chartered Accountants, Mr Frederick Whinney, was therefore nominated with power to associate someone else with him in the work.[50] Having regard to the circumstances, he chose me; and he and I were soon hard at work on the accounts of the various departments of the Woolwich factories.

It was in the year 1887 that I was elected a member of the Council of the Institute of Chartered Accountants in England and Wales. I had been a member of the Institute since 1880, while it was formed under Royal Charter; and before that, since 1870, a member of the London Institute of Accountants, a body which jointly with several provincial societies of our profession, enrolled themselves in one society under the charter granted to professional accountants in 1880. My old master William Turquand was the first President, R. P. Harding.,[51] the first vice-president; and when I joined the Council, Mr Whinney was president with Mr Deloitte, vice-[president]. Mr Price was on the Council from its commencement in 1880 until his death.

There is no doubt that the extended Institute was of great benefit to the profession. There were many matters of vital interest to us requiring discussion and settlement, and there had been before little or no common action amongst us for our general good. The larger firms were also to some extent jealous of one another – all were comparatively of recent growth, and we were seldom brought into touch with one another; and this feeling of jealousy arose simply from want of good fellowship which would naturally spring from better acquaintanceship. The work of the Institute in arranging for the examination and the admission of articled pupils, in dealing with undesirable members, and in discussing the many difficult matters of principle which turned up in the daily business of all of us, soon brought us together, and the Institute found itself doing excellent work. We met in 1887 in rooms which we hired in Copthall Buildings and the examination of our candidates took place in such rooms as we could obtain for the purpose: but we looked forward to the time when our funds might be sufficient for acquiring a house of our own. The work of the Council was shared by various committees. I was placed on the Examination Committee before I had long been a member of the executive, and found the selection of suitable questions, and the classification of the merits of the candidate's answers, a most responsible and difficult task.

The year 1888 passed away much as its predecessor, the chief event in the household being Nicholas joining Willy at St Davids, Reigate, in May. In business I was hard worked. The investigation with the Departments at Woolwich was concluded early in the year, the report of Mr Whinney and myself being signed in March. I was by no means satisfied with this piece of accountant's work, but it is possible that I should not have done better if I had a freer hand. The report did not make use of the opportunity, which the drawing up of it afforded, to point out how the very great cost of account keeping of the departments might be made productive of greater and more useful information than is the case. Great labour is taken to ascertain the exact cost of each article passed into the store of the Commissionary General, and of the disposal of such articles afterwards; but there is no general annual statement showing in money values to what services of the State the amount spent in materials and wages has ultimately to be allocated on the issue of these stores, or to what extent the reserves of finished material have been strengthened or drawn upon within the twelve months. Mr Whinney and I were both called upon again to give evidence before the Committee.

In January [1888] I was asked by Mr (afterwards Lord) Goschen, then Chancellor of the Exchequer, to assist the Treasury in carrying out some changes in the account keeping of the dock yards of the Admiralty. .... It brought me into touch with Mr Jackson (afterwards Lord Allerton),[52] then financial secretary to the Treasury, and Sir R. E. (afterwards Lord) Welby,[53] his assistant; also with Mr Richard Mills, then in the Treasury but afterwards Comptroller and Auditor General, and Mr Gordon Miller, accountant to the Admiralty under Sir Gerald Fitzgerald,[54] the Accountant General to the Navy. Of Mr Mills and Mr Miller I saw a great deal, and appreciated the kindliness of both, and was a witness of the great ability with which the latter discharged his heavy duties. The report which Mr Mills and I drew up was sent in May 1889 but in July 1888 we drew up a preliminary report, after receiving a letter from Mr W. H. Smith, who was then First Lord of the Treasury, somewhat pressing me in the matter. I find I wrote to Georgie from Hyde Park to Feldemore on the 5th July, expressing the interest I felt in this work: –

> I have come on early from work, for instead of being a long time at the Treasury settling Mr Mills's and my joint report on admiralty matters, I found the draft which I sent to Mills this morning practically approved by him with some verbal improvements, and we had nothing to jaw about. I thought how different it was with Whinney! I think that good man Miller enjoyed his visit to us. I am sure he is an earnest worker, and it will be a real pleasure to me if I can help sometimes; and in this matter it is really helping to put the nation's house in order! I hardly had time yesterday to tell you that I spent most of the morning with the secretary to the Admiralty (Mr Forwood) and the Comptroller of the Navy, and had an open time with both.

The affairs of the New British Iron Company now in liquidation occupied me much during the whole year. I had the assistance of Messrs Freshfields & Williams as my legal advisors.

On the morning of the 23rd [July, 1888] I write from Kendal: –

> The morning yesterday was threatening, but my clerk Wyon,[55] and I set out from Rigg's Hotel in the dog cart about 9.30, hoping for better weather. We got out at the beginning of the Fox Howe Road at Ambleside and walked straight away to Easedale, keeping to the West Side of Rydalwater, along Loughrigg Terrace, and down Mr Bulmer's drive. It poured with rain in Easedale and

all attempts to keep ourselves dry were given up, but we had a most pleasant walk. It was muggy and warm but the hills were all clear from cloud. We then made for the Nab, calling however at Hengh Folds to see if John [W. Richardson] was there; and found him with his sister Caroline, Dr Gregory White and Miss Dendy at early dinner. We went on to the Nab where kind Mary Elizabeth [Waterhouse], my cousin, took compassion on us, and found a man's Sunday clothes in duplication, into which we got and dined while our own were being dried.

At Kendal, when engaged in the audit of the Bank of Westmorland, I always paid a visit to the shop of an old furniture dealer named Wells, and generally found something on which to expend the amount of my audit fee. He generally had some good Chippendale or old cane seated chairs for 10/- each or so, and I laid up some of these in anticipation of the enlargement of Feldemore. The old grandfather clocks came from him . . .

Feldemore was becoming so favourite a home, that we began to think of the desirability of completing the house, which was now hardly large enough for our needs. The hall, drawing room and library, with good bedrooms over, were under consideration; and George Redmayne was revising his rough original ideas with regard to these in order to adapt them to our more clearly defined wants. The lodge has been spoken of as in course of being built. It had been planned to afford, in addition to the quarters of the gate keepers, accommodation for two or three persons, who might be in need of a few days holiday, and not have the means to obtain healthy and quiet quarters. Some of the women attending the Working Women's College, with which dear Georgie was, with her friends Miss Martin and Mrs Lionel Lucas, connected, saved up a little money for an annual holiday, but found no economical or satisfactory way of spending it. The quarters and the lodge were to afford these or others equally without means, refreshing rest for a fortnight or so, at little, or no cost to themselves.

CHAPTER XIV

1889–[1891]

The year 1889 saw the beginning of the work of the additions to Feldemore. Tenders were asked for from several builders, and Mr John Chappell of London, a builder of some reputation, was selected. He was then building a huge house for Colonel North, the successful speculator and financier, at Eltham in Kent. The west side of our house and the front door were after a while necessarily closed to us, and consequently during this and the succeeding year we were not able to solicit visits from our friends as fully as we should have liked.

A trip to see our estate in Norway, which I had been planning for 1888, but which we were then unable owing to my business engagements to carry out, was now arranged for June [1889]. . . . Landing at Bergen, we visited Voss-wought and Eids, then by Bergen and Molde, where we stayed two nights, to Halsven, Swenningdal and Feldbeckmo on our estate. Here we all greatly enjoyed ourselves.

The year [1889] was a very full one so far as business was concerned, audits springing up among the private banks. These concerns were beginning to find themselves at a disadvantage as compared with the joint stock undertakings that prided themselves on the stability exhibited by their published balance sheets; and were considering the propriety of themselves circulating statements of their affairs among their customers. Several private banks, therefore, asked that balance sheets should at any rate be prepared, leaving the publication of the same to be considered afterwards. Our visits for this purpose had to be conducted somewhat in secret, for the investigation of a bank's affairs by a public accountant might give rise to an impression totally at variance with the fact. Our work was therefore done occasionally after office hours. I find I wrote to Georgie on the 30th July on my way back from a country bank: –

> I wrote [to] you yesterday from the train on my way down to London. It was queer to see the reception given to me and my

clerk by the partners in the bank. They had never called in auditors before, and we first had a very solemn tea at the home of one of them – and then devoted the evening to the books at the bank. We got to be very good companions by 12.30 when our work was done.

Messrs Berwick & Co. of the Old Bank, Worcester, were the first as a private bank to publish their balance sheet. I spent a day or two with them in September, staying the night with Sir Edmund Lechmere at his house, 'The Rhydd', on the Severn, near Malvern; their future accounts were all signed by my firm. Almost all other private banks fell into line as to the publication of their accounts within two or three years.

Some other interesting work given me was in assisting the Lancashire County Council in the work of allocating receipts and expenditure between the boroughs and urban districts of the county under the new Local Government Act. The matter came before Lord Derby, as umpire in the following year.

On the 14th December [1889] I find the name of Matthew Gage in our visitor's book. I had been introduced to Mr Gage in July when he had come over from Riverside,[56] a year or two before – and who he thought would assist him in raising money for the irrigation of land and the cultivation of oranges at that place. Wilson [Crewdson] introduced him to his uncle, Theodore, who though somewhat indisposed to assist Mr Gage at first, was won over by his persuasive powers to take up his project. Some confirmation of the propriety of Mr Gage's calculations and proposals was obtained by my partner, Mr Sneath, during a visit to America in the autumn; and having obtained promises of sufficient financial support, my brother made arrangements to go out to California with Wilson Crewdson and judge matters for himself. He accordingly sailed with Wilson and Mr Gage on the 21st December.

The progress in the building of the extension at Feldemore was not so rapid as we had hoped. A difficulty arose in getting the bricks specified, and after some delay others were substituted. But I was beginning to learn that in building, estimates neither of time nor cost could be closely depended on; and though I fear I showed my annoyance repeatedly at delays and extra expenditure, this work was of so much interest to me that I was not much affected. I think the roof was on before the winter was far advanced.

When we came back to London after Christmas, influenza went

through the house, and left me with slight congestion of the lung which prevented my going to business until 13 January [1890].

I find a letter from Mr Kendel about this date referring to my candidature for membership of the Garrick Club. I also find letters from Mr Fletcher, ... my kind friend Mr Snagge, then a county court judge, our friend Colonel Brackenbury, and Arthur Cecil referring to my candidature. I forget who proposed and seconded me; but think Mr Peter Williams of Freshfields firm, was one of the two. It was interesting on my admission by the committee to see what members had kindly backed their recommendation by signing their names on the leaf of the Candidates Book set apart for the purpose.

The only other club of which I was and am a member is the City of London Club in Old Broad Street, which I joined I think in 1867, being kindly nominated by George Grenfell Glyn, afterwards Lord Wolverton. I appreciated the benefit of the change of scene for half an hour in the middle of the day when able to go there for lunch. The men I met there, generally sitting at the same table as myself, were a very pleasant set: E. L. Beckwith, Sir Samuel Canning;[57] F. F. Back, a great gardener, who lived in the house, Sir Richard Moon used to live at Harrow; Francis Ince, Henry Samuel, S. S. Josephs and Charles Linds, all old University College School fellows; and J. H. Pember, Cecil Boyle's partner, were amongst those I used to sit by most frequently, chiefly in the earlier years of my membership. Our introduction to Morton Latham was through the City of London Club.

I find in my business diary under the date 19th June [1890] an entry after recording an afternoon's work at Euston, 'To Brasted'. This referred to an outing in response to an invitation by Mr William Topping that his colleagues on the board [of the L.N.W.R.], and certain of the officers, including the auditors, should dine with him at his house, Brasted Park, near Sevenoaks. The long summer evening, the beauty of the house and grounds, once the residence of Louis Napoleon, and the kindness of the host made the evening a very pleasant one. The journey also to Sevenoaks through from Euston over a variety of junction lines to the west of London was instructive. The full board meetings at Euston were held monthly, the country members generally staying two or three nights at Euston Hotel and making the Thursday evening of the board week the occasion for a dinner open to any member of the board who liked to put his name down, and to any friend he liked to bring. The auditors were kindly included in the arrangement. In the summer the dinner, instead of being at the Hotel was sometimes arranged for some country place – such as Richmond and Maidenhead; and occasionally invitations, such as Mr Topping's, were received, which it was a pleasure to accept. I often went to the Euston dinners ... Sir Richard Moon was very seldom present, preferring a quiet dinner with Lady Moon; but on nearly every occasion men distinguished in various walks of life were present as guests. About twenty or more in number were generally at table. Lord Rathbone was perhaps the best story teller, and when he brought with him, as he often did, his old friend and college companion, his honour Judge Snagge, the laughter was almost continuous.

Home [summer of 1890], with all the interests of the extension to the house, now nearing completion, seemed all that was wanted for the holidays. There was much doing also in the way of boys' cricket, and Willy was in request for local teams with the Du Boulays, Kensleys, Powells and others, at Cranleigh (where Sir Richard Webster, now (1890) Attorney General, had built his home some three or four years back, and was a great supporter of the game), Wotton, Ockley and Bramley. .... I found much to do in arranging the details for the new building, fireplaces, tiles &c, and the groundwork around the house. I had H. E. Milner, the landscape gardener, son of the gentleman who had advised me in 1878, down for one night in August. It was late when he arrived, but there was a glorious moon, and he soon made up his mind how to advise me, viz: to have a large rectangular space in front of the house, corresponding with the good elevation which George [Redmayne] had designed; the entrance to it from the drive and the exit from it to the stables balancing each other on their respective sides.

The year that had closed [1890] had been an important and very busy one so far as my work was concerned. The publication of the balance sheets of private banks was followed by a series of amalgamations between them and the large joint stock banks competing with them; and there was scope for services in arranging the terms of amalgamation. Others of the joint stock banks came to us for their audit – Lloyds Bank, then a Birmingham institution, of which my old friend, Howard Lloyd,[58] was general manager, made use of our services, Stuckeys also came to us, and I had a run down to the head office at Langport on the 7th May to spend a night with Mr Stuckey and arrange details.

Towards the end of the year, I had a most interesting piece of work arranging the terms of amalgamation of Prescott, Cave & Co. of Threadneedle Street, my cousin's firm of Dimsdale, Fowler, Barnard & Co. of Cornhill, Messrs Miles, Cave, Baillie & Co. of Bristol and Messrs

Tugwell, Brimer & Co. of Bath. I had to report upon the profit earning power of each business, and this without creating any suspicion as to what my visits to the banks were for. At Bristol, where it was thought I might be recognized by old friends, though most courteously entertained by the partners, I was put for my work in a 'first floor back', and the blind drawn down at midday. I spent a pleasant night at the house of Mr Fenton Miles on the further side of Durdham Down.

The [London &] North Western Railway work, in the doing of which I was glad to feel I had the confidence of the chairman, continued to take much time. But I grieved to think, and to be told, that Sir Richard Moon's advancing years would lead him to give up control of the company. He had made up his mind to retire at the meeting held in February 1891. I [received] two letters, from him, referring to the use which my half-yearly books of account were to him.

A committee had been formed under the chairmanship of the Hon. St John Brodrick,[59] then member of the Guildford division of Surrey, and Financial Secretary to the War Office, to consider the appropriation of stores and store houses as between the Army and Navy; and I was asked to take part in their deliberations. We had some interesting evidence submitted to us, and then in the course of the year visited, in company with the various officials, the dockyards and stores at Woolwich, Portsmouth, Plymouth, Chatham and Deptford. The work was of considerable importance and I was interested in the decisions arrived at. These seemed to give satisfaction to those most interested.

Another matter of business was the amalgamation of hotels under the Gordon Hotels Company Limited. Gordon was a man of great commercial ability, and impressed me very favourably. He had acquired, partly for his private residence, and partly for re-sale, the magnificent estate known as Bentley Priory, near Harrow. He gave some of those connected with the formation of his company a dinner there in July. I find I wrote to Georgie the day after: –

> I had a pleasant trip to Bentley, finding Alfred also a guest. It is a most gorgeous place, but one feels a regret that the old home of a noble family (Duke of Abercorn), and the residence of Queen Adelaide, should have fallen into the hands of a hotel proprietor, however much one may like and esteem the man. Alfred and I were close to each other at dinner, being divided only by Mr Burnand (*Punch*).

We did not get many jokes out of our neighbour. I remember his saying that he felt like a bridge between two Waterhouses. Perhaps he felt his situation a little damping to his spirits.

In the same month [December] on the 18th I had an interesting call by appointment from the old Duke of Bedford[60] who desired the services of an accountant in the audit of his country estate accounts. At his request I looked into the account keeping of his own estate office, and the methods of check already adopted; and I wrote [to] him that the existing methods seemed so good that I was doubtful whether any further supervision by me of accounts so detailed and voluminous would justify the payment of the fee which I should be obliged to charge. He replied that it was for him to judge that and I was instructed to proceed with the work. He was a most kind and liberal landlord, but most particular about the accounts, liking to have a balance sheet for the year ready for his inspection within a day or two of its close.

Before I pass on to relate our life in our enlarged house, it may be fitting to record a few things about its building. The spaces which George Redmayne had left for mottoes in the hall, drawing room and library gave me great concern. I wrote to John W. Richardson for advice, and he, ever ready in such a matter, immediately proposed one of his own coining: –

> 'At focus sic cavitas' (As the hearth so may love glow). This seemed most appropriate for the hall. . . . For the drawing room I had seen, when going over Mansfield College, just built at Oxford, a line which I was told was from Seneca and I thought would serve admirably – 'Nulli boni sine socio jucunda possessio est', which I translated to my own satisfaction: 'of no good thing is possession pleasant without a companion', and considered it might be held to refer to the enjoyment of music and other nice things in the drawing room in the company of ladies and others.

CHAPTER XV

[1891]

Theodore and Maria, braving a terrible London fog, came down with me to Feldemore on the 2nd January 1891. My brother was weak and required some nursing. He was much interested in the new rooms – the library pleased him much, as also the organ which Georgie was able to play sufficiently well to give us all great pleasure.

In the middle of March [1891] Georgie and I found ourselves able to set out for a real holiday in Italy, taking Theresa with us, who had an invitation to stay for a while with the Kopfs.

After our return from Rome Georgie seems to have felt somewhat burdened with the thought of social and other duties which she feared she was not fulfilling, and with all that had to be done for a new house &c. I was also very much away from home on business [1891], and she felt Theresa's absence much. She writes in her diary, Sunday 19th April, that she could not conceal the oppression under which she laboured when Sir Thomas and Lady Farrer were calling, and says: –

> So I talked with Lady Farrer about it, and had such a nice, helpful time. Two things she said to help me much. One, that we must not faint even though there may come moments and longer when one has, as it were, to go underwater – another, not to quarrel with oneself.

On the 15th May, dear Theodore came down to Feldemore to stay over Whitsuntide. His asthma was very trying. He had difficulty in breathing and was prevented from taking exercise.

On the 22nd May our cousin Sir Robert Nicholas Fowler died after a few days illness. . . . I had seen Robert recently upon the amalgamation which took place of his firm with that of Prescott, Grote & Co., but he left the arrangements much to his partners. He was a man whom all liked and many loved. He had found time to visit us at Feldemore in 1885, bringing two of his many (ten) daughters, who formed a charming home circle.

My dear brother Theodore's condition had been so critical that, on the 14th October [1891], I went down to Bournemouth, whither he had been taken from Yattenden, to see him; and found him seriously ill. . . . We had a telegram on the 17th [November] to the effect that the end appeared very near. We came up to London immediately [from Nottinghamshire], and I pressed on to Bournemouth. The last train to that place had left, but I followed the mail bags and got out with them at a little place on the main line not far from Poole – I secured a precarious seat on the rounded top of the mail cart, which after a long drive through Poole took me into Bournemouth about 4 a.m. I found my dear brother had slightly rallied, and he gave me a welcome. His strength was however passing away, and he quietly and unexpectedly sank on the morning of the 30th November.

My brother's death was a great loss to us all. . . . For myself, I shall perhaps never know how much I owe to his affection and example during the ten years or more that we lived together before my marriage; and to his constant interest in me, and all that belonged to me, since. His love for our children was very great, as was their love for him. The kind advice which he gave me in business affairs to the end was of inestimable value to me, and as I looked to the future I hardly knew how I should get on without him.

Mr John Belcher,[61] architect, and now an R.A., was engaged in 1891 upon the buildings of the new Chartered Accountants Institute in Moorgate Place, for which he has competed in a limited competition, my brother Alfred being one of the judges. His design was highly approved, and as I was on the building committee of our council, I was much interested in the work, and was glad to find the architect not only excellent in his profession, but very pleasant to have anything to do with.

In business the year [1891] was a full one; country bank audits and amalgamations coming thickly on the top of other work, and necessitating many runs into the country. I find my business journeys were as follows: – January 16–17 Bonsile & Co., Worcester staying with Mr G. E. Martin at Ham House, Upton on Severn; 18–22 to York, Darlington, Alderley and Crewe; February 24, Oxford; March 2–3 to Southport about the West Lancashire Railway; 4th to Oxford; 27–28 to Ipswich, Ransome Sims & Co; April 25–29 to Preston re Lancashire County Council; May 4–5 to Norwich about Gurney's Bank, staying with S. G. Buxton at Catton; 6–7 to Nottingham and Pleasley; 20–21 to Winchester to Deane & Co., the bankers; June 10–12, to Norwich and via Peterborough to Newcastle to Hodgkin & Co.'s bank; July 8–9 to

Saffron Walden, Gibson & Co.'s bank; 16–17, to Bristol and Bath, Oxscott & Co.'s branches; 20–24 to Liverpool, Alderley Edge, Crewe &c. and Kendal, staying with J. Swainson at Stone Cross, and to Newcastle; 30–31 to Leighton, Bassett, Son & Hains staying with Theodore Hains; August 5 to Huntingdon, Veasey Bisborough & Co.; 11–12 to Darlington, staying with D. Dale; 24 to Lewes, Old Bank; 26–27 to Birmingham, Lloyds Bank, staying with Howard Lloyd at Cannon Hill; October 8th to Bedford, Bernard & Co.; 23 to Lewes (Old Bank); November 7 to Lewes; 16th to Mansfield, Hollins & Co.; December 10–11 to Norwich, Caley & Co. I am afraid these constant absences from home cannot have been pleasant to dear Georgie, but she never complained about them. The change was good for me, and new work was always pleasant. I could also sleep well in the trains.

At Euston the year was marked by the retirement of Sir Richard Moon, and the election of Lord Stalbridge as his successor in the chair of the North Western Railway. The meeting in February at which he retired was the occasion of a very eloquent little speech from Mr David Plunkett (whom I have previously referred to by his later and better known name Lord Rathmore) expressing the admiration of himself and his colleagues for Sir Richard Moon. Mr W. H. Smith, then First Lord of the Treasury, proposed a vote of thanks to him for his great services to the railway. I [retained] a copy of the proceedings of the meeting . . . in which I see the chairman was kind enough to refer publicly to my work for him. . . . The new chairman had a big lesson to learn when he took office, but his great knowledge of men and affairs generally, his universal courtesy and good humour, combined with his high family connections; soon led him to acquire the friendship and support of all around him. He did not however delight in my books of account in the same way as his predecessor, not having been brought up to love figures. He professed, however, to be a willing pupil.

When in Rome in March, I was very much pleased to receive the amended holograph letter from the first Lord of the Admiralty[62] . . . as in [the report] I tried again to bring before the notice of the Admiralty what had appeared to me a defect, or at any rate an opportunity lost, in the account keeping of the department: –

Admiralty, White Hall
March 16th 1891

Dear Sir,

The very laborious and useful work you have undertaken on more than one subject connected with naval matters, and the great administrative good that has ensued from your recommendations has come so prominently under my notice that you must allow me in the name of the naval service to thank you for what you have done. The details of dockyard and ordnance administration are so technical and self contained that few outsiders of ability and experience care to master them, or make practical suggestions for their improvement. Your labours and the authority your name carries have been most useful to the Admiralty and, interested as I am in trying to put naval organisation on a sound and self-working basis, I feel it is only due to you to say that changes for which the Board of Admiralty may publicly be credited, are largely due to your individual work.

Believe me to be yours truly,
George Hamilton.

Edwin Waterhouse, Esq.

My reply was as follows: –

Rome 22nd March 1891

My Lord,

I have to acknowledge your most kind letter of the 16th which has been forwarded to me. It has given me much pleasure to have taken part in planning some of the recent re-arrangements at the Admiralty, involving changes the benefit of which will I believe soon be apparent. But I think you have attributed too large a share in any results that may have been already attained to my individual efforts and recommendations. Mr Forwood and his co-adjudicators quickly appreciated how the desired ends might be obtained and the heads of most departments rapidly took up the suggestions made. It will be upon them I think that credit for any benefits that may be brought about should chiefly rest, for these cannot result without very labourious detailed work; carried out, for a while at any rate, in the face of constant difficulty. If I can be of any further service I shall be very glad.

Perhaps I may state what struck me most in a review of the account keeping of the Ordnance Store Departments. This was that all the labour bestowed on keeping an account of the *cost* of stores, whether made in the 'factories' or purchased, was thrown away so soon as these stores passed, as practically all did, into the hands of the Commissary General of Ordnance, so that all connection between *money voted* for stores, and the money value of *stores issued* to the Army and Navy was lost, as well as the possibility of representing in the only intelligible summary form, viz. – that of £.s.d., how the stores account from time to time stood. The vast number of different articles puts difficulties in the way of their account keeping, but having already the amounts of individual articles, and the initial costs, the entering of money values, can only be a question of clerical staff, and that not a heavy one.

The recent changes in Naval Store Department may perhaps make it possible for this defect being remedied so far as naval stores are concerned; and when you have set the example the War Office might follow suit.

Again thanking you for so kindly referring to any assistance I may have been able to give in this interesting and most important work.

I am, my Lord, very faithfully yours,
Edwin Waterhouse

The Right Hon. Lord George Hamilton

CHAPTER XVI

1892–1893

The London life went on much as usual until Easter when the boys coming from school on 12th April, the move was made to Feldemore on the 13th, and the Haas came to spend Easter with us.

The building of the Institute of Chartered Accountants on the site secured for it in Moorgate Place was now being pushed on with, the foundation stone having been laid during the presidency of Mr J. J. Saffery. Mr Welton was our president for 1891–92 and at the expiration of his year of office, my fellows on the Council did me the honour of electing me, without any previous training as vice-president for the post. The appointment was likely to throw more than usual responsibility on its holder, as, during the year of office our new building would have to be inaugurated, and it was naturally the desire of the Institute that the occasion should be made use of to bring our profession a little before the public. I saw no reason however to refuse the honour paid me, and relying on the help of many kind colleagues, more especially that of my friend J. G. Griffiths, of the firm of Deloitte & Co., who was appointed vice-president, I accepted the post. Mr Griffiths was an older member of the Council than myself and our positions should have been reversed but he made some excuse for preferring it otherwise. Much had of course to be done in the arrangements of the new dwelling place of the Institute and some of the decorations were matters of much interest.

A magnificent frieze around the building representing industries and arts was being carved from designs of Hamo Thornycroft; while Mr Bates, also an R.A., was made responsible for [the] other stone adornments of the building, lower and more conspicuous to the eye than Thornycroft's frieze, in which he [Bates] was particularly successful and which have given me pleasure to look at ever since. As Thornycroft was a friend of my brother Alfred's, he was not a stranger to Georgie and myself, having dined perhaps on more than one occasion with us at Hyde Park Street. I was an intense admirer of his beautiful figure of Diana, executed, possibly at Alfred's suggestion, for the Duke of Westminster and placed in Eaton Hall. There is no duplicate of it, nor cast, so far as I am aware; but he gave a photograph of it to Georgie which we greatly prized.

My office as president relieved me of the duty of being an active member of the Examination Committee of the Institute, the work entailed by which was more than a man, otherwise very busy, could easily get through. The last examination in which I took part as examiner involved the careful study and placing of seventy four sets of answers, a most difficult task, especially in respect of those which were not clearly above or below the qualifying standard. Perhaps a still more difficult matter for me was the thinking out the questions to be put. My old school fellow at University College, Mr G. W. Knox, was for many years chairman of this committee, and I feel the Institute owes him a deep debt of gratitude for all the hard work he gave the matter. On Saturday 30 July [1892] I invited the London members of the Council for the afternoon and early dinner at Feldemore. Some twelve came and we had a pleasant afternoon though I fear many of them felt the loss of time involved in coming to and fro.

Our friend William Lidderdale of the London house of Rathbone & Co., who was governor of the Bank of England in 1890,[63] when the house of Baring was in such difficulties, and was instrumental in averting a very serious financial crisis at that time, was an intimate friend of his colleague at the Bank, Mr Henry Hacks Gibbs of Aldenham. The young ladies, his daughters, had described to Mr Gibbs, the beauty of our orfes fish, and suggested that they would adorn some ponds he had been making in the wonderful gardens he had laid out at Aldenham. So this led to an interchange of compliments, our gardener, Crump, taking down a canful of fish, and returning with an assortment of cretons which completely stocked our little store. Then Mr Gibbs wished us to come to see the ponds and a kind invitation came that we should bring Theresa and spend a Sunday at Aldenham with our mutual friends Mr and Mrs Lidderdale and their daughter, May.

In the autumn of 1892 I was asked to assist in an investigation into the manner in which the Salvation Army had expended the funds raised for 'Social Work', in response to the appeal made in the book, *In darkest England and the Way Out*. It was thought I could best render help as a member of the committee which was composed of Sir Henry James (afterwards Lord James of Hereford), Lord Onslow, Mr Walter Lang, Mr Sydney Buxton, with Mr C. E. Hobhouse as secretary. The examination of the accounts fell to my share of work, and on these I reported to the committee. I certainly was not impressed with the success of the Army's work at their farm at Hadleigh, nor were my sympathies largely evoked with regard to the general manner in which the huge sums of money entrusted to the Army were dealt with. Our investigation covered only the social work however. But the description given by Mrs Bramwell Booth as to her work in the 'slums' of London was deeply interesting and to me touching. Sir Henry James and I were by chance the only two members of the committee present when she narrated some of her experiences, and from what Sir Henry said afterwards I found that he too recognized how engrossing her work must be to her, and that only strength from the unseen could enable her or any one to get through it.

Amongst the visitors to Feldemore during 1892, which have not been already mentioned were ... in November Mr and Mrs Frederick Seebohm of Hitchin and my friend I. J. Merz of Newcastle Seebohm had been a friend of my brother Theodore, who valued his friendship highly for his literary powers and tastes, his interesting conversation and the kind affection shown him. I had been brought into contact with him in connection with the audit of his bank, Sharples & Co., and enjoyed my business visits to the Hermitage, Hitchin. ...

We [Edwin and Georgie] returned to London [after Christmas at Feldemore] on the 18th January [1893], when London work and engagements began again, the fortnightly concerts at Dannreuthers in Orme Square being amongst our pleasures. ...

On the 18th [February] I went to the Hague with Theresa, who had been invited to stay some time with her friend Miss Marie Hubrecht. Though very busy with audits I managed to get a day at the Hague and one in Amsterdam, where Mr Hubrecht, a privy councillor, procured us admission to the wonderful picture gallery on a day when it was closed to the public.

On the 15th April [1893] our neighbour Mr Leveson Gower stayed a night with us, meeting Mr and Mrs E. J. Halsey, whose son Lawrence had in 1890 come into our office as a pupil.

The arrangements for the opening of our Institute building were occupying our minds much at that time. As president I had to address the annual meeting held for the first time in our own Examination Hall, and to preside at a dinner to which I and others invited many of our friends; the Lord Chancellor, who happily was my old college friend, Farrer Herschell, being at my invitation our principal guest. In all these arrangements I was greatly helped by my vice president, J. G. Griffiths. As the hall of the new Institute was not large enough for the 260 persons or more whom we wished to accommodate we secured the beautiful hall of the Merchant Taylor's Company for the dinner. I was in much fear about my address and the speeches expected from me in the evening at the dinner. The address was written and in type before its delivery, which was a great help, and my little speeches were so far as they could be committed to memory. On the afternoon of the same day, the 10th May, the Imperial Institute was opened by the Queen at Kensington, a function which may have prevented some of our friends from accepting our invitations; but I think all who accepted came except Mr Lidderdale who wrote to explain that he went by mistake to the wrong house! ... As our guests could not see our building when meeting at the Merchant Taylors Hall, we gave them some idea of the exterior by an etching by Mr Fulleylove on the pretty programme of music for the dinner; and not a few of these guests joined many others on the following evening at a conversazione and dance in the Institute building, to which Mr Lidderdale, to make up for his mistake the preceding day, came with his two charming daughters. Dear Georgie was present in a gallery during the dinner, and helped me welcome the guests on the following evening.

This [Friday 30 June] was the last day of the half year – and I had to be late in the City at bank audits.

On the 5th October [1893] I invited the country members of the Council of our Institute to spend the afternoon and dine here [Feldemore]. Including Griffiths, who kindly came to help me entertain them, fourteen came. I think a walk up Holmbury Hill with Willy was the most successful part of the entertainment.

In the spring of the year [1893] I received a letter from Mr Harrington Wright asking on behalf of the Overseers of Westminster monthly meeting, which, if any, of their meetings for worship, I attended; and in the event of the answer being in the negative inviting my 'serious' consideration to the position of being a 'nominal member only of a Christian community'. I would add the letter which I wrote in reply on the 4th June 1893, as giving the views which I then held, and from which after an interval of some years, I see no reason to draw back: –

The subject of your letter of the 27th April has had my careful thought. I understand you ask me to consider whether if I do not attend any meetings for the worship of the Society of Friends, it is fitting that I should continue 'a nominal member only of the Christian community'.

For many years I have been a member of the Church of England, attending the services of the church which in this place is near at hand. I do not suppose I am within easy reach of Westminster, or of any other meeting more than three or four Sundays in the year. On these Sundays, if spent in London, I generally go to a neighbouring church. For many years prior to my marriage I attended meeting[s] – I fear often without edification for I found it generally impossible to control my thoughts. I liked however to be associated with and to worship with those who held the views in which I had been brought up, views which were so dear to my own loved father and mother.

But when I joined the Church of England I did not feel that I was leaving 'Friends'. No doctrine really dear to 'Friends' seems to me inconsistent with membership in the Church; and no doctrine of the Church of England which I found it necessary to subscribe to on joining it, was inconsistent with all that I have been taught to love as a Friend.

Indeed the opposition which I feel to some of the 'externals' of the church – matters of really no importance, unless they are allowed to take the place of, or interfere with, essential and life-giving beliefs – has I think increased the love which I have for the simplicity of the tenets of Quakerism. But I like to think and to foster the feeling that my religion is something deeper and wider than any church, and that an endeavour to hold the faith as it is in Christ Jesus need not prevent my claiming fellowship with Friends and with churchmen. I did not put myself on to the Register of Friends – if I had, I should perhaps consider whether, not attending meeting, I ought not to ask that my name should be taken off. . . .

The reply which I had to this letter was from Bevan Braithwaite. . . . He seems to have gathered from my letter – I think quite wrongly – that I had been meditating sending in my resignation to the Society. I ventured to set him right as to this, and his second letter of the 2nd January 1894 followed. The correspondence was renewed in July 1894, Percy Bigland then writing that Bevan Braithwaite and he were appointed by the monthly meeting to visit me. We were then just setting out for Scotland, and the matter was adjourned till later in the year. I seem then in response to an enquiry to have given a choice of two days for our meeting, but have no recollection of anything further in this matter, until I received a letter from Bevan Braithwaite of the 12th December 1894 stating that Friends had favourably received the report about me.

The year [1893] was a very full one in business. The railway and bank audits took me away from London much more than before. One important matter in London was the reconstruction of the London Bank of Australia, which had to ask the forebearance of creditors amounting to some £6,000,000. The matter was entrusted largely to Messrs Freshfields and myself. Years of drought and bad seasons, following a period of inflation of values, had brought affairs in Australia to a very low ebb. Sir James Garrick[64] was chairman of the bank, and, though not a man of wide experience in finance of the kind, was able to carry his way with creditors and shareholders by the confidence inspired by his frankness and the exceptional gentleman-liness of his personal character. His brother, Mr Alfred Garrick, was also on the board. Another interesting matter was my appointment as representative of the Bank of England on the committee of inspection of the South American & Mexican Company, one of several compa-nies for the formation and failure of which the Trustees and Executors Corporation was to a large extent responsible. Mr George S. Barnes, the official receiver, had the matter in hand.

CHAPTER XVII

1894

My absences from home on business were as frequent as ever, and must have been very trying for dear Georgie. But she recognized their necessity and never complained. Even when I had not to be away from London, my work required so much of my time that when our headquarters were at Feldemore I was obliged to be two or three nights in the week at Hyde Park Street. This intensified the pleasure of a Saturday holiday when I could get it.

The second year of my presidency of the Institute of Chartered Accountants was about to close and I was giving a president's dinner in the hall of the Institute to which I and others of the Council asked our friends. I was no doubt busy the night before preparing the speeches I had to make. My chief guest was Lord Randolph Churchill,[65] whom I had interviewed by appointment, and given some particulars of our Institute, the health of which he was kindly willing to propose. He said he would give us at the same time some political 'spice', and I looked forward to something that would please and amuse. But the poor man was in very failing health, and as soon as he arrived I saw something was the matter. His speech was evidently an uncongenial exertion to himself, and consequently painful to his hearers. He said things about the Army and Navy Services in connection with my work for his committee of investigation into Woolwich methods which had been better left unsaid, especially in the presence of the Accountants General of the War Office and Admiralty, who were my guests on the occasion, and who were in no way responsible for the state of things to which he referred. Indeed, they had been of great assistance in the investigation, and had turned most willing ears to the recommendations of the committee. In my reply to the toast I tried, but I fear not very successfully, to lessen the harshness of somethings which he said. I believe that this was about the last speech he ever made. He was then suffering from the disease which led him in the hope of recovery to set out very soon after for a trip round the world. But he grew rapidly worse and returned in haste from India, dying in January 1895. Among my other guests were His Honour Judge Snagge and Sir J. W. Pease,[66] and they by their speeches were very helpful in putting the company at their ease again. Mr St John Brodrick, of whom I had seen something as a member for the Guildford Division of Surrey, and as Financial Secretary to the War Office, was unable to carry out his intention of joining us.

A contemplated trip to Baireuth early in August [1894] was given up owing to my being so tied by my work at the time, but we looked forward to a holiday stay at F. Bowman's house at Garramor which he had kindly let to me for a few weeks from the middle of August [plates 34, 35]. On the 10th August I had the pleasure of receiving at Feldemore a party of my L. & N.W. Railway friends. They were a company of seventeen – thirteen directors, my colleague Edward Lawrence, F. Harrison, the general manager, F. Mason, solicitor and F. W. Webb of Crewe. ... They came by special train to Dorking, whence I brought them here, via Coldharbour – many going to the top of Leith Hill on the way. Lord Stalbridge was not able to come with the others, having he said much to prepare for the half-yearly meeting to be held on the morrow, but he was good enough to follow by a slow S.E.R. train with Mason, and got here in time for dinner.

On October 11th [1894] Willie took up his quarters at New College, Oxford.

A provincial meeting of our Institute was held in Liverpool on the 18th and 19th [of October]. I went down ... and dear Georgie joined me for two more nights at the hotel. The Lord Mayor of Liverpool and the Liverpool members of our Institute gave us a very kind welcome. ... I read a paper 'On some Aspects of Liquidations under recent Legislation'. I had accepted the invitation of Mr Ismay to spend Saturday afternoon and night at Dawpool. ... At Dawpool I was very kindly received by Mr and Mrs Ismay,[67] who happened to be alone in the very magnificent and beautiful house which Mr Norman Shaw[68] had designed for [them]. I was intensely interested in this and the lovely things which, with his great wealth, he had placed in it.

The year 1894 was a very full and important one for me so far as business was concerned. The trouble arising in connection with the insolvent condition of the Land Securities Company Ltd were made known to me early in the year; and on the 30th March I was appointed receiver on behalf of the debenture bond holders, and soon after liquidator of the company under the supervision of the court. The company had an interesting history. It was one of the first to be formed after the passing of the Joint Stock Companies Act in 1862 for the purpose of advancing money on the security of landed property, and having power to issue within prescribed limits, mortgage debentures against the security thus deposited with them. The Land Registry office was made the depository of the deeds, and the Registrar of that office certified, under an Act passed in 1865, that the mortgage debentures as issued were in order. At the time of my appointment the company had about £2,000,000 of such debentures outstanding, but many of the securities held were old and of a very unrealizable character; and the business of the company could not be continued without injustice to many concerned. The causes which led to such a state of things are given in a report which I addressed to the creditors and shareholders on the 30th April. It became my duty to call up the £650,000 of uncalled capital, and great hardship resulted to many of the shareholders. The position was also greatly complicated by the existence of two classes of creditors, the bondholders, and a comparatively small body of unsecured creditors, who had a right to rank against the uncalled capital jointly with the bondholders' claim that might ultimately prove to be unsecured. Soon after my appointment I applied to the Court to sanction a scheme of arrangement bringing all parties into line; and I had the satisfaction of obtaining consent to my proposals, with slight modifications, in December. By this the liquidation was very greatly facilitated and forwarded. Schemes of arrangement, however, were not in favour, for the court, and especially our friend Sir Rowland Vaughan Williams,[69] the judge in bankruptcy, was fearful that such schemes lessened its hold upon directors and managers who had failed in their duty in the past, and were sometimes pressed upon its acceptance in order to prevent actions for misfeasance from being brought. I had some difficulty in removing such an impression. Matters in this respect were left unaffected by my scheme, and in course of time the fullest investigation was made, and all reparation found under the circumstances possible, obtained.

The liquidation lasted ten years, and I finally closed it only by transferring certain assets very difficult to realize to another company. All my reports during the ten years have been bound in a volume as a history of this, to me, very important work. I should not have been able to carry it through as satisfactorily as I did had it not been for the cordial support of Mr J. H. Burroughes and Mr Robert Vigers, two members of the committee of inspection whose advice was of the greatest value; and the kind co-operation of Mr Hood, the registrar of the court. Ashurst, Morris & Co. were my solicitors, Frank Crisp and Mr Jno. Stevenson, of that firm, having the matter in hand.

In March [1894] I joined at the request of my old master Alexander Young[70] and Mr John Morris, his adviser, the board of the reconstructed Trustees, Executors and Securities Insurance Corporation, and became for a while Deputy Chairman under Young. The Bank of England and the South American & Mexican Company were interested in the Corporation, and I consulted my friend Mr Barnes, the liquidator of the latter and chief official receiver, when taking this step.

I also annex [a letter] . . . from the Duke of Devonshire[71] referring to our previous correspondence in December 1890, and asking me to undertake some work in connection with his Eastbourne property in conjunction with Mr (afterwards Sir Richard) Farrant, whom I knew having been connected with the Artizans' Dwellings Co. (see p. 104).

On the 20th July my business diary records a visit to Trentham [Stoke on Trent]. The young Duke of Sutherland[72] as a member of the L. & N.W. Railway board had included the auditors in an invitation to his colleagues to spend a night at Trentham. It was a gentleman's party, but we were introduced to the Duchess.

Reginald John Smith, a college friend of my nephew Wilson Crewdson, had married one of the daughters of Mr George Smith, the publisher, of the firm of Smith Elder & Co., and the young couple had come to live next door to us on the south, a house that had for sometime previously been occupied by a Mr Louis Floersheim, a London financier of some repute, and years before by my parents' friend, Miss Benson. My acquaintanceship with Reginald Smith brought me into the notice of his father-in-law, who asked me to assist him in the management of a huge business into which he had, without any great seeking on his part, come into, and shared practically with only one other person. This was the Apollinaris Water business, and the story, which he told me and others of the way he came into it, is worth recording. It was somewhat as follows. Amongst his friends was Mr Ernest Hart. Dining with this gentleman one night, a German water was offered to the guests which so pleased Mr Smith's taste that he asked whether he could procure some for consumption in his own house. He was told that it came from a spring in the Ahr valley near the Rhine where Mr Hart had drunk and liked it on the spot, and that a certain gentleman in the City was the agent for the proprietors in England. Mr Smith ordered some of the water, and was satisfied that it ought to prove a very popular beverage of the kind. He had heard of fortunes being made out of German waters and had, he told me, occasionally in the past when publishing profits were low, put off an expenditure proposed by Mrs Smith which seemed to him a little extravagant by telling her that it had better stand over until they had bought their German 'spring'. So he thought his time might have come, and mentioned the matter to a very keen business friend of his, a Mr Edward Steinkopf. This gentleman shared his views as to the excellence of the water and the two called on the London agent to make enquiries. They found that he was practically the owner of the spring. He extolled the purity of the water, dwelt upon its increasing popularity and sought to impress his hearers with the extraordinarily large sales he was effecting. This he put at some 200,000 bottles (or something of the kind) a year, and expressed the view that they were possible of expansion. Mr Steinkopf immediately offered to buy over one million bottles if he might have the right to take the full overflow of the spring without further payment. The bait took. The immediate profit was too good to be refused, and a bargain was struck on some such lines. A company was formed, Smith and Steinkopf being practically the only shareholders and directors, each with an equal interest. Before long they were making fabulous profits. But one half of these did not satisfy Steinkopf. He was the chief manager, and an able one, and he wanted a good sum as a first charge for his services. Mr Smith was very liberal but did not see his way to go the full length of his partner's wishes, and the occasionally held board meetings were not harmonious. Mr Smith had power to nominate another director to sit with him and he asked me to be his nominee. The business was within a year or two sold to an extended company, so I was not very long on the board, but it was a very interesting and responsible position while it lasted. I find the story of Mr Smith's acquisition of the business is referred to in the sketch of his life prefaced to the supplement (No. XXII) volume of the thin paper edition of the *Dictionary of National Biography*, the bringing out of which was one of the chief works of his life.

Other work which occupied me in 1894 was a member of the London Finance Committee of the Chicago Great Western Railway, of which our friend Mr Lidderdale was chairman, and Mr A. F. Wallace, one of his colleagues at the Bank of England, and Mr Howard Gilliat, other members. The company had got into financial straits and the committee was very helpful in assisting in reorganizing its finances so that after a while its prospects were greatly improved.

There had been so many scandals in connection with public companies, showing fraud in their inception and formation, and dereliction of duty on the part of promoters and directors, that in November the Board of Trade, under the presidency of Mr James Bryce, desired to consider the possibility of amending the Joint Stock Companies Acts, and appointed a departmental committee to enquire into the subject. Lord Davey was chairman and the members, Sir Joseph Chitty, Sir R. Vaughan Williams, Sir W. H. Houldsworth, M.P., Sir A. K. Rollit, M.P., Mr Buckley, Q.C., Mr F. B. Palmer, Mr John Smith, the Inspector of Bankruptcy, Mr A. F. Wallace, Mr John Hollams, Mr Frank Crisp, Mr G. Auldjo Jamieson and myself. ... The committee had a heavy work before them, and we met for sometime thrice a week, at 4 o'clock or so, at the Board of Trade offices. It was not till the 27th June 1895 that our report was completed.

CHAPTER XVIII

1895

Arthur Hugh Lister was one of the Lyme Regis family, and after learning to be a Chartered Accountant in our office, was with us for some time as a valued assistant, until he was wanted to take up a family business. This, however, did not suit him, and he began life again, taking up the medical profession, to which he bids fair to be an ornament, following the example of his more than distinguished uncle.

On the 5th July I dined at the kind invitation of Paul Bevan, who was secretary of the club, with him and his colleagues of the 'Odd Volumes'. He also had been one of my articled clerks, and was in 1895 in partnership with Mr Woodthorpe.

[Edwin Waterhouse quoted his wife as writing on 12 September 1895 that she had consulted their local doctor who] 'has reassured me a great deal again. He has prescribed what he trusts will remove the pain, or at any rate make it less acute, so I hope to meet you without any groans tomorrow'. [The initial diagnosis was rheumatism.]

In business I was very much occupied with the liquidation of the Land Securities Company and other current work. An amalgamation of Gurney & Co. of Norwich with Barclay & Co. occupied me towards the end of the year. The committee on the Joint Stock Companies Acts sat until June.

CHAPTER XIX

1896

[Edwin Waterhouse quotes from his wife's diary for Friday 10 January 1896, in which she recalls the previous evening spent in at 13 Hyde Park Street with her husband, Theresa and Willy:]

> I am so happy we had that dear evening at home together yesterday. Perhaps I ought not to say 'at home', but I think of all the associations of that room. It will always have a loving corner in my heart. . . . The doctor has just been, and is quite willing for me to begin baths tomorrow [she was staying at Droitwich Spa]. He is quite encouraging. He really investigated me *most* carefully and thoroughly, and wants to mend my *general health*. How that has failed, I cannot tell. Perhaps I never husbanded it as I ought.
>
> Sunday 12th. A tiny turn – after service, but found walking impossible, pain quite bearable and lameness too – but an inexplicable oppression on my chest exhausts me after a very few minutes walking.

A letter [from Georgie] of the same day reads: –

> . . . I seem almost to have lost my own identity, and wonder what has become of the person I used to know under my name. Now, if it be God's will, I should like to find only the best part of her again someday.

On Saturday 18th [January] I was able to fit in a visit to Droitwich at the time of my audit of the Worcester Old Bank, and spent the night at the Raven Hotel. On the Sunday I went with Theresa to Worcester Cathedral and we lunched with Mr Cherry at Henwick. I returned to London from Droitwich in the evening, having to do a day's work in London before going north on L. & N.W. Railway work on the Monday.

She [Georgie] left Droitwich on Thursday the 6th [February], caught a glimpse of Willy at Oxford Station in passing, and was welcomed by Nicholas at Gomshall, Theresa having to stay in London owing to a cold, and my Euston work keeping me in town.

On the 11th [March] Dr Phillips was led to believe that the suffering undergone by dear Georgie was due to something much more serious than rheumatism, and advised me of an immediate operation to ascertain the extent of, and if possible, remove the cause of the trouble. Mr A. Pearce Gould was accordingly called in and on the 12th after a surgical examination under anaesthetic, I was informed that the disease, which had it been known of, could not have been arrested, was quite beyond the surgeon's power to remove or mitigate, though there was no saying what nature itself might effect. All that dear Georgie could now do was to conserve her strength as much as possible and await the result of a conflict between her own powers, supported by her faith and courage, and the inroads of a terrible, deadly disease.

She kept in touch with all that was going on, saw much of the children, and some callers, coming down sometimes into the drawing room for part of the day, being carried as she could not walk. On the 18th [March] Sir Joseph Lister[73] confirmed the opinions expressed by the other doctors, taking as Phillips reported a 'gloomy' view of the case.

I was again at Feldemore on the 21st [March] meeting George Redmayne and King the builder about the contract for the new wing to the house. I was in great doubt whether the building should be allowed to proceed.

[From Georgie's diary] April 16th: 'It is a mere trifle, but I just made a note of my great dislike of heavy mourning apparel. I have always taken my own line in this matter since before 1883, when, and since when, I never wore or bought an inch of crepe.'

The sad days and weary nights passed on, with, it may have been, some intervals of less pain than at other times, but without anything to show that the disease was not making unchecked progress. The weakness of our dear patient daily increased; and, though the restlessness consequent upon this and the terrible pain was diminished by opiates, she appeared to be gradually sinking.

The nurses called me three times to her room during the night of Sunday [10 May], the end seeming near, but she passed through Monday apparently without much pain or consciousness. I had written on Sunday to stop the men coming down to work on the new building, and all seemed hushed waiting for the solemn summons. At 4 am on Tuesday the 12th I learnt there was little if any change but at 6 o'clock

I was called in, and sent for Theresa, Willy and Nicholas. At 6.30 the spirit of our loved one quietly passed to the God she loved and to the precious child that had gone before her. As we turned to leave the room the words, 'Precious in the sight of the Lord is the death of His Saints' fell from my lips.

The funeral was arranged for Saturday 16th. On looking back it is wonderful how we were all helped from giving way to the feeling of poignant grief which filled our hearts. To myself the sense of dear Georgie's condition of peace and rest after all the suffering she had gone through – and which I believe she largely prevented us from witnessing or being conscious of – filled me with thankfulness. My thoughts went back to a conversation we had in Grasmere Lane, shortly before the days when we pledged ourselves to each other, about the power of resurrection in natural as well as spiritual things, and the life to be won by death. I remember quoting the words of Him who is our resurrection and our life, 'Except a corn of wheat fall into the ground and die, it abideth alone, but if it die, it bringeth forth much fruit'. Such words, which now seemed spoken to me by her could not fail to help me in my depths of sorrow. I wished to place them on her grave; and they are there, on the tombstone designed by dear Alfred with the ears of wheat running around its edge.

[Edwin received many letters of sympathy, including those from Joseph J. Saffery and John G. Griffiths, council members of the Institute of Chartered Accountants.] Other members who also kindly wrote to me, to most of whom dear Georgie was slightly known, were my old schoolfellow G. W. Knox, Ernest Cooper, Frederick Whinney, Charles Fitch Kemp, A. A. James, John Gane, Walter Fisher, William Edmonds and W. B. Peat.

CHAPTER XX

1896 continued and 1897

As I write this, it is 1910, some four years since I commenced the self-imposed task of putting down some record of this life, not so much myself, as of the grandmother and mother to whose influence, prayers and goodness, I and my dear children owe so much. The task has been of interest to myself, and of profit, as enabling me to recognize, even more clearly than before, the goodness and mercy which have followed me. Whether it may ever interest others, or whether any reader will ever get so far in the narrative as to read this, I am doubtful. One good has resulted from my work in the destruction of a large amount of correspondence, which might, from the mere fact of its continued existence, have caused some trouble in the future.

A little change for Theresa and myself seemed desirable, so we planned a short stay in Switzerland among the wild flowers of spring. Nicholas and Dorothy Walton were to come as our companions . . .

[Returning to England at the end of June] my business occupied me much, but I was at home at Feldemore as much as I could be.

Ellen was due at St Andrews on the 23rd [September] and Theresa and I went with her, all staying a night in Edinburgh on our way. On the way south I had business in Darlington so I stayed with Theresa at Hulton from the 25th to the 28th. On Sunday the 27th we went to the meeting at Guisbrough and in the afternoon called on Alfred and Helen Peace at Pinchingthorpe, and saw Alfred's collection of the results of his African big game shooting. On Monday I went to the Raby Estate office on business for Lord Barnard, and was shown something of the magnificent castle by old Mr Scarth, the agent.

The last three months of the year [1896] were spent between London and Feldemore, where much work was going on with the new wing to the house. With Willy and Nicholas at New College and Ellen at St Andrews, I had only Theresa and Valentine to bear me company. In November we spent two nights in Oxford, to the great pleasure of the brothers, Willy being in lodgings in the High Street, and Nicholas in the new buildings of his college.

In business though there was not much fresh work, I was fully occupied during the year. An investigation into the account keeping of the Works Department of the London County Council, by a committee of the Council under the chairmanship of Mr Melvill Beachcroft,[74] occupied some of my time in December, being appointed one of the assessors of the committee jointly with a Mr Gruning, a surveyor.

On the 15th March [1897], I paid one of my business visits to Oxford, taking Theresa with me who was so glad of the opportunity of seeing her brothers. I dined on the 16th at Mr Cannans, then as now, secretary to the delegates of the Clarendon Press, in his nice house adjoining the Botanic Gardens and I find I have noted as amongst the guests – the Vice Chancellor (Magrath), the Rector of Exeter (Jackson), the Master of Pembroke (Price), Mr Russell of Christchurch, Mr Morell, the solicitor, all with their wives.

My business work in the spring kept me much at the office but I managed to get to Feldemore for two if not three nights after working days. Monday and Wednesday nights were generally spent in London, where I made up arrears of work by long days at the office, usually dining at the Garrick Club on my way to Hyde Park Street.

On the 7th June [1897] Professor Bartholomew Price, the Master of Pembroke College, wrote to me that at his proposal the Hebdominal Council had, in recognition of my services as auditor of the University Accounts for the last fourteen years, resolved to confer an honorary M.A. degree of the University upon me. ... Other letters from Professor Price followed which led to my attending early on 1st July to receive the honour at the hands of the Vice Chancellor.

The days of our beloved Queen were being lengthened out and arrangements for the celebrations of the 60th Anniversary of her accession to take place on Sunday the 20th June were under discussion. Willy desired to remain in Oxford. Ellen was at St Andrews, but Nicholas came up and I obtained excellent seats for him and Valentine in the yard of Charing Cross Station as guests of the South Eastern Railway. ... Everything passed off happily; and having regard to the immense crowds, practically without accident or drawback. The sight of the aged Queen as she neared the end of her long drive was very touching.

A naval review was held at Spithead on Saturday the 26th. I took tickets for Theresa, Margaret Vaughan Williams, Nicholas and myself on the *S.S. Opliss* of the Orient Company, a company with which I had been connected as auditor since its formation. We embarked at Tilbury on the Friday, saw the magnificent sight and the illuminations next day; and on the Sunday, after steaming through the fleet, crossed to Havre, visiting Rouen from that place on Monday, and reaching the Thames again on the Tuesday morning.

Willy ... passed his examination satisfactorily, though without the 'honours' which perhaps might have been his if he had adhered to his original intention of taking up the branch of science which first attracted him. It was arranged that after our autumn holiday he should come, as we had for long intended, into our office as an articled pupil.

The new wing of the house at Feldemore, though the billiard room was not made full use of until after Christmas, was open for occupation early in August [1897], and the furnishing, electric lighting &c. of the new rooms were matters of much interest.

[Returning from a holiday in Norway] Nicholas soon went to New College for his second year, and Willy began regular work in the City as my pupil, making 13 Hyde Park Street his quarters during the week.

The year [1897] was a very full one so far as business was concerned. The London County Council matter occupied me much on the top of current audit work, for the first three months. After April I was interested with the management of the affairs of the Colonial Company Limited, for which I had been auditor for thirty years or so, being appointed chairman of a committee of conference with the board, then receiver for the debenture holders, and finally liquidator. It was a pleasure to work with such good and pleasant men of business as Messrs Neville and Frederick Lubbock, notwithstanding the good management of whom, the company had from circumstances quite beyond their control got into difficulties. Frank Preston, the chief clerk to the company, was also of great assistance to me. After considerable trouble the company was reorganized.

Another important concern which came into my hands was the Aranco Company Limited, a concern possessing a railway and coal mines in Chile. This also after some years of liquidation was by my exertions again placed on its feet to the satisfaction I think of all concerned. The Land Securities Company continued to occupy much of my time.

In June I was asked by Lord Herschell to assist him in a little matter [in relation to the Society for the Prevention of Cruelty to Children].

CHAPTER XXI

1898

The year 1898 opened to me with a trembling sense of the possibility of what might prove a great joy to myself and a benefit to us all. Our life in the meantime continued much as before – William, who had been articled to the firm in September taking up his work in London, Nicholas going back to New College, Ellen to St Andrews, while Theresa and Valentine . . . went up to London quarters in Hyde Park Street about the middle of January.

[Having discussed the possibility of proposing marriage to Helen Caroline Weber with Kitty, his sister, Theresa and Willy, Edwin Waterhouse] felt it necessary at once to ascertain my fate and . . . posted a letter that night to 4 Blomfield Crescent, asking permission to call on a personal matter of importance. . . . The interview which was granted me on the Monday morning though it did not secure the absolute promise I desired justified a strong hope of success. Theresa kindly arranged to go the next day to add an expression of her desires to my own, and rejoiced my heart by telegraphing to the City that she had had a 'delightful interview'. I had to go to Darlington that night on the business of Pease & Partners, and to attend an appointment on the Wednesday with Sir Joseph Pease, Sir David Dale and J. W. Richardson, my brother-in-law. I stayed with the Dales for the Tuesday night, and feared that I exhibited more than usual absence of mind. At their house I received the letter from Theresa which . . . prepared me to anticipate the full joy which was even then awaiting my return. [Miss Helen Weber had agreed to the betrothal.]

Dear Georgie and I had known the Weber family since our marriage, Mrs Weber being the eldest daughter of F. W. Benecke of Denmark Hill. Indeed Dr Weber and Georgie's father had been acquainted, possibly from very early years, in Trieste. My early friendship with Charles Benecke and his family led to a very friendly relationship between Georgie and the Denmark Hill family, and Dr Weber being resident in Green Street up to the time of his death in 1886, we often met him and his wife and children. He used to take exercise before breakfast in Hyde Park, and was known as the 'running doctor'. Mrs Weber, in later life, was a great invalid, and her daughters, Helen and May, who lived with her, and were among Georgie's chief friends, would have been oftener with us had it not been for their constant attendance upon her. She died in 1890, and soon after her death the daughters moved with their brother, Lewis, to 4 Blomfield Crescent, and we then saw them frequently.

Helen and I were married at Christchurch, Lancaster Gate at 9.30 am on Easter Monday, the 11th April [1898]. That church is a favourite one for weddings, and the rush of matrimony immediately following Lent and Easter made it necessary for us to choose either a very early or a very late hour. . . . There were present in addition to all our dear children, Mrs Thöl, my sister Maud, Wilson and Mary [Crewdson], the James P. Thöls, the Gilmans, and many of Helen's friends, including some of her Shepherd's Bush acquaintances.

Leaving London by a morning train Helen and I found ourselves at York for a lovely afternoon service in the dear old minster, and the next day found us enjoying in absolute privacy the hospitality of Mr and Mrs George Macmillan at their little retreat Bolton House Farm in the Danby Dale, Yorkshire, which they had most kindly placed at our disposal for ten days . . .

On the 25th June when my partners J. G. Fowler and Mr Wyon were with us for the Sunday, we entertained on the Saturday the office staff at a kind of garden party and early dinner. We sat down 52 in number in the cellar room which I had decorated some little before with French landscape wallpapers &c. for ball suppers and similar entertainments. The names of those present on the occasion [were: Messrs Bass, Brocklehurst, Bulman, Bywater, Cooke, Elwell, Evans, Farmer, Fort, Fowler, Garrett, Gooch, A. H. Hales, Hallett, Halsey, Hughes, Hawtree, James, Johnston, Just, McDermott, Majestic, Martin, Masters, Mellors, Mordaunt, North Smith, Parkhouse, Pawlyn, Pettigrew, Pollard, Price, Reed, Rogers, Rocke, Seale, D. Smith, Smyth, George Sneath, W. C. Sneath, Stainforth, Stephenson, A. W. Wyon, White, together with William Waterhouse, Nicolas Waterhouse, Miss Weber, Miss Theresa Waterhouse and Mrs Helen Waterhouse].

The 31st [December 1898] being a Saturday, I was able to get home after the cash audit at the Banks. The year had been a busy one. The Aranco Company, the Land Securities Company and current audits, which annually increased in number, taking the bulk of my time. Special matters of business during the year included an examination into such accounts as were rendered of a new process for smelting refractory ores, in which Mr Frank Bevan, Mr Wilberforce Bryant and others were interested. Mr Lidderdale, after careful consideration and advice, became interested in the process, which seemed to promise great results, and consented to be chairman of the company formed to work it. But the man who had introduced the matter to my friends proved, in the course of two years or more after the expenditure of a large amount of capital in putting up the necessary apparatus, to be an unprincipled villain, and large sums of money were lost.

I had an interesting matter entrusted to me by Mr Robert Perks, the well-known solicitor and M.P., who had for years been a kind business friend. He was concerned for the estate of Mr Walker, the contractor, and had with extreme ability, and very much to the advantage of those concerned, carried on sundry contracts which were current at the time of Mr Walker's death, the profits arising to many hundreds of thousands of pounds. The question arose whether these profits belonged to the corpus of the estate as inherent therein at the time of Mr Walker's death, or whether they, or a part of them, were due to a subsequent period and therefore the property of those entitled to the income of the estate. Mr Perks took the bold but simple course of settling the matter by an Act of Parliament, under which the question was, with the consent of all the parties, referred to me for settlement.

I think this was the year when I was first entrusted with the audits of Huntley & Palmers of Reading and of J. J. Colman & Co. of Norwich.

On the 11th August [1898] I find an entry in my business diary referring to an 'auction' for offices in the City. We had long been looking out for quarters which might suit us better than 44 (previously 13) Gresham Street; and soon after Horace Pyne, to the great grief of his friends, died in 1897, I made enquiries as to the house in Frederick's Place, Old Jewry, which he had for long occupied. I found that our friends, Maples, Teesdale & Co., who had taken over his business, were keeping on the offices. But in the course of a year or two they found it convenient to remove all books and papers to their own offices which were immediately opposite in Frederick's Place, and they wrote to me and others that the house was vacant and named the rent they were asking. My partners and I were aware of its fitness for our require-ments, and we sent round a letter by hand accepting the offer made. Unhappily others were desirous of becoming the tenants, and Messrs Maples & Co. found themselves rather in a difficulty as to whom to favour in the matter. They entrusted their interests to their neighbour, Mr Robert Vigers, and he decided to have a kind of informal auction in his private office. When the time arrived only two persons turned up, a young solicitor acting for a well-known firm in which he was a partner, and myself. The other would-be tenants had not been quite prepared to accept the terms offered, or were otherwise ineligible. Whilst waiting for our summons to Mr Vigers's room my competitor claimed that his position was impregnable, as his firm had accepted the offer made [to] them in its very terms immediatcly on receipt; and consequently there was a contract in writing which must bind the lessors to them. I pretended to differ from him, and drew from him, when before Mr Vigers, a stronger repetition of his argument, and then asked what should be done if two persons accepted the offer in the terms proposed to thcm; 'Oh, the letter which arrived first would carry the day' was the reply 'and we sent ours by return of post'. 'I think', said Mr Vigers, turning to me, 'that I received yours by hand'. It was pleasing to me to beat my friend on his own ground, especially as I learnt afterwards that his partners were by no means anxious to change their offices.

We soon made arrangements to move in, the change being effected in March 1899, and never regretted the step. Though soon small for the requirements of the firm, it was nice to have a house to ourselves with housekeeper &c. The house was an old one, my room on the first floor having a nice 'Adam' fireplacc and mantelpiece. The lease contained a stipulation that we should 'uphold' the premises, a term the meaning of which was made clear to us, when we discovered that there being no proper foundations, and the subsoil, mud, we had to underpin the structure.

On the 9th November I was arbitrator in a somewhat interesting dispute, and the meeting was for the convenience of the counsel engaged, held at the Royal Courts of Justice, one of the unoccupied courts being made use of for the purpose. I find I wrote to Helen in the evening from Hyde Park Street, 'I have had a hard day's work, the streets crammed with sightseers and Lord Mayor's day bothers: – and in the next court to mine I had the Lord Mayor and the Lord Chancellor – sounds well, does it not.' The use of one of the judge's courts for a private arbitration is not unusual I think, for the Committee or other rooms available in the building are so dark and inconvenient. On another occasion, similar to the one above mentioned, I was amused by one of the Counsel, I think it was Mr Carson, afterwards Solicitor General, addressing me as 'my lord', possibly by mistake, but more probably to amuse or gratify me, for I was sitting in the Registrar's seat on the lower storey.

I had for some years been one of the auditors of University College, Gower Street, part of the time jointly with my old friend John Hennell. At the annual meeting of the College in 1898 they did me the honour of admitting me to [a] life governorship. My dear brother, Theodore, had been elected to the much higher position of a Fellow in 1867, our friend John F. Rotton being treasurer of the College for many years.

The year 1898 saw the billiard room [at Feldemore] furnished with a table. None of us knew anything about billiards but the boys and I soon began to knock the balls about. I had in the previous year procured some of the furniture for the room and the corridor leading to it: the tapestry on the walls, the curtains and most of the upholstery having been provided and put up by Morris & Co.

I cannot close the record of the year without referring to the increasing trouble of heart arising to myself from the difficulty I had in adapting myself to the ritual which Mr [A. C.] Hayes had been gradually introducing into our church services. Knowing that any endeavour to secure a return to the simple ritual adopted by Mr Shearme would be useless, I had for years past, so far as I was able, to shut my eyes to the prostrations and other practices which were repugnant, as I believed, to the feelings of many others besides myself; and seldom ventured to raise a protest. But on one occasion – I think it was in 1897 – I was a witness in the vestry of what seemed to me very ungentlemanly pressure upon our friend Mr Vatcher, who was staying with us and had kindly undertaken with Mr Hayes's full concurrence to preach. Mr Hayes handed him a stole of a bright colour and intimated that he must wear it. Mr Vatcher objected strongly, saying that having always been accustomed to black, he should not feel himself comfortable in anything else.

[Edwin Waterhouse quoted a letter that he wrote to Mr Hayes on the same subject when Mr Vatcher visited the following year to give another sermon:]

> I entirely agree with what you say as to toleration, but I do not see why a clergyman should not be the first person to set an example in this as in all other things taught by Christ, even in his own building and towards another clergyman. ... I have prayed too, but I feel I have need not so much to pray for peace as for God's Holy Spirit and greater knowledge of his Love. I feel that love often, not so much in church, as in my daily life, even in my City

work. Oh for a bigger sense of what it means, and that I may guide my thoughts and words and deeds by it! Is not a man's religion far deeper than his church?

I should not wish now, in 1911, to add to what I said in the above letter about my work, an expression of thanksgiving and praise for the constant answer to the liftings up of my heart in reference to business matters – for preservation from the temptations which might so easily, and did I fear in some cases, overcome me, and from the mental worries which over anxiety about one's actions or apparent failure therein, is sure to bring about. The fact that my partners allowed nothing to stand before the honour of our business name was a great and abiding cause of the ease with which our business was carried on, but the mental prayer for guidance as one crossed the threshold of the office door in the morning was helpful, and as fitting as the thanksgiving customary when sitting down to meat.

CHAPTER XXII

1899–1900

We made Hyde Park Street our headquarters until Easter, but I was frequently at Feldemore for Saturday and Sunday. January was a busy month for me, for in addition to the work at the London Banks, my diary records visits to Hodgkin, Barnett & Co. at Newcastle, the Union Bank at York, Benricks at Worcester, and for the first time the Wilts & Dorset Bank at Salisbury, where I had been appointed auditor with Mr Alexander Young. These audits and the railway work kept me not a little from home. We moved our offices to 3 Fredericks Place, I think in March.

William, who was articled to the firm in the autumn of 1897, was now beginning to take part in its work, and had a seat in my room; Nicholas continued at Oxford. The three girls were all with us.

[Mr Jacob A. Forrest obtained Edwin Waterhouse's permission to marry his daughter, Theresa, on 24 April 1898. Mr Forrest was vicar of St Saviours, at Shepherd's Bush.]

[The couple married on 22nd June at Holmbury St Mary, the service being performed by the suffragan Bishop of Southampton. The wedding presents were displayed in the billiard room at Feldemore where the reception was held.]

The visit of [Joseph] Kopf [whom Waterhouse had previously met on a visit to Rome] and his daughter was very pleasant to us. He enjoyed the drives when Helen took him through the Surrey lanes, which he greatly admired; and his trips to the British Museum and the other art collections in London . . .

As a birthday present for me, he promised me a copy in bronze of the relief of my head [plate 37]. This duly came to hand and, having the marble [version], I gave it to the Institute of Chartered Accountants to hang in their committee room. Kopf and his daughter left us on the 11th July.

I had planned to stay in Scotland for our autumn holiday, in which Jacob and Theresa were to join us. Having some work to do for the Duke of Sutherland, I enquired of his London agent, Mr Wright, if he could recommend a furnished house for a few weeks in the Dunrobin district. He spoke very highly of a farm house, Kirkton, near Golspie, and without seeing it, I engaged to take it. The L. & N.W. Railway meeting was on Friday the 11th August, and we spent the Saturday at Feldemore but pushed on to Perth on the Monday. Here I had an appointment with Mr Auldjo Jamieson, who wished to see me about one of his sons coming into our office, and came over from Edinburgh for the purpose. We reached Kirkton after a tedious journey on the Tuesday to Mound Station which was about a mile from the farm. . . . My chief pleasure was in walking along Loch Fleet, and watching the innumerable sea and other birds which abounded on the shores and in the woods. . . . On the 18th September Helen, George [Redmayne, who joined them towards the end of the holiday] and I went to Pitlochrie, the rest of our party taking [the] train through to the south. Ellen took Valentine to St Andrews to begin her school career there . . . and Nicholas, having now taken his college degree and left college, took up his work at the office with Willy, the two making 13 Hyde Park Street their chief resting place.

As we desired a change of house in London, I began on our return from Scotland to look out for something to suit us better than 13 Hyde Park Street. Our twenty-one years lease had some time previously run out and we were continuing as yearly tenants only. The house did not suit Helen owing to the strong morning light of its east outlook, almost equalled by the glare of the afternoon sun on the white paint of the houses opposite. Having no stable also, the necessity of finding accommodation for the horses, carriage and man, whenever we had them in London, was a drawback. My attention was drawn to 33 Sussex Gardens, facing north in a line with Oxford and Cambridge Terraces. It seemed to meet our moderate requirements, and was in good condition, having recently been done up to meet the taste of its last occupier, an architect. We arranged for the transfer of the lease, and carried out the move from No. 13 early in the following year [1900].

On the 21st November [1899] I went with many others from Euston to the funeral of Sir Richard Moon, who died at the age of 85 at Copsewood Grange, near Coventry. The funeral was at Binley Church. It was a sad occasion and a little wanting in beautiful music and such homage as could be paid to a life of such strenuous, successful and unselfish work.

After our return from Scotland, we had a pleasant visit of three nights in October from Wilson and Mary Crewdson, Arthur Davey and his wife being here for a Sunday at the same time. Davey, the son of Lord Davey, had studied accountancy in our office, and had married Miss Iona Robinson, an old friend of Helen's. The visitors book also records a Sunday in October spent with us by the Hon. G. Colville, who had been appointed secretary to our Institute of Chartered Accountants.

[Edwin Waterhouse referred to 'an excellent clerk of mine, Mr A. E. Williams, who for long had conducted much of our work in Newcastle and Darlington', but who subsequently 'was tempted from our firm's employ by an advantageous offer from the North Eastern Railway, and now stands very high in their confidence at the head office of that company'.]

All this time and for months past our hearts were full of South Africa [the Boer War] and all that was going on there. The war cast a great shadow over the land, arising from the ignorance and miscalculations of those who ought to have known better. Disasters which should never have occurred had followed one another in rapid succession, and it was not till Lord Roberts took command that one was able to breathe freely again. We had not many friends in the Army – the time was terrible for those who had – Claude Waterhouse, my cousin Crewdson's eldest son, was in the action at Magersfontein, and three times wounded.

During the last few days of April [1900], spent mainly at Feldemore, I was laid up with a slight attack of gout. . . . William, however, was poorly . . . and I remained in bed. Dr Cory saw him next day and his illness, which was attended with a high temperature, soon proved to be pneumonia of a virulent type. [Dr] Phillips kindly came down from London to advise, and all that could be done was done to arrest the progress of the disease. But all without avail, and after some days of patient suffering the dear boy's spirit passed away on the 10th May, and on the 14th his body was placed beside his mother and sister.

Dear William's death was a great shock and blow to me and to us all. He had ever been a most dutiful and affectionate son and a most loving brother, always good and patient and unselfish but taking perhaps a too questioning view of things to allow his surroundings to give him the pleasure they might give; and in an almost too earnest desire to do the wisest thing falling with a certain amount of indecision. . . . I looked forward to his developing, in time, a strong personality, full of goodness and truth, and ready to serve God with a big muscular frame and loving heart. But it was not so to be.

I left . . . on Sunday afternoon [20 May 1900] to take the night train via Stranraer to Belfast, where I had an appointment with Mr Pirrie on the affairs of his (Harland & Wolff's) huge shipbuilding yard, the accounts of which he desired me to audit. I was intensely interested in all that I saw and in the management of the magnificent offices.

In the autumn of this year [1900] there was a general election and Mr Brodrick and Mr Henry Cubitt were again returned for the divisions of the county in which Shere and Abinger respectively stand. The Conservative Party was so strong under Lord Salisbury's leadership, and our member's seats appeared so safe, that there was very little excitement or political feeling evident. . . . I went down to Shere to vote on the evening of the 9th October. . . .

Helen was obliged to take things quietly, and suffered much at times from neuralgia. She consequently did not move to London as usual in November.

Business during the year [1900] was heavy as usual, and though I was now entrusting much of the work in the North of England to others, I was a good deal away from home. In November I was kept some days in court during the hearing of the action brought by the Earl of Portsmouth against Sir J. W. Pease, and gave evidence as to the facts. The Earl was successful but I felt much sympathy with Pease, and it seemed to me that greater care on the part of the legal advisers two or three years before in connection with the transaction in which he was interested, both as trustee for his niece, Lady Portsmouth, and as a member of his firm, would have protected him from having the sincerity of his actions called into question.

CHAPTER XXIII

1901

On July 5th dear Helen's suspense was brought to an end by the birth of a stillborn child. Her recovery was fairly rapid, although she suffered much from neuralgia, and a nervous depression which continued for a long time.

My brother Alfred's visit to Feldemore postponed till early in August did not take place. He had another attack of heart weakness early in the month. . . . Further news from dear Flo of the 9th made us anxious, showing that dear Alfred was suffering from a paralytic seizure [stroke], which while the doctors [Sir Thomas Barlow] gave all the encouragement they could, was of a most serious nature.

Nicholas had a business trip to Cologne. . . . In business the year was an active one chiefly in connection with matters of old standing. . . . In August I was asked by the War Office, the Hon. St John Brodrick being then secretary of state for war, to join a committee on the organization and accounts of the ordnance factories. Mr F. W. Webb of Crewe was chairman, Mr H. S. Carrington and Mr A. T. Dawson (of Vickers, Son & Maxim) [were] other members, and we were assisted by my clerk, Mr H. J. Morland,[75] who rendered a useful report to the committee in his own name. The report of the committee was issued in September 1902.

CHAPTER XXIV

1902–1903

The year 1902 opened much as its predecessor. Leonard Redmayne, and afterwards his father, came to Feldemore for two or three days early in January, and after that we all went up to 33 Sussex Gardens until Easter. I was much away on the January audits, but was able to get down to Feldemore on Saturdays and Sundays to see how the work there was progressing.

Poor Mr Lidderdale was suffering from a most painful and incurable disease, which he bore with the utmost courage and patience. I had been meeting him for some years past on the affairs of the Chicago Great Western Railway, he being the chairman of a committee of bond holders of which I was a member. Howard Gilliat and Alexander F. Wallace were also members, as also Sir Charles Tennant at the time of his death, when his son, Sir Edward, took his place.

I was deeply grieved when at Pontresina [on holiday] to learn by a private letter from Sir David Dale, dated 24th August [1902] that the banking firm of J. & J. W. Pease had failed to meet their engagements. This firm acted as bankers for several large undertakings, such as the Collieries and Ironstone Mines (Pease Partners Ltd) and the Middlesbrough Owners Estate Ltd, for which I had many years been auditor; and Sir David, who was the most active director of Pease Partners, thought I ought not to be ignorant of what had occurred. ... The catastrophe was a terrible one. I felt intensely for my kind friend, Sir J. W. Pease; and next for my equally kind friend Sir David Dale, who, though having nothing to do with the bank was, owing to his great financial ability, an old and valued adviser to the Pease family; and was now, through the concerns with which he was connected, more especially the North Eastern Railway and the Collieries, deeply affected by the failure – while his grief at his friend's most unexpected calamity and all the consequences ensuing to others, was very great. Of this I am confident, that if the balance sheets of the banking firm had been for some time past submitted to Sir David's examination and

169

criticism, the catastrophe would have been prevented. I think I may say that if the accounts of the bank had been subject to the audit of my or another firm of Chartered Accountants, entailing a due comparison of its assets and liabilities, the condition of things which led to the failure would not have arisen. It was a dangerous thing to establish such a 'bank' without more than usual precautions against the abuses which might follow. But, started as practically a family business, to employ the surplus funds of one family concern to meet the requirements of another, it seemed at its inception a simple and useful institution; and for this purpose it was started by Joseph Pease, the father; the chief, possibly the only, outside account at that time being that of the Stockton & Darlington Railway, of which he had followed his father, one of its founders, in the office of Treasurer. But some of the businesses outgrew their family character and from them large deposits of what was practically outside money were received. While large funds were thus freely placed at their disposal, applications were made to the banking firm in later years for financial assistance by some of the less successful concerns in the neighbourhood, and for charitable purposes which, having regard to the reputation for very great wealth in which Sir Joseph Pease was, as I believe he thought truly, held, it was hard to refuse. Such a course once entered upon, it was difficult to stop, and there is no doubt an accumulation of accounts arose on the bank books which should never have been allowed. A firm stand might have brought things round, but it was easier with [the] assistance of friendly bankers in London to let matters drift, in the expectation that, with one or two profitable years in the coal and iron trades, financial ease might result. This might have been the case, but the success of the action of the Earl of Portsmouth largely drew upon the resources of the bank and family, and suddenly it was found impossible to raise the funds needed to meet the proportion of the North Eastern Railway dividend falling upon Darlington, the monies already provided by the Railway having gone elsewhere.

I have described the aspect which this most unhappy affair presented to my mind, because it was one of the most painful experiences of my business life, and was so sudden and unexpected as to need more explanation than seemed to me to be given of it at the time. I do not think it would have occurred if Pease had not to some extent shut his eyes to the net which the relationship of the 'bank' and his various other concerns was gradually drawing round him. If he had had a good independent bank manager or even a strict audit, things would have worked differently. I wish also to record that, though I audited the accounts of the collieries and mines and some other undertakings in which the family was largely interested, I had no knowledge of the affairs of the 'bank', and was never consulted with regard to them. I remember however having frequently drawn attention to the large cash balances belonging to the collieries undertaking, which were allowed to accumulate in the 'banks' hands when they might have been properly made use of in discharging the debenture deed of the collieries undertaking.

Sir David Dale's anxieties at the moment of failure were very largely increased by the serious illness of Lady Dale. Notwithstanding what he writes in his letters, she passed away before the end of the year, a terrible loss to him.

I never discussed the matter of the failure with Pease; indeed I do not remember that I met him to converse with after the event. He went to reside in Falmouth, and died the following year. . . . He was one of the most valued friends of my family and one of my oldest, best and kindest business friends – a man whom to know was to admire and love. . . . I cannot imagine his failing in courage to face any situation, and believe that nothing more than, it may have been reprehensible, thoughtlessness brought him and his friends to this great trouble. How great is the worldly wisdom of the command to 'owe no man anything, save to love one another' and if monies are to be held by any for the convenience of others, as is the case with bankers in regard to their customers' deposits, there should be no limit either to the care exercised in their investment, or, subject to due regard to the privacy of individual interest, to the publicity given to the character of the assets representing them. If J. & J. W. Pease had, like most of their brethren, published their balance sheets, the probability is that they would now be doing well for themselves and for others.

[A further dispute with Mr Hayes, the rector of Holmbury St Mary, prompted Edwin Waterhouse to write to the Bishop of Winchester on 26 May 1902:]

> Mr Hayes has disappointed his parishoners. Small alterations and innovations in the directions of ritualism have recently been followed by practices which are distinctly distasteful to I believe the bulk of the congregation. I may mention among these a large increase in the number of the celebrations of the Holy Communion, at one of which held once a month at 10 am, on Sunday the schoolchildren are invited, if not enjoined, to attend as spectators; and the use of incense at or after the same service, professedly, it is

only fair to add for fumigatory purposes ... while the addresses from the pulpit are to a large extent exhortations to make use of the sacrament as the means of salvation.

While in London we had a change of horses. One of Mr Burdett Coutts's pair immediately on our arrival at 33 Sussex Gardens became unaccountably ill. [Mr Coutts then exchanged these for 'a magnificent pair, larger and more beautiful than the first'.] I wrote [to Mr Coutts] telling him that I had called the horses 'Burdett' and 'Coutts', and that I should always like to tell my friends the liberal way in which he had treated me. Sometime I might be able to pay the further £100 [because of the superior quality of replacements], especially if the horses turned out well, and my L. & N.W. Railway dividend increased. Mr Burdett Coutts was at this moment, in conjunction with Mr Nathaniel Spens,[76] Lord Brassey and Mr George Peel, making a vigorous attack on the L. & N.W. Railway with relation to the absence of ton-mile statistics in the accounts, the ascertainment and publication of which he and his friends believed would lead to great economies in working and increased dividends.

The event to us of the spring was the engagement of dear Nicholas and Audrey Lewin. Nicholas had passed his final examination in the Institute, and arrangements could be made with the firm to secure him an income – so the marriage was fixed to take place in August.

A matter of interest to ourselves and our neighbours arose in the early months of 1903 with regard to the water supply of the district. Mr F. E. J. Blackburne, a very pleasant and useful neighbour, who now lived at Hazel Hall ... found his neighbours in Peaslake very badly off for water, the wells being shallow and often giving out, and to some extent contaminated by surface impurities. He accordingly moved the District Council of Guildford to provide a public supply at the cost of the parish. ... The authorities admitted the necessities of the case, and at Mr Blackburne's initiative the Rural District Council appointed a committee of persons interested to consider the circumstances and report. I was appointed and was chosen chairman of the committee. ... I think the Council was glad to be free of the responsibilities of the matter, and the committee's suggestion that a private company should be formed to do what was necessary under arrangements with the Council for taking up the roads &c. was therefore pressed forward, and the Hurstwood Water Company Ltd was registered on the 28th July [1903], the directors being Mr Blackburne (chairman), Mr Bray, Mr Edlmann ... Colonel Fraser of Nestey and myself.

In April [1903] I was elected at the suggestion of Lord Farrer, who was chairman, a member of the Abinger Parish Council.

We were deeply grieved to hear in February of the death of Joseph Kopf, after a short illness, at the age of 76.

In March I suggested to Mr Brodrick, then Secretary for War, that I might be of use as a magistrate: and he at once communicated with his father, Lord Middleton, the Lord Lieutenant of the county.

On the 22nd August Nicholas and Audrey were married at Abinger Church, Jacob Forrest [Theresa's husband] officiating. There was a large gathering at Parkhurst after the ceremony, the afternoon being a beautiful one.

After a short honeymoon, he took his bride to a little house he had bought after much looking about, in the Victoria Road, Kensington, No. 73 subsequently changed to 71.

Ellen and Valentine went for their autumn holiday [1903] to Drewsteignton, near Chagford, on the edge of Dartmoor, the Merrimans being their companions. ... Their lives at home were fully occupied. Every Monday they went to London for the night, spending the evening at a club for factory and working girls at Lambeth, in which Mrs Bennett took a great interest – and then a day or two more were devoted to violin, singing and drawing lessons.

During the later months of the year [1903], the affairs of the Riverside Trust Company, of which I had been chairman since 1892 – having joined the board soon after dear Theodore's death in 1891 – were giving the directors considerable anxiety, more especially in respect of their relations to Matthew Gage, the original vendor. This gentleman, having entirely disappointed the board in his conduct of the company's business as manager in Riverside, had at an early period resigned, or been superseded in, his office; and had, since that event, for years taken up an attitude of antagonism against the directors in London, complaining that the board had not contributed the full amount of capital necessary for the company's development, and had failed in its engagements to him. There was no basis for these complaints, but he brought actions against us in the Californian courts, prejudicing the company's business in the sale of lands and its welfare generally. Early in 1900 we came to what should have been a binding agreement with him under a deed of arrangement, which we thought would cause him to work in harmony with us, he being largely interested as a shareholder in the company. But he was at his old games again, and it was evident in 1903 that he was seeking to gain control of the company. He held a very large voting power in respect of some deferred shares, and it was clear to us that if he succeeded in winning over to his views one or more of our largest shareholders the coalition might succeed in turning us out as a board, seizing the reins and dealing as they liked with the property. Once in office they might arrange a foreclosure on our lands to the exclusion of our bondholders who had no mortgage registered in California perfecting their security. Mr Gage's deferred shares and one block of preferred were pledged for a cash advance to a San Francisco bank, the other block of preferred shares to an English gentleman named Newton, who held a large amount of preference shares in his own right. With Mr Newton's help, Mr Gage could command a majority of voting power, and we became aware that Mr Gage was seeking with Mr Newton's assistance to get himself installed as general manager in Riverside with full powers.

He evidently had in view the raising of money on our orange properties, but we happily were able to check his action in this direction by placing a mortgage covering our debenture debt on the California Registers. But we found it useless to oppose the coalition which he had formed against us in London; and we had to submit to Mr Newton, Mr Caldicott (Mr Newton's agent) and a Mr Brinsmead being placed on the board in the seats of three existing members, who retired in their favour. Wilson Crewdson and I retained our seats. The only thing we could hope for was that the new directors, as business-men, would after a while at any rate, become, as we had become, aware of Mr Gage's true character, and withdraw the support which they were at the moment giving him. This happily came about even sooner than we had thought possible. Mr Newton, owing to ill-health, was unable to attend the board meetings, and Mr Brinsmead was appointed in his absence. At the first meeting, with Mr Brinsmead in the chair, Mr Gage produced a power of attorney for the company to execute, which would have transferred all the functions of the board to Mr Gage himself. Mr Harrison, our solicitor, of my brother's firm, pointed out that the execution of such [a] document would lay the members of the board open to action by the shareholders for derelic-tion of duty, and time was allowed for consultations with counsel. In the meantime it became apparent that much of what the new members had heard about the past history of the company was contained in a letter written some weeks before by Mr Gage to one of our share-holders. A copy of this letter when asked for could not be refused. It was found to be full of mis-statements and false charges; and before our next board meeting Mr Harrison, with Crewdson's assistance, had prepared and was able to read such a reply to it – backed by a file of original documents in support of what he had to say – that Mr Gage's mouth was shut. He was, of course, supplied with a copy of Mr Harrison's statement, but before the next board meeting took place, he had started back to his house at Riverside, of course without the power of attorney with which he had hoped to astonish our agents. The confidence of Mr Newton in him was naturally shaken. That gentleman soon after went out to Riverside hoping to benefit his health; and when there was impressed more by the excellence of the management as set up by ourselves than by Mr Gage's ability to effect improvements in it, and no more opposition arose either from Mr Newton or his agent, Mr Caldicott. Mr Newton retired from the board which from ill health he had never been able to attend, and soon after died. Mr Brinsmead remained chairman until June 1904, when I was re-elected to that office by the board. We therefore were in dread that another attempt might be made by Mr Gage to get the reins into his own hands, but we had comparative peace for two years. I shall hope to take up the story of our company again in 1906 [p. 182].

CHAPTER XXV

1904–[1905]

On Monday the 11th [January 1904] about 10 am we were able to give thanks on the birth of a sweet boy: such a gift from God that we named him at once, 'Theodore'. I being also glad to carry on the name of my dear brother. . . . All went on well with both mother and child, and I went about my January audits with a light heart.

On the 19th September [1904] I took Ellen and Valentine to Plymouth for a night, spending a most interesting day in going over the dockyard, and the battleship 'King Edward VII', which was just completed; and in seeing the works for the huge new docks at Keyham. A few days before we had met by chance in Exeter Cathedral my old friend, Gordon Miller of the Admiralty, and hearing of our intentions he sent a letter to the superintendent of the dockyard, which secured us much kind attention and the use of the admiral's steam launch.

[To protect the waste lands in the village of Holmbury St Mary from the dumping of refuse, Edwin Waterhouse helped to form the Holmbury St Mary Village Association in June 1904, of which Edwin was the trustee, and served as chairman of the committee.]

The later months of the year were to some extent occupied by the arrangements for closing the liquidation of the Land Securities Company, particulars of which were given earlier [p. 146], when the company came into my hands in 1894. I had realized the assets and paid the proceeds to the bondholders as rapidly as possible but there remained a few properties – notably a mortgage on a leasehold wharf repayable by instalments spread over a long series of years – most difficult to value or sell. I desired that the bondholders should form themselves into a new company, and take over these assets at a valuation likely to yield a profit, thus closing the liquidation and giving them a saleable security. The circular embodying this scheme of arrangement was issued on the 29 December 1904, and approved at a meeting of those interested on the 10 January 1905. The company taking over the remaining assets was then registered, and arrangements made for the transfer of them on the 25th March. The taxation and costs kept the matter open for a short time longer. The final account showed that with the £148,000 received in bonds and shares from the new company, the creditors had received during the liquidation £1,565,702 or 77¾% of the capital (£2,014,589) of their bonds; while a further £287,662, or 14½%, had been paid them by way of interest. My estimate of the return of capital had been between '70 and 80%'. The bonds and shares in the New Company were easily saleable; and with my assistance, a market was formed at par for a large number of small holdings, thus simplifying the register.

Another death which took place early in 1905 was that of Mr George E. Martin of the Worcester Old Bank. ... He and Mrs Martin were most kind and hospitable people, and I had been repeatedly to their beautiful place, Ham House, near Upton-on-Severn, when engaged on the annual audit of the bank. The bank was after a while absorbed by one of the large joint stock concerns, and the audit, so far as I was concerned, came to an end.

The law relating to joint stock companies seeming to require further amendment, Mr Gerald Balfour, President of the Board of Trade, appointed early in the year a committee, under the chairmanship of Sir R. J. Reid, to consider and report upon the improvements that might be made therein; and he asked me to render assistance as a member of the committee. ... I found several of my friends on the committee including Mr John Wreford Budd, the solicitor of Austin Friars, Mr (afterwards Lord) Faber, director of the L.N.W. Railway, Mr F. B. Palmer the K.C., who was on the similar committee, of which I was also a member, appointed by the Board of Trade in 1894, my friend Mr G. S. Barnes, Mr Warmington, K.C., who was at University College School with me in 1856; and, subsequently appointed, Mr Felix Schuster,[77] Mr (afterwards Sir) Edgar Speyer,[78] Mr Worthington Evans and Sir William Holland were other members of the committee. Our deliberations were lengthy, many of my afternoons were required in our meetings, and it was not until June 1906 that our report was complete. It had then to be addressed to the president, Mr Lloyd George – as another result of the change of ministry in 1905, our chairman being called to the woolsack in December, Mr Warmington took his place on our committee. The report and proceedings of the committee are bound up with those of the 1894 committee and form a volume in the library [at Feldemore].

In June [1905] I was the guest of the directors of the L. & N.W.

Railway and the L[ancashire] & Y[orkshire] Railway in a little trip to Norway on the S.S. 'Duke of Connaught'. . . . Lord Stalbridge was taking his son, so Mr Theodore Julius Hare asked that his son, Marcus, who was in our office, might be spared from his work to go also; and this led to my suggesting that I should be accompanied by Nicholas, a favour which was most quickly and kindly granted. . . . All the company turned up, except Mr Ismay, Mr [E.] Nettlefold,[79] and Sir G. Pilkington[80] among the directors, and Mr Thornhill and Mr R. Turnbull among the officers . . .

[The 'List of Passengers' gives the auditors as being J. S. Harmood Banner M.P.,[81] J. E. Halliday and E. Waterhouse.]

[On 22 August 1905, after a protracted illness Alfred, Edwin Waterhouse's brother, died; Edwin was now the last survivor of seven brothers and sisters.]

To me dear Alfred has ever been a pattern brother, ever full, I am sure, with longings for my welfare – ever ready with advice when asked for, and that sound and to the point. I do not think he was naturally devoid of strong feeling. I am reminded of one or two incidents of my boyhood in which he may have shown some heat of temper – but he soon learnt to rule himself as to set us all an example in his calm judgement and humility.

Dear Alfred had thought fit to put my name in his will as one of the Trustees, but having regard to the full competence of the others appointed, viz. Bessie, Paul and Amyas . . . I did not take up the duty. . . . Dear Maria's [who had died very shortly before Alfred] estate was easily disposed of – after various legacies the residue passed to Wilson and Gwendolen. . . . Wilson . . . kindly handed to me many articles which he thought I should specially value, and the volumes of my mother's journal then passed into my hands.

A symptom or a feeling of a little over fatigue had induced me to consult our good friend Napper and at his recommendation I made up my mind to withdraw from the firm at the year's end, thus reducing my responsibilities. This has been to a certain extent made easy when our articles of partnership was last revised by arranging the terms on which anyone of us should he so think fit might retire.

During the month of November I was considerably exercised in regard to a possible variation in the methods of account keeping of the London & North Western Railway, which had been so safely followed for so many years under the late chairman and his co-adjutor and friend, Mr Henry Crosfield; and which had ever since my appointment in Mr Crosfield's office been continued, as fitting the finance of a railway of its standing. A proposal was made with regard to a matter of account affecting the locomotive department, which seemed to me to mix up capital and reserve in a manner likely to lead to error. The proposal, however, seemed to meet with the approval of the officers concerned and possibly also of members of the committee, a recently appointed one which dealt with half-yearly balance sheets and other matters of account. My colleague Mr (now Sir) Edward Lawrence and I were asked to attend a meeting of that committee on the 17th November at which Sir F. Harrison, the general manager, and others expressed views in favour of the course proposed. But as senior auditor, being given the opportunity by the chairman Lord Stalbridge, I spoke very strongly against it, so far I think as to amuse some of the directors by my expressions. But they had effect, for a counter, and what seemed to me an unobjectionable proposal put forward by myself was accepted, and I was requested to join in drawing up a minute which would give effect to it.

But the incident opened my mind to the fact that, as was very natural owing to the passing of time, and consequent changes in the directorate, even the members of the committee on accounts had but little knowledge of the system on which the North Western Railway for more than 50 years had governed the relations of capital and revenue, a liberal expenditure to the advantage of capital being defrayed out of income. Mr Crosfield had in 1868, when the accounts of several railway companies had been called in question and found wanting, written a somewhat full and reassuring circular with regard to the North Western finance, which was issued to the shareholders and gave great satisfaction. This circular I had often referred to as a guide to myself, and it occurred to me that a similar statement of particulars, dealing with the much larger figures and more numerous items of the present day's accounts, could not fail to be of interest to all who had to do with North Western finance.

I accordingly prepared a memorandum of some length, the facts for which were to a very large extent all contained in my last half-yearly book of account, and after getting the approval and signature of my colleague, who at the time was somewhat seriously ill at his home in Liverpool, I had it typed and sent to the chairman on the 7th December with a line suggesting that at any rate it might be put into the hands of the members of the accounts committee and leaving the propriety of any further publicity being given to it to his discretion.

The memorandum, though regarded as a very private document, was printed; and the distribution of copies, limited at the chairman's suggestion to members of the board and the principal officers, effected the object intended by it, bringing before the minds of those in control the sound financial methods of the railway in the past, and showing how these had originated and been maintained; and moreover letting it be known that on this subject, at any rate, the auditors could speak with knowledge.

In November Nicholas started with his wife for a trip in America, more especially to visit those with whom he hoped soon to be connected in partnership, and to have a glance at Riverside, in which I and others of the family were much interested. They had time also to see some of the sights of America. After spending some time with the members of the firm in New York and Chicago, he wrote [to] me a long letter giving his impressions of the management and staff.[82] This he posted on his arrival at the Grand Canyon, Arizona, on the 22nd November [1905], the conclusion of the letter being as follows: –

> In writing to you I am first putting down matters as they strike me (a total outsider to the country) after having the opportunity of talking with three of the partners here, and of glancing through their offices and books. We have received the warmest hospitality and kindness in New York and Chicago from the partners and from their wives; and we are enjoying ourselves immensely. . . .

They returned on the 28th December, having spent Christmas day on the S.S. 'Majestic' in mid-ocean.

CHAPTER XXVI

1906

The circulars announcing my retirement from the firm went out on the 1st January. I annex a notice relating to it, and to Nicholas's admission into the partnership which appeared in *The Times* the following day:

Partnership Changes

Messrs Price, Waterhouse & Co. announce that Mr Edwin Waterhouse, being desirous of partially withdrawing from the active business practice which has occupied him for more than 40 years, has retired from his position as a member of their firm. He will continue, however, to conduct those matters of business in which he holds a personal appointment, and will remain available for purpose of consultation. The firm will be continued under the same name of the remaining partners with the addition of Mr Nicholas E. Waterhouse A.C.A. the son of the senior now retiring.

I had many kind and complimentary letters from my business friends congratulating me on my being able to take the step; and out of them I have selected ... those from Mr Gamlen at Oxford, Sir David Dale, Mr James Stuart of Colman & Co., Lord Stalbridge and my old friend Joseph Swainson of Kendal. I add also letters from Lady Fry, Mr Radcliffe of Liverpool, and my kind good friend Edward Lonsdale Beckwith now of Eastbourne.

I also [received] a letter dated 24 April from A. Lowes Dickinson[83] referring to a kind gift and still more valuable address from the partners and many of the staff of the American firm. The articles referred to were duly received and the address – a very nicely worded one – bearing 26 signatures now hangs in the library, while the piece of plate, a very large and heavy salver, too heavy indeed for use, is stowed away in a place of safety.

Though my work in railway and bank audits, undertaken in my own name and requiring attention at the beginning of the year, kept me busily occupied for some weeks, I immediately felt the relief in being concerned with nothing but my personal work, and before long a certain amount of pleasant freedom resulted.

The condition of the labour market and the large amount of unemployment were exercising the minds of our politicians and early in January [1906], I was asked to associate myself with the committee of which the Revd Russell Wakefield was chairman appointed to deal with the matter in London. I found it impossible however personally to render the assistance in financial matters which the committee deserved.

Sir Edward Lawrence's severe illness continuing, and being of the advanced age of 81, he thought fit to resign his position as one of the auditors of the London & North Western Railway. He had long suffered terribly from rheumatism and gout for many years, bearing his afflictions with singular bravery and cheerfulness. Mr Henry Wade Deacon, also of Liverpool, was proposed as auditor in his place. I had the pleasure of making this gentleman's acquaintance at the general meeting of the company on the 16th February when he was appointed.

In June [1906] fresh trouble arose on the Riverside Trust Company. We learnt by cablegram from our good friend and legal adviser in Riverside, Mr I. G. North, that Mr Gage was on his way to England, with the intention as he believed of again endeavouring to obtain control of the company by redeeming the shares in the hands of the executors of the late Mr Newton. Mr North urged us immediately to purchase the shares ourselves and thus prevent Mr Gage from again obtaining, with his other holdings pledged in San Francisco, a majority of the voting power. On Tuesday, the 26th June, I went up specially to London to meet Crewdson and Harrison and discuss what was possible. We saw the desirability of the course suggested by North, but we knew that owing to the foreclosure action of the executors of Newton now being complete they were not in a position to sell. But the necessity of checking Gage's action was clear to us all and it occurred to me that what could not be done on this side with the Newton shares might possibly be done by Mr North on the other side with the shares in the hands of the San Francisco bank. I told Crewdson that he and I were bound to do all we could to protect the shareholders he had introduced into our company and that I would find £5000 towards the purchase of the 900 deferred shares that carried so much voting power if he would pay a like sum; and I advised our cabling to North to proceed that same evening to San Francisco and ascertain whether the purchase were possible. I think the idea of making a bid for the deferred shares may have presented itself to all three of us, but I was the first to suggest the means. Crewdson agreed and we cabled North. He was at San Francisco the next morning, and we learnt within a few hours that the bank could and was willing to sell, but that we must take the 400 fully paid up shares as well, and that $90,000 would be required. The cash was cabled to him on Friday 29th, and we requested him to make the purchase in the name of Crewdson and myself. He wired, however, asking that the name of some wholly independent person might be given as that of the purchaser so Crewdson and Inglis (Harrison's partner) came down to Gomshall on the morning of the Saturday, and we had a consultation in the arbour at King's Gardens at the Hammer, thus allowing them to take the next train back to London. A name was chosen and cabled to North and we learnt within a week of our meeting on Tuesday the 26th that the purchase was completed. The transfer came over in due course and we were free from the terrible fear that somehow or sometime the large voting power held by Gage, in respect of these 'B' shares, would be used against us again in the same way as it had been in 1903. Our board too was again working harmoniously for at the general meeting held in March 1906, Mr Brinsmead retired by rotation; and, not being duly proposed for re-election, his seat became vacant, and was afterwards filled by the election of Mr Harrison. Mr Caldicott, a man of sound business talent, continued with us, as representing the large interests possessed by the Newton family.

Mr Gage did not hear of the sale of his shares in San Francisco until he returned home after an apparently unsuccessful attempt to redeem the shares held by the Newtons. He immediately commenced an action against the bank alleging fraud and conspiracy with ourselves in the sale to our nominee. The bank brought a counter action for the recovery of the balance still due to them.

I was then [December] engaged in reading through my mother's journals, and had formed the idea of printing some extracts from them for the benefit of a few. . . . I also had in thought the putting down of some recollections of my own life – a thought which has resulted in these volumes, and I had written to Bessie [Alfred's bereaved wife] asking if she could lay her hands on any early sketches of dear Alfred's which might be of interest as illustrating my mother's life.

On the 20th December [1906] there was a meeting of the committee of the Chartered Accountants' Benevolent Association of which I was president, at which I was able to announce the munificent gift of £2000 for the purposes of the association from W. B. Peat, then president of the Institute, sent to me a few days before.

CHAPTER XXVII

1907

[Edwin Waterhouse decided to give up the tenancy of 33 Sussex Gardens in February 1907.]

At the end of February we moved some of our furniture in London to Feldemore; some went to the rooms at No. 1 Campden Grove, where May Weber lived, which Ellen and Vauly had taken as London quarters for themselves; and some was given away. Valentine made arrangements for sharing a studio with a friend of hers on Campden Hill. On leaving Sussex Gardens I had to pay very heavily for dilapidations. My predecessor from whom I had taken the residue of his lease had put in expensive things more to his taste than ours, in the way of parqueterre floors and gilt flock papers, which not being high class in quality showed considerable depreciation. For this I had to pay. If before the surveyors had come in, I had taken up the floors and put up simple papers, so as to revert to the condition of things when the lease was granted, I believe I should have done much better.

I find a letter from J. Wigham Richardson of the 11th March ... it refers to Cecil [Moresby] White, Rosie's eldest surviving son, going out to the firm of Price, Waterhouse & Co. in America. He had been working for years with a brother of his father's, a District Auditor for the Local Government Board in Yorkshire. There seemed no prospect of a future before him in this, and I had been trying unsuccessfully to get him a post in Canada in the Bank of Montreal. The firm kindly found an opening for him, and he went on the 6th February. Having no London house, I now seldom spent a night in town, working [on] such business as I had from Feldemore. ... On the 30th April I attended the dinner of the president of our Institute Mr W. B. Peat, and stayed with the Shearmes at 18 Cleveland Gardens. This was the occasion when Mr Peat told me my speech, which was a poor and halting one, was not 'up to sample'. He had formed too high an opinion of my powers that evening in Liverpool.

Another death occurred in May . . . that of our kind old neighbour, Mr Leveson Gower, at the age of 88. His son George . . . did not care to reside at Holmbury, and the place was sold; the house with immediately surrounding grounds being bought in 1908 by Mr Joynson-Hicks, who distinguished himself by securing North West Manchester for the Unionists against Winston Churchill the same year.

On the 11th July Helen and I joined the annual excursion of the Surrey Archaeological Society, I having become a member at the suggestion of my friend, B. L. F. Potts of Holmbury St Mary. We joined the party in our own carriage at Merrow, where we examined the very interesting old inn 'The Horse and Groom', and the church and then went on to West and East Horsley churches, and to West Horsley Place, a most interesting old house.

Nicholas availed himself of the audit of some branch banks in Cornwall for a change for himself and his wife.

On the 30th August Helen and I took Theodore and his nurse to Felixstowe, where they were going to stay a month with Theodore's godfather, Mr Vatcher. . . . I was much interested in seeing Sir Cuthbert Quilter's huge place at Bawdsey. Quilter was not at home, but the Vatchers showed us the wonderful rock garden facing the sea, on an artificial cliff, huge in its length, and magnificently furnished with plants. . . . The enormous house itself looked dreary and absolutely wanting in taste, as also the immediate surroundings, which had evidently not borne the impress of the same hand as the gardens.

While Theodore was with the Vatchers, Helen and I paid a visit to the English Lakes, which were new to Helen. Leaving Felixstowe on Monday 2nd September and spending a night at Crewe on the way, we spent from Tuesday to Saturday at Rigg's Hotel, Windermere. On the Wednesday, after wiring our intentions to Brantwood,[84] where the Arthur Severns were living, and receiving a welcome in reply, we drove by the ferry to [the] Waterhead Hotel, Coniston, a new drive for me. . . . The house and grounds are very interesting, having been left much as they stood at the time of Ruskin's death in 1900. Driving home via Ambleside we got out at Skelwith, and walked along the familiar Loughrigg Terrace and Rydal Lake to Pelter Bridge, all unspoilt since 1868.

Helen was then a little tired, but we pushed on to our cup of tea, and the carriage that was waiting for us in Ambleside, and reached Windermere after a most delightful day. The next day was devoted to Grasmere and Hengh Folds . . . .

Motorcars and motorbuses were ruining the district wherever they could find footing on a high road. The churchyard at Grasmere had the contents of a huge motorbus thrown out upon it, just as we arrived on foot; and the simple grave was thronged by ignorant and uninterested people. 'Who was Wordsworth?' 'Why! Don't yer know?' 'He was the man as made Grasmere.' A drive over Kirkstone [Pass] to Ullswater, and a trip by steamer to Pooley Bridge occupied us on the Friday, after which we changed our quarters to the Lodore Hotel, which like Rigg's, we found very comfortable. The summer had been and was [so] dry that there was little or no water in the falls, and they did not answer Southey's celebrated description of them. On the Monday we had a lovely drive over Honister [Pass] to Buttermere and Crummock [Water], coming home by Newlands. We met a huge party of Newcastle Co-operatives as we neared our hotel, who were provided with sleeping quarters in a kind of barn under Catbells, a most pleasant looking set. Then on Tuesday with the help of the convenient electric launches belonging to the hotel, we explored Keswick and called at Fawe Park[85] by water – a house built by my brother Alfred for Mr James Bell, now occupied by Middleton Fox, who married his eldest daughter. . . . The following day we paid a visit to Shap and Shap Fells, where we found the air of the moors delightful but the hotel not sufficiently tempting. The next day we went to Watendlath and Rosthwaite, and on the 13th over Catbells to Portinscale. Lodore was very pleasant, but the weather was hot and the low situation not bracing enough for us.

On the 21st October Ellen and I went down to York to embark next day on one of the most delightful sea excursions we could imagine. Helen and I had been asked to join the 'Mauretania' on its first voyage from its birthplace on the Tyne to Liverpool for delivery to its owners. But Helen's inability to face the sea and the sea air led me to ask to be allowed to bring Ellen instead, a favour kindly granted. We joined a large party on the 22nd at Newcastle Station and soon found ourselves on the huge ship at Wallsend. Many other guests arrived; and after some waiting one was conscious that some electric button having been pressed, the mammoth ship was on its way down the river, with a hardly perceptible motion among the tugs and boats that accompanied it and amidst the shrieking of steam whistles and sirens, supposed to evidence joy and good wishes on such an occasion. The wharves and sides of the river were black with people cheering and waving as the great boat of which they were so fond passed away from them never to come back. . . . The autumn sun was now just setting, and we were passing into the lovely opal of the eastern sea, a much more fitting home for the giant ship than the river that had been its cradle. At the mouth of the river there was a training ship and the boys had manned the yards. Suddenly the din of the tugboats ceased, and nothing was heard but the sweet voices of the boys rising on the air with a 'God save the King', one of the most beautifully effective things I ever heard. I confess it brought the tears to my eyes.

The weather was perfect, and the one complete day at sea passed marvellously quickly. There was so much to see in the ship, the engines, the turbines, the magnificently equipped saloons and cabins, staircases and lifts. . . . Early on the 24th we were at the mouth of the Mersey. Considerable fog came in, and as suddenly cleared, revealing the Liverpool docks in brilliant sunshine under a deep blue sky.

In business I had a year [1907] of comparative quiet, though the work in connection with some personal appointments continued and one or two matters were referred to me individually. The arrangement of terms in the amalgamation of some very large coal concerns was an interesting and pleasant piece of work; as also the successful advocacy of the views of the International Mercantile Marine Coy before an arbitrator, in a dispute with another concern of great magnitude. I was also called in by the London County Council to advise them again on matters relating to their Works Department. Our old member of parliament, St John Brodrick, was, as Lord Middleton, filling up spare time as a member of the council, and wrote to me on the subject.

I also find a letter from my old pupil Leonard W. Just, the youngest son of my old tutor, who after his time with Price, Waterhouse & Co., had gone out to Canada to seek his fortunes as a Chartered Accountant there. He was doing well in Montreal.

CHAPTER XXVIII

1908

The beginning of the year, as the close of the preceding one, was occupied by the correction of the proofs of the book containing the extracts from my dear mother's journals, the compiling of which had given me so much pleasure and profit. At George Macmillan's suggestion, I asked R. Clay & Son to do the printing, and was quite satisfied with the result. I ordered 100 copies for private circulation and early in January I was able to issue some of them, and I continued to give others away as I found persons likely to value them.

January and February [1908] were occupied somewhat with the audits to which I still had to give my attention, and some nights were spent in London, chiefly at Euston or Garlants Hotels.

[30th January 1908, Edwin Waterhouse attended the annual dinner] ... given by the Board of the South Eastern Railway to the officers and friends of the Company. I happened to sit by a Mr Kenneth Grahame,[86] secretary to the Bank of England, of which institution the company's chairman, Mr Cosmo Bonsor, was a director. I discovered that Mr Grahame's name was familiar to me as the author of a charming little book about and for children, 'The Golden Age'. We had a pleasant conversation, and finding he knew something about Quakers, I told him about my mother, and afterwards sent him a copy of the 'Extracts' to read. I annex the letter which accompanied the return of the book:

> I am now returning to you the copy of the 'Extracts' which you were so very good as to give me a sight of and which I have read with great interest and pleasure. The serene and quiet atmosphere of it all is most appealing and in strange contrast to the troubled and lurid effect of – for instance – the recently published 'Father and Son'.

Valentine had to find fresh quarters for her work, and her friends advised her to take a studio of her own. It seemed to me that the studios of some young lady artists, consisting often of a single room, approached direct from the street or a public staircase, exposed them to the intrusion of persons whose company they might wish to be without, and of others whose names and business at any rate should be notified before admittance was granted. She therefore had some trouble in finding a room which would meet with my approval. Two joint studios taken with a friend, with some reliable old servant to watch the door would have met my wishes. She found, however, some suitable rooms in the house of a sculptor, Mr Hope-Pinker of 22 Avonmore Road, Kensington. These had a private door and approach; but arrangements were made that the entrance to them to any one but Valentine herself, should be through Mr Hope-Pinker's own front door, giving her the advantages attaching to an inmate of the house. Mrs Hope-Pinker resided at their country home, but one or two daughters lived in the Avonmore Road [residence].

At the end of July [1908] I went down as usual to Liverpool and Crewe on my railway work, and spent a night with Alfred Ashworth at Horsley Hall. . . . I came home from the North feeling poorly, and a weakness in the eyes soon developed itself, resulting in my seeing everything double. I consulted Sir Thomas Barlow and W. J. Lister, and they insisted on my using my eyes as little as possible, and spending a very quiet time at home or elsewhere. This was trying to me as the L.N.W. Railway dividend was about to be considered, and I got it into my head that the old stage methods of finance were about to be discarded, and a new and dangerous system introduced at the insistence of a high official of the company. A statement setting forth many of the to my mind necessary reserves of the company was being circulated with a view apparently of questioning whether some of them might not be applicable to dividend. I wrote a very strong letter from home on the 3rd August to my colleague, Mr Wade Deacon, setting forth my views, and I went up with Helen to the Euston Hotel on dividend day, that I might be within reach if wanted. I was glad to learn that my fears were groundless. Whatever may have been in the mind of the official referred to, it was not put forward for serious discussion, and the accounts were drawn up on the same safe system as had prevailed in the past. Parkhouse, the chief accountant, brought them to Feldemore for my signature on August 12th and stayed the night.

On the 3rd September my cousin, J. H. Paul Bevan, died after a painful illness from which he had long been suffering. He had, after leaving my office, practised accountancy in partnership with a Mr

Woodthorpe, and a little article appeared about him in 'The Accountant':

Paul Bevan, M.A., F.C.A., F.S.A.

We deeply regret to announce the premature death of the talented and promising member of the profession, Mr Paul Bevan, partner of the firm of Woodthorpe, Bevan & Co., chartered accountants of Leadenhall Buildings, London E.C. John Henry Paul Bevan was the only son of William Bevan, in his day a leading solicitor in the City of London, and was a grandson of Paul Bevan, of Swansea and London. He was born on the 29th August 1860, and was educated at Wellington College, afterwards proceeding in 1878 to King's College, Cambridge. . . . He was articled, after he had taken his degree, to his relative, Mr Edwin Waterhouse, of the firm of Price, Waterhouse & Co.

The only business, other than the few audits to which I attended, that came to me during the year was an investigation into the affairs of the Underground Electric Railway of London, which I was asked to join by Mr (now Sir) Edgar Speyer and his friends; more specifically with the view of considering the prospects of a scheme for the reorganization of the company's finances, which had reached a very low ebb. Liabilities in the way of redeemable bonds to the extent of some millions sterling were maturing in the course of a few months, and the circumstances necessitated an application to the court. [Edwin Waterhouse was appointed chairman of the advisory committee, its other members being: Mr J. Spencer Phillips, chairman of Lloyds Bank and deputy-chairman of the North Staffordshire Railway Company, Mr Marlborough Robert Pryor, a director of the London and India Docks Company, chairman of the Mexican Railway Company, a director of the Sun Insurance Office and chairman of the Sun Life Assurance Society, Mr Thomas Skinner of 77–81 Gresham House, Old Broad Street, and Mr John Bathurst Akroyd of the Stock Exchange firm of Cazenove & Akroyds, while Mr Lynden Macassey was the secretary.] I found Mr Spencer Phillips and Mr Marlborough Pryor most pleasant, helpful colleagues. With the assistance of Mr Speyer, Sir George Gibb and others our work was made easy, and we were able to join in a report, which seemed not only to satisfy the court as to the desirability of the arrangement proposed, but to meet the views of all the parties intended. The company has steadily progressed since.

CHAPTER XXIX

1909

[Edwin Waterhouse refers to] two pleasant letters from Lady Fry, referring to other matters than the little subscription which she was in the habit of writing for each January. The arbitration which Sir Edward Fry had so kindly undertaken in a matter between the London & North Western Railway and some of their workmen, was most ably conducted, and enabled matters to go on for a while on a friendly footing, though the men and their leaders do not seem to understand the nature of the agreement. I also annex a letter from the Metropolitan Railway with reference to the relinquishment of the audit of that railway after 36 years service:

> Metropolitan Railway Company,
> Secretary's Office
> 32 Westbourne Terrace,
> London W.
>
> 22 January 1909
>
> Dear Sir,
> ... I am now desired by my Directors to notify you that the following resolution was unanimously passed at a meeting of the board on the 19th instant: – 'Resolved – that the Directors receive the resignation of Mr Edwin Waterhouse with much regret, and desire to place on record their high appreciation of Mr Waterhouse's services to the company during the thirty-six years he has occupied the position of one of the auditors, and of the valuable assistance and advice which has been so readily afforded by him in connection with the company's accounts throughout that period.'
>
> Yours faithfully,
> N. H. Brown

The constant friction which arose between Mr Hayes [the Rector of Holmbury St Mary] and myself in relation not only to church matters but also to the affairs of the 'Hollybush', of which the churchwardens were joint trustees with the Rector, made me desirous of relinquishing that office. I accordingly after careful consideration wrote [to] Mr Hayes some time before our Easter Vestry [meeting] that I did not seek reappointment, and I had his letter of the 22nd March in reply [in which his resignation was accepted by the Revd Hayes].

I had a most interesting visit to Bethesda and Bangor. Mr A. E. Young, Lord Penrhyn's agent coming over for us to Capel Curig in his motor and then showing us the quarries – all the arrangements there were most interesting to me, the vastness of the whole concern and the piece-work system running through all the processes to which slate is subjected ensuring the best results from each block of slate quarried. The place seemed excellently managed and much harmony to prevail, possibly the result of the lessons learnt by the men in their foolish strike and contests with Lord Penrhyn,[87] a few years ago, a trouble which gave Mr Young much anxiety and probably affected his health.

At Whitsuntide I was kindly invited by my friends, the Andersons, managers of the Orient Line of Steamships, to a little boat trip on the 'Orsova', one of the five huge new steamers for the Australian service. Nicholas, who was taking my place in the audit of the Orient Company's accounts, was also asked. There were more than 200 guests (no ladies), not a few of whom I knew. We left Tilbury on Saturday, 29th May, for Plymouth, coming back on the Monday. The picking up of a man who somehow managed to fall overboard off Cowes was the most exciting part of the trip.

I must also record the visit on December 1st of Mr Alfred Crebbin, a gentleman residing in Colorado, recommended by Mr Dale Shaw, as a very clever man of business likely to assist us in the settlement of some long standing questions between the Riverside Trust Company and the Gage Canal Company, a corporation which supplied our lands with most of the water required by them. Mr Crebbin came over from America to confer with our board, and was entrusted with the negotiations which he carried out very successfully the following year. While in London, he spent a night here, and impressed Helen and me very favourably as a most upright as well as a most able man.

Another death during the year [1909] was that of Mr Parkhouse, the Chief Accountant of the London & North Western Railway, since the retirement of Mr Whittle. He was a man whom I always held in the highest esteem. ... His chief clerk, Mr Isaac, was appointed to the vacant office.

CHAPTER XXX

1910

The begining of the New Year, as the end of the old, was marked by political warfare, the budget of the Asquith ministry provoking much resentment. A general election took place in January, and though little of a politician, I felt compelled to do what I could in our village to support Mr W. E. Horne[88] and Col. R. H. Rawson,[89] the Conservative and Unionist candidates in the Guildford and Reigate divisions of Surrey. I am glad to think that in each case the seat was regained from the radicals, who had held them since 1906. Mr Horne came with Mrs Horne to dine with us before a meeting at our schoolroom in which I took part as one of his supporters, and he impressed us very favourably.

I recorded my vote for my old schoolfellow, Sir Philip Magnus,[90] who held his seat for the London University, and for the Unionist candidates for the City of London, where the citizens' Conservatism was clearly expressed. But the general result, while it gave no working majority of Liberals over Unionists, did not do much or anything to deprive the ministry of their powers so long as they were able to carry the Irish Nationalists with them by promises of Home Rule, a promise which was to be redeemed as soon as the powers of the House of Lords had been crippled so far as to prevent effective opposition. Then followed the Parliament Bill with its inflammatory speeches even by members of the government, trying to set class against class and to provide antagonism between the people and the peers; a time of great unrest, the end of which is not yet (1912) in sight.

The early part of 1910 was also much occupied with the affairs of the Riverside Trust Coy. Gage had brought an action against the Bank of California for having, as he alleged, improperly disposed of the shares held by them as security for his debt, while the Bank had a counter action against him for payment of a balance still due. He came over to this country in order to examine on commission certain persons, including Crewdson and myself, whom he no doubt hoped to be able to prove guilty of the fraud and conspiracy of which he had accused us.

Mr North came over about the same time to render assistance to our solicitors and to those who represented the Bank of California on their side. He arrived in London early in January and immediately called on Messrs Waterhouse & Co. in Lincoln's Inn. But he was seriously ill, having left home when unfit to travel, and was reduced to a very low ebb from a fatiguing and sleepless voyage. He was unable to attend our board meeting on the 6th January and took to his bed at his hotel on that day. Though most carefully looked after by an assiduous doctor, and by kind Wilson Crewdson ... he sank; and on Sunday the 9th passed away. ... We knew that by making use of various pleas and delays we might indefinitely postpone Mr Gage's enquiry; but as we had nothing to conceal, it seemed better that the enquiry should come off at once, and the fullest information afforded. The examination was therefore fixed for the 28th January at the American Consulate. Several counsel of repute and various solicitors were engaged, and I was interested in finding that Gage's case was in the hands of my friend, Mr F. Edmund Bray, a rising young barrister, quite able to do justice to Gage's contentions ...

I, as chairman of our company was put into the chair, and after a little questioning, I was gradually led up to the subject of the purchase of the shares from the Bank, evidently looked upon as the result of a deeply laid and very long considered scheme to deprive Gage of his interest in the Company. ... I took the opportunity of going back to 1903 when the possession of the same shares had given Gage the control of our affairs and led to his nominees being placed for a time on our board. [Edwin Waterhouse then outlined the acquisition of the shares in 1906, p. 182.] Crewdson following me in the chair had but had little beyond confirmation to add to my statement. Shortly afterwards we signed the notes of our evidence, and so far as the commission and charge of fraud were concerned, the matter appeared to be at an end.

The London & North Western Railway audit work, in the detail of which I was now much helped by Mr Leale, an experienced clerk of the firm, and other audits occupied me as usual in January and February.

On the 3rd May I looked in at the Royal Academy to see Valentine's picture, 'The Witch Wife', which had been given a very good place on the line in the last room. The subject was somewhat ambitious, but well treated, and the colouring good. I was quite proud of her success.

The rest of the year [1910] was spent so far as Helen and I were concerned, somewhat quietly at home. I had little of business to occupy me, except the half-yearly audit of the L. & N.W. Railway.

On the 4th August I went down to Southampton at the invitation of our neighbour, F. J. Mirrielees,[91] and spent the night on the [R.M.S.] 'Balmoral Castle', accompanying a large party – mostly coming down from London by a special train next morning – in a cruise round the Isle of Wight the next day. The boat had been beautifully fitted up to take the Duke and Duchess of Connaught to South Africa, and several entertainment trips were being made by it. ... I was amused at the conversation of my fellow travellers, who happened to be the Rt Hon Alexander Carlisle of Harland & Wolff, Sir Henry Lucy, better known as 'Toby' of *Punch*, and a Mr Laycock of Sheffield.[92] The two last were warm in the praises of a particular port with which Laycock's cellars were apparently well fitted, bought from an over accumulation at Chatsworth, while Carlisle, seemingly a teetotaller, was equally strong in favour of a 'tea-meal' with the ladies, such a dinner as we had just had on the steamship being a hardship and an unusual occurrence for him. He looked the strongest of the three, and is, I am informed, much looked up to in the huge workshops in Belfast, mainly owing to his 'command of language'.

Illness kept me at home for a few days in August so I was unable to attend the L. & N.W.R. meeting on the 12th or to be present at the directors' dinner on the 10th.

On Tuesday 15th November Helen and I went to Uppingham that we might just see the place as a possible school in the future for Theodore.

The year had been full of political excitement, and was not to end without another election. The returns for supertax and 'form No. 4' in respect of lands, gave great and it appeared useless trouble in the filling up. I had about 50 of the latter, one for each cottage or holding to send in. They went [off] in August 1910 but as yet (June 1912) I have heard no more of them. But I was quickly assessed in respect of supertax. On the 24th August there was an imposing Unionist and Primrose League gathering at Netley Park ... there was no doubt about our loyalty to the Conservative Party, indeed the polling might have shown a larger majority in each division had we not been so sanguine.

[Coming to Feldemore as a guest], Prebendary Carlisle thought that I might assist him in a professional capacity in his great work, and I consented to act as consulting accountant to the Church Army, as a kind of referee in any matter of doubt or difficulty relating to the accounts. This resulted in my making some slight alterations in the form of the published accounts, which have I think added to their clearness.

Business in the City was getting, so far as I was concerned, very small indeed, with the exception of the few audits which I continued with the assistance of the clerks of the firm, and of Nicholas who was fast supplanting me in the affections of my business friends. I had a pleasant little matter to attend to for Alexander Wallace and his partners, and another for my old friends the Alexanders of Lombard Street, who desired a change in the constitution of their company.

During the year 1910 I compiled, mainly with the purpose of making these records more complete, a list of the descendants of my grandfather, Nicholas Waterhouse of Everton.

CHAPTER XXXI

1911-[1912]

The New Year opened to many with feelings of alarm and distrust. The radicals had lost little or nothing at the polls and the government with the help of the Irish vote was contemplating the carrying through of measures disruptive of the constitution and the existing order of things, without further consultation with the electorate.

On the 15th February when in the garden at Feldemore with Helen we saw an aeroplane for the first time, making its way as we thought from Brooklands to Brighton. Miss Foxwell and Theodore also saw it. It seemed to be three or four hundred feet above us, and was travelling at a rapid pace, making a great and unpleasant noise. . . . Not long after four passed over here on the same track. Since then to the present time (August 1912), I have not seen another.

We had many guests [at Feldemore] in May and June, amongst them the Macmillans; Mr J. B. Cooke of Crewe Works, the newly appointed mechanical superintendent of the L.N.W.R. and his wife; Mr and Mrs F. H. Dent, he being the new general manager of the South Eastern Railway, a son of the late Admiral Dent of Holyhead; Mr [Gilbert Henry] Claughton [Chairman of the L.N.W.R. in succession to Lord Stalbridge]; Paul [Waterhouse, son of Alfred], Lucy and their daughter Rachel; and Francis Fox. My acquaintanceship with the last named dated from 1872 or thereabouts when I used to stay at Saltburn, where he lived in a house built for him from my brother Alfred's designs. He was the younger brother and partner of Sir Douglas Fox, and both were and are distinguished as civil engineers, from work in many parts of the world. I had met Francis Fox in a South Eastern Railway train on my way home one afternoon in the spring, and he greatly interested me in telling me of his then occupation in giving Winchester Cathedral a sure foundation, a work which was nearing completion; and in developing afresh a Cornish mine, which had come to grief 60 or 70 years ago, owing to the difficulty the then proprietors had in dealing with a large amount of refractory material from which they could not extract the copper or tin. This ore Fox discovered like pitchblende, some of which from the radium in it, proved to be worth more than £2000 per ton. His visit to us for a night on the 9th June was in fulfilment of a promise made to bring and show us some specimens of the ore and the radium extracted from it. We found him not only most interesting owing to his scientific knowledge, but most anxious to promote the knowledge of Christ.

[Edwin Waterhouse obtained seats from the L.N.W.R. to watch the Coronation from their offices in 35 Parliament Street and on the following day at Charing Cross Yard from the S.E.R.]

Helen, to whom a crowd was always a most ugly thing and much to be avoided, would hardly have thought of going up for the day had it not been for her desire that Theodore should be a witness of a great historical event.

The following morning Valentine and I went up by the 8.40 train to Charing Cross; and had an excellent view of the interesting procession from the seats erected over the tobacconist's shop at the entrance gate to the station yard . . .

Winston Churchill, as Home Secretary, made himself somewhat conspicuous and objectionable in the way he drove about over the route. The troops, especially the Colonials, made a fine and interesting spectacle.

[In July Edwin Waterhouse visited Liverpool Cathedral.] I had the good fortune to meet Mr Scott,[93] the architect, on the spot, to whom my family name was well known through my brother. I very greatly admired his work so far as it has gone, especially the Lady Chapel which being complete is put to cathedral uses. We went upon the scaffolding round the huge east window of the choir.

On the 9th August [1911] when I spent the night at Euston Hotel on L.N.W.R. business, the thermometer was close upon 100 degrees in the shade, and we had a succession of cloudless days following it. On the same day (9th August) the dock and carmen strike broke out and soon after the general railway strike was declared, commencing the 17th. . . . On the 10th was the division of the House of Lords on the Parliament Bill, adding to the anxieties of all thinking persons.

One event, however, of the present year must be here recorded – the death on the 21st August 1912 of my brother-in-law, George T. Redmayne.

[At this point in 1912 Edwin Waterhouse decided to end *His Story*, though he subsequently took up writing again, and attempted to summarize recent developments:]

Before I take leave of my story, I will endeavour to outline the circumstances of the hour – our family life, and the condition of things around our house. .... It has been a generation of change. It has seen the development of the telephone and electric light, the invention and, with singular speed, the introduction with almost universal use of the motor car, driving our old omnibuses and cabs off the streets, and superseding in nine cases out of ten, the pair horse carriages which used to be the mark and pride of the well-to-do. Our country roads are now full of the dust raised by the broad rubber wheels of the engine driven vehicles, of the smell of their petrol, and of the sound of blatant trumpets which warn others of their dangerous approach. And within the last few years the horrors of the aeroplane have come upon us.

Such questions as these fill one's mind at the moment; a time of great political perplexity and strife, and of social upheaval. The strikes of the carmen and railway men of 1911 have been followed by the coal strike of this year, paralysing industry in practically all its branches, for all are more or less dependent on coal. But the community at large was affected by it as well as the employers of labour, and the wide resolve not to be coerced by the ignorant and self-seeking leaders of the workers in a particular trade had its effect; and after weeks of great distress in many homes, the using up of hard-earned reserves, and the loss no doubt to a considerable extent of the trade of the kingdom, work at the collieries was slowly resumed. More recently a strike at the London docks, causing great privation and even starvation among many workers at the East End, was overcome by the sternness of the dock authorities.

A weak government also pledged to obey the behests of their Nationalist supporters, after having with the help of these Irish allies, passed an ill considered and badly drafted Health Insurance Act upon us, are now pressing forward measures for the disincumberment of the Empire in their scheme for Home Rule for Ireland, and for the disheartenment, if not spoliation, of the Church of England in Wales by its disestablishment; and all this with an emasculated House of Lords, their promises of reform and reconstruction of this body being ignored. The outlook is uncertain and dark, foreign affairs and our relations with one or more great continental nations being by no means free from anxiety, and this at a time when our means of defence and our powers of influence have been brought comparatively low, by a grudging outlay for the last few years on our army and navy. There is however one bright feature in the outlook – the growing attachment to the mother country of our colonial brethren and the growing possibility of a closer union with them for purposes of trade and defence.

[Helen Waterhouse] lives a busy life, giving not a little of her time to the little lad whose welfare she has so much at heart. After breakfast, which follows our prayers in the hall at 8.30, she devotes one or two hours to household work and correspondence, and at 11 o'clock takes a walk, generally to see a villager, or her guests in the lodge or orchard cottage. In the early afternoon she likes a drive, calling on a neighbour, generally taking Theodore and Miss Foxwell with her; and after that there will be games with Theodore in the garden, often broken in upon by callers. In the evening we now generally sit in the billiard room, where she reads while Ellen or Vauly and I play in our fashion with the balls. For myself, I find plenty to fill up my time with. Indeed, the days seldom seem long enough for what I want to do in them. Not a little time is spent in the garden or grounds, and the writing of these pages has filled many odd moments of late. The little business I still attend to has taken me to London at any rate one and sometimes two days a week. This occupation will be curtailed when, as I intend, I give up the audits of the National Provincial Bank of England, the Wilts. & Dorset Bank, and the London & North Western Railway at the general meetings of each to be held next year. I have already given informal notice of my retirement, and am hopeful that my place in each may be taken by Nicholas, but this is beyond my power to arrange. The directorship of the Riverside Trust Company, with the slight weekly duties of the Life Association of Scotland, and the fortnightly ones of the South Eastern Railway will then be the only matters to take me from home.

Nicholas has now been a partner in the firm since my retirement in December 1905, and has from what I can gather gained not only in experience but in the confidence of his seniors in the firm and his business friends. He has a quick way of getting through his work without being worried, and a pleasant manner with all.

[Edwin Waterhouse lists his friends in the neighbourhood, noting that many of them have commissioned architect-designed houses with landscaped gardens. However, the rural nature of the countryside is being disturbed.]

Peaslake village has been much enlarged by new buildings, both of cottages proper and week-end residences. Lord Ashcombe has been willing to part with land on building leases, and recently Purser's Farm, the property of a City charity, has been in the market in lots. The result has been that some very beautiful sites for mansions have been spoilt by the erection of a lower class of dwelling than they are worthy of.

[Edwin Waterhouse mentions] a pretty little house at the edge of Hurtwood, 'Southcotts', no doubt originally a cottage, and for some time occupied by Mr and Mrs C. N. Williamson, the novelists, [which] was sold by them two or three years ago to Mr Mark Gregory, who had been known to me for many years; first, as looking after the affairs in Ruabon of the New British Iron Coy, which I wound up; and afterwards as a director, jointly with Professor Ayrton, of a manufacturing company in South Wales, of which my firm were and are auditors.

Peaslake is rather a nest of suffragettes. I have been told that there are fourteen ladies there of very advanced views, among them Mrs Brackenbury and her two daughters, all of whom were convicted recently of breaking shop windows in London for the purpose of advertising themselves and their cause.

I cannot end the story of my three score years and ten without some general retrospect. . . . I have described only hours of sunshine, and left the cloudy days out of the record. There have been some times of doubt and difficulty, some seasons of depression, some business anxieties. Mistakes have been made, and sins have to be deplored. But to dwell on these, even if they had not been mercifully few, and had not already largely passed out of memory, and the sins forgiven would not be of interest or use. Mine has been a singularly happy life . . . and this mainly owing to the love which has been showered upon me by my parents, my brothers and sisters, my childhood and specially by those dear women whose lives have been linked with mine . . .

In business too I have been connected with men whose character has strengthened my own sense of upright dealing, and with whom it has always been a pleasure to work.

But while thus testifying to the smoothness of my life, I am deeply conscious of my own shortcomings. . . . I have been guilty of sharpness of temper and tongue, not only towards subordinates, but towards most near and dear to me.

A review of the preceding pages – now extended far beyond my original intention to ten big volumes – easily discloses the fact that my relations with our present rector have cast a shadow over the later years of our life at Feldemore.

APPENDIX
1913-1917

2 September 1914

About two years ago I brought my record of seventy years or more to an end. I prepared an index of persons and matters referred to, and a table of the contents of each chapter composing the record.

I write on the 2nd September 1914; and what have I to say? For about a month this country has been engaged in an awful war which has enveloped Europe in flames, and plunged a large proportion of it into desolation under the sword. ... The German Kaiser has thrown off his mask, and causing a quarrel between his Austrian friends and Serbia as an excuse, is seeking, with the military machine he has been training for a quarter of a century for the purpose, to enforce his despotism of 'blood and iron' upon Europe.

It is extraordinary how with these things at our doors, almost within the sound of cannon in our ears, our daily bread is given us day by day, and our life goes on much as usual in the quiet and peace of lovely Feldemore.

But we hear little of what is going on for the newspapers are kept without news, except what a governmental Press Bureau may vouch-safe, or occasional correspondents supply under rigid censorship. ... The train service of the country was hardly thrown out of gear for public traffic while [the British Expeditionary Force was being sent to France] ... although all the railways were, and are, in the hands of the military authorities; but the constant rumble of trains at night through Gomshall eastwards evidenced something very different to usual.

Lord Kitchener, happily now minister at war, is appealing naturally for recruits, and his call is being bravely responded to by rich and poor. ... Relief funds, and organizations for ascertaining distress and distributing relief, and for nursing, are being arranged in every district. ... The Prince of Wales set in foot the National Relief Fund, which has accumulated £2,000,000 during the three weeks or so for which it has been open. Price, Waterhouse & Co. undertook the correspondence arising on the receipts gratuitously and Halsey[94] and Nicholas have been continuously in charge as Hon. Accountants at York House, St James's. They have many willing helpers, and a very large staff from the General Post Office to assist, but are often at work till nearly midnight.

The enemy amongst us is constantly in our thoughts. Spies abound and German waiters and servants are naturally suspects. Railway bridges and points have to be guarded. Boy scouts and other willing helpers, including Theresa's boys, have been used for the purpose.

What may be at hand for us we know not. There is a strong conviction that civilization will in the end prevail, but the struggle with the powers of evil may be long protracted, and may entail untold misery. ... As Lord Kitchener points out, it may be a question of staying power, and in this we and our allies may have, in the long run, the advantage. Germany's forces, though enormous, have a limit. She is putting all her manhood under arms, and as the war goes on their numbers can but diminish, while the resources of the allies, with the vast population of Russia; the assistance of our colonies; and, as it is trusted, the willing enlistment of the mass of the men of these islands, should afford in time a fighting force sufficient to break the German despotism however strong it may have grown.

For the term 'holy' to be applied to a war, it must be one for the advancement of God's kingdom against the powers of evil. This may well be the case with the war in which we are now engaged, but one of its effects may in God's mercy be the purification of the nations, and a turning to God, of which the English may stand in as great a need as others. The pleasure seeking and selfishness of so many, the vanity and folly of our pastimes (evidenced by the thousands who look on at a football match), the neglect of the sabbath and church, especially among men, have brought the spiritual life of many, even if it can be said to exist at all, to a very low ebb. It may be that a time of trial to lead us to repentence and a change of life is to be ours.

It is now my intention to narrate the chief events of our home life during the last two years, but I shall have to refer again to the progress of the war.

1913

A considerable diminution in the audit work which remained to me took place within the year. On the 21st January I was due at Salisbury on the Wilts. & Dorset Banking Company's audit but I did not attend owing to ill health at the moment. I should have retired at the time, but

Mr Devenish, the last general manager, and now a director, suggested my postponing this action for twelve months. Nicholas made my excuses, and did the work for me. On the 30th January I attended the meeting of the National Provincial Bank of England in London, and had the pleasure of hearing Nicholas appointed to the office which I then resigned.

At the London & North Western Railway . . . the audit committee of shareholders had been informed that my name would not be put forward for re-election at the expiry in February of my two-year term of office. Mr Ernest Moon, now Counsel to the Speaker, learning that Nicholas aspired to the office, kindly sent for him.

The audit of the Danish Gas Company was given up [in October 1913. Edwin Waterhouse mentions] a kind letter from the chairman, Sir Corbet Woodall – who as an intimate friend of Colonel Lewin and, often at Parkhurst, occasionally gave a visit to Feldemore – referring to my resignation and the appointment of Nicholas in my place. In December I asked that I should be relieved of the duty of Chairman of the Parliamentary and Law Committee of our Institute, a position which I had held for many years, and I fear not very satisfactorily of late. My colleagues kindly assented to my request, and very unexpectedly presented me with a very beautiful old cake basket of silver in token of their appreciation of my services.

At the beginning of 1914 I resigned the audits of Alexanders & Co. Ltd, and the North London Railway. The firm [Price, Waterhouse & Co.] were appointed auditors to Alexanders, and at the general meeting of the North London Railway, Nicholas was chosen as my successor.

[Edwin Waterhouse had held the post of auditor to the N.L.R., a subsidiary of the L.N.W.R., for eight years on his retirement.]

I have also to record the death of our builder, and old acquaintance, George King, on the 18th January [1914]. His two sons, William and George, continue the firm in the old name of W. & G. King and promise to make good men of business.

The year 1914 up to the outbreak of war . . . was marked by great political strife and grave political anxiety. While the follies of the Land Valuation (Finance Act 1910) Act had for sometime been pressed upon us, and the irritation caused by the badly considered National Health Insurance Act, 1911, was only very slowly subsiding, the anticipated disruption of the Empire by Home Rule in Ireland and the spoliation of the Church by Welsh Disestablishment were never absent from our thoughts. Various matters were also brought forward by the Government with the object on the surface of ameliorating the condition of the working classes, but considered by their opponents as simply methods of obtaining popularity among unthinking people and securing their votes.

[War having been declared on Germany,] for the first few days or weeks it was a terrible nightmare, and our hearts were full of dread. By the end of the first month one began to realize that events could not follow each other at any rate with the speed which the enemy had hoped for or anticipated.

Some twenty of our villagers have joined the forces; or after having been selected, are preparing to do so in the training camps. Among the latter is Willy Hobday, whose health, after eight years of apprenticeship and service at the Crewe Engineering Works, entirely broke down. Being advised that he must seek outdoor occupation, a call to take up his duties in the Territorial ranks, came opportunely; and his health has already been largely benefitted by the new and active life.

31st May 1915
The awful war goes on – now for more than 300 days – but the months seem to bring it no nearer to its end. . . . On each side the losses have been enormous – the allied troops, British and French, Belgians and Canadians and other colonials, have all shown the utmost bravery, and the spirit of Kitchener's new army is all that can be desired.

Our allies have been setting us an admirable example in the marshalling of their resources, both public and private, for the full equipment of their armies. French and Russians have submitted cheerfully to measures, such as the total prohibition of the sale and consumption of absinthe and vodka, as may ensure the fullest output from their factories of military material, and in other ways forward the successful prosecution of the war. In Great Britain, the ignorance of a very large proportion of the working classes of the immense issues at stake, their consequent apathy and thoughtless endeavours to procure, during a period of high prices and wages, holidays and pleasures for themselves, have led to an increased consumption of alcohol in some manufacturing districts. . . . While abuse of alcoholic drink has, as ever, been one of the causes whereby the full output has been restricted, the present situation points to a wider evil – viz. the slackness in the public interest exhibited not only among some sections of manual labour, but also among the salaried and commercial and monied classes. While the response to Lord

Kitchener's appeals for men for his new armies has been surprisingly good ... far more are required, and a strong feeling in favour of conscription, or at any rate of universal military training, is being aroused, as the only way of bringing home to the minds of the unthinking a sense of their duty to the state. Men are required not only for the ranks, but for industrial service in the manufacture of material, more especially of explosive ammunition of which the past rate of production has proved inadequate to meet the enormous consumption of projectiles, which is one of the features of the present struggle.

16th June 1915

A large number of the staff of Price, Waterhouse & Co. have entered the forces, and are either training for service or are engaged in the war. The firm are intending to print from time to time and for private circulation, a Bulletin,[95] as a record of facts and experiences of interest to the staff. The first number, dated February, gives the names of 56 men serving in the forces from the offices of the firm. I think Nicholas himself would desire to serve, but his various appointments would make this difficult. He is now much occupied as a member of a semi-official committee for assisting English prisoners of war.

Life in London continues to some extent affected by the war, in the putting out of lights at night, and other precautions against aeroplanes &c., but here the days pass much as past. The price of meat and some other things have gone up considerably, those of beef and mutton about 40 per cent. Bread having gone up in price seems now on the decline again.

Nicholas has managed to be with us frequently at the weekend, coming down by motor for a few hours. . . . He has also devoted himself to me on the occasions when I have gone up to London on business; but these are getting few, as I have given up the chairmanship of the Riverside Orange Company, kindly taken up, to the benefit of all, by Mr Inglis, and I have little now to take me to the City.

It is February 1916, eight months since I wrote the above. . . . The war, which occupies almost all our thoughts and prayers, now in the 19th month of its horrors, seems to have made in the interval but little progress towards its desired end.

The great recent act of the government, fully endorsed by Parliament, is the scheme of conscription adopted to supplement voluntary enlistment. While enforced military service is so contrary to English ideas, the feeling in favour of a vigorous prosecution of the war, and the taking of any step likely to secure this, rendered the scheme acceptable to the minds of all but a very few.

Munitions of war appear to be provided for in the vigorous arrangements made by the Ministry of Munitions ...

Our expenditure, including some assistance in money to our allies, has been estimated at £5,000,000 a day.

29 February 1916
I gave up the presidency of the Chartered Accountants' Benevolent Association on the 29 June [1915], and my seat on the Council of the Institute in July [1915] and more recently [January 1916] I have resigned my office as auditor to the Dean and Chapter of Westminster Abbey. ... I am glad to say that Nicholas was kindly chosen to fill the vacancy on the Council and to follow me in the audit and Choir Stall at Westminster. He has been a great help to me in the Riverside Orange Company, where they have kindly appointed him a director.

The firm of Price, Waterhouse & Co. got into their new building at 3 Frederick's Place in the autumn, but the first time I paid a visit to it was on the 3rd November [1915]. They kindly gave me a painting made of the old offices before they were pulled down. It hangs in the library.

29 August 1916
Since the beginning of July both our allies and ourselves have been able to take up the offensive, most especially on the Somme, driving the enemy yard by yard out of the carefully entrenched ground long occupied by them. Though the gain in territory is but small, the fighting has proved the excellent spirit and valour of our young troops.

23 September 1916
On the night of 24 April [1916] Joseph Gurney Fowler, senior partner in my old firm, died after a short illness. ... He had for a long time occupied the position of Treasurer of the Royal Horticultural Society and took a great interest in gardening generally. He had excellent business abilities and the firm will feel his loss severely.

Nicholas and his partners, with an office staff depleted by war, have been very busy with a large amount of ordinary accountant's work supplemented by work for the government in the settlement of accounts with railway companies and traders and the ascertainment of 'excess profits' liable to taxation, while Nicholas has had important personal work on a committee formed at the instance of the War

Office to ascertain and provide for the wants of prisoners of war in the enemy's country. His work for the Prince of Wales' Relief Fund, and Princess Mary's Fund is now practically closed. He has been able to continue his very acceptable visits to Feldemore about once a week. . . . The following are extracts from Nicholas' letters during the last six months:

13th March: 'we continue to get more work, and I am glad to say that we have come to fairly satisfactory arrangements with the military authorities as to exemptions. The individual partners in W. Peat & Co. and P. W. & Co. are to undertake to attend at the War Office to advise as to the prices to be paid to contractors for goods to be purchased on the basis of their costs. We should have power to make, or instruct local accountants to make, investigations where it seemed to us necessary. The advisory work would of course be honourary.'

6th April: 'I had an interesting interview today with Mr H. of Skinningrove,[96] chiefly as to his arrangements with the government to enable him to increase steel output, so as to be independent of Germany in this respect after the war.'

25th April: 'I have just heard from the office of poor J.G.F.'s [Fowler's] death. . . . I wonder who will take up his position with Railways and Government Control. His first report was completed only last week. He was also on the government committee dealing with excess profits claims.'

20th May: 'Have been very busy all this week, mostly at the war office. . . . Wyon, Dickinson and Garnsey[97] also spend much time at the Munitions Ministry, where I expect they are most useful.'

20th June: 'The War Office work is getting very heavy, and I do not feel that I give as much time to it as I ought, but I have some first class clerks there jointly with Sir W. Peat.'[98]

8th September: 'At the War Office today, Lord Derby, as representing Lloyd George, sent for me and asked if I would be one of two of our committee to join a new committee with full power to act in any way it thought fit without reference to the War Office. . . . The new committee is to be ostensibly "Red Cross" [a welfare committee to deal with British prisoners of war].'

16th September: 'I think I shall have a lot of work in connection with the new committee and can only hope it will be useful. . . . The system of accounts to be devised will necessarily be elaborate as we shall buy provisions in bulk and pack and despatch them, probably many thousand parcels a day, and it will be necessary to keep strict loss accounts. I shall of course act in conjunction with the accountant of the Red Cross, whom I know well, and we must have a competent paid staff.'

When I made up my private accounts for the year ending 30th June last, I found that, with super tax, thirty per cent of my gross income had gone in imperial taxation. The percentage cannot fail to be much more during the current year [1916] when a 5% income tax, if not more, will rate throughout. This at a time when owing to the war not a few investments fail to produce any return, must be very trying to many, and must make it very difficult to meet the high prices of the necessaries of life.

15 June 1917
Our life at Feldemore has been very quiet during the last nine months. Helen and I have not been away even for a night; my health, owing to increasing years, makes home the best place for me. We have had but few visitors, travelling being difficult and discouraged by the government. Nicholas, however, has been able to be with us pretty regularly once a week to dinner . . .

The hand of death has been busy amongst our friends; some of our oldest neighbours have passed away, while the roll of honour of those stricken down in the war lengthens.

NOTES

1 Richard Lane (1795–1880) was the foremost architect in Manchester in his day, and was the first president of that city's architectural society. A designer of churches, chapels and public buildings, he favoured the Greek Revival style. Alfred Darbishire, another Quaker who served his articles with Lane, described his master as a gentleman and a scholar but added that the 'the firm of Lane and Alley Limited had a touch of humour in it, which certainly did not suggest genius or high art' [Alfred Darbishire, *An Architect's Experience, Professional Artistic and Theatrical*, Manchester (1897), p.21]. When Alfred Waterhouse had completed his training with Lane he left for the obligatory tour of the Continent with his school friend Thomas Hodgkin, whose sister he was later to marry.

[RIBA Biography File 'Richard Lane'; H. Colvin, *A Biographical Dictionary of British Architects 1600–1840*, London (1954), p. 502; Sally Maltby, Sally MacDonald and Colin Cunningham, *Alfred Waterhouse 1830–1905*, London (1983), p. 6.]

2 The Great Exhibition of 1851, intended to show off Britain's industrial and commercial might, was housed in the innovative glasshouse designed by Sir Joseph Paxton and called the Crystal Palace. Examples of manufacturing in all their variety were arranged by nation and by specific activities such as, mining, iron manufacture, machine tools, and hardware.

[Robert Hunt, *Hunt's Hand-Book to the Official Catalogues . . . of the Great Exhibition*, 2 Vols, London (1851).]

3 Following this first visit in the summer of 1854, Edwin Waterhouse took at least another five holidays in the Lake District. In August and September 1856 the Waterhouse family stayed at Nab Cottage, overlooking Rydal Water. (p. 63), and two years later spent their summer vacation at Thorny How, Grasmere (p. 65, see plates 15, 16 and 17). Although wealthy families living on the fringes of the Lake District had begun to build summer houses there during the last quarter of the eighteenth century, the area did not become a popular resort for the middle classes until the mid-nineteenth century, when the construction of the railways facilitated travel from centres of population such as Manchester and London. The branch line, for example, from Oxenholme (on the route from London to Carlisle and Glasgow) to Windermere had been opened in April 1847. The transformation brought by

Notes

the railways is alluded to by Edwin Waterhouse when referring to Rydal Water as a 'delightful spot, then comparatively quiet as, compared with what it is fifty years later' (p. 63). When he returned to the Lakes in 1907, having previously been there in 1888 (p. 126), Waterhouse was upset by the influence of motorbuses and motor cars (p. 186). Whilst holiday-makers had for the most part been well-to-do for the greater part of the Victorian period (being able to afford the cost of accommodation and able to spare several weeks away from work), the artisan and thrifty worker was beginning to visit at the turn of the century. In 1907 Edwin Waterhouse recorded meeting 'a huge party of Newcastle co-operatives' who were sleeping in a barn some miles outside Keswick. Alfred Waterhouse, whose architect's practice was originally based in Manchester, won a number of commissions to build villas for the middle classes wanting a summer or retirement home amongst the beautiful fells and lakes. These included Rothay Holme (1854–56) and Fawe Park (1856–58), both near Derwentwater, whilst another early commission was the Keswick Art Gallery (1856).

[*The Discovery of the Lake District* (Victoria and Albert Museum, 1984), pp. 28, 106–07.]

4 University College School, founded in 1830, was soon accommodated within the buildings of the college itself, and among its first headmasters were Henry Malden, Professor of Greek, and Thomas Hewitt Kay, Professor of Latin. It was a remarkably original institution: there were no compulsory subjects and no rigid form system. Most boys were taught Latin and French and many learnt German; other popular subjects were chemistry, English and physical geography. Religious knowledge was not included in the curriculum and flogging was banned.

[Hale Bellot, *University College London 1826–1926*, London (1929), pp. 170–71.]

5 Sir Edward Fry, P.C., F.R.S., F.S.A., (1827–1918) the second son of Joseph Fry of Bristol, was educated at Bristol College and University College London, where he became a close companion of Theodore Waterhouse (whose diaries and correspondence he edited in 1894), having already met the Waterhouse family when they lived at Sneyd Park, through his father's friendship with Alfred Waterhouse Senior. Called to the bar at Lincoln's Inn in 1854, he became a Q.C. in 1869, a judge of the High Court in 1877 and Lord Justice of Appeal in 1883. Knighted in 1877, Sir Edward Fry retired in 1892.

[W.T. Pike (Editor), *Bristol in 1898: Contemporary Biographies*, Vol. 1, Brighton (1898), p. 86; *WwW*, Vol. II, p. 383.]

6 Lewis Fry (1832–1921), son of Joseph Fry of Bristol, married Elizabeth Pease in 1859. He qualified as a solicitor but entered Parliament as a Liberal Unionist in 1878, as member for Bristol; he subsequently sat for North Bristol (1885–92 and 1895–1900). Lewis Fry chaired the parliamentary committee on Town Holdings (1886–92), and was pro-Chancellor of the University of Bristol.

[*WwW*, Vol. II., p. 384]

7 Having entered the firm of William

Notes

Bevan, a City solicitor and brother of Mary Waterhouse, Theodore Waterhouse decided to seek an academic education. As his mother wrote in December 1856, 'our dear Theodore having concluded to study at the University and then return (D.V.) to his uncle's office, instead of remaining there until he can be articled, there being no vacancy at present. It seemed a thing rather quickly determined on . . . but his father did not see his way to oppose it, neither indeed did I, though it took us a little by surprise'.

[*Journals of Mary Waterhouse, op. cit.*, pp. 124–5]

8 Sir Julian Goldsmid (1838–1896) became a member of the Senate and was briefly Vice-Chancellor (1895–6) of the University of London. Called to the bar at Lincoln's Inn in 1864, Goldsmid sat as a Liberal Unionist M.P. for Honiton (1866–68), Rochester (1870–80) and St Pancras (1885–1896). He served as a Vice-President and Treasurer of the Council of University College, and gave £1000 towards the foundation of a University of London Library.

[Negley Harte, *The University of London 1836–1986*, London (1986), pp. 125,144.]

9 William Turquand (1818/19–1894) in January 1861 at the time that Edwin Waterhouse joined Coleman, Turquand, Youngs & Co., was one of the leading accountants in the City. His father was one of the first official assignees to be appointed under the Bankruptcy Act of 1831, and William was himself recorded in 1846–47 as holding such a post at 13 Old Jewry, London. Having then set up in private practice, for while in partnership

with a Mr Edwards, Turquand then joined the Scots brothers, John (d.1888) and Alexander Young (d.1907), to form the firm of Turquand, Youngs & Co. Like the other successful accountants based in the City, Turquand was a specialist in insolvency work and handled many of the major bankruptcies of the period, including Overend, Gurney & Co.

[*The Accountant*, Vol. XX, No. 1008, 31 March 1894, p. 290; *DBB*, Vol. 5 (1986), pp. 582–4; Edgar Jones, *Accountancy and the British Economy 1840–1980, The Evolution of Ernst & Whinney*, London (1981), pp. 34, 42, 43, 48–9.]

10 Rt. Hon. Herbert Hardy Cozens-Hardy (1838–1920), educated at Amersham School and University College, London, where he was a fellow, became a bencher of Lincoln's Inn. He was Liberal M.P. for North Norfolk (1885–99). In 1899 Cozens-Hardy was appointed a judge of the Chancery Division of the High Court of Justice, a post he held until 1901, when he became Lord Justice of Appeal. Serving as Master of the Rolls from 1907 to 1918, he received a peerage in 1914.

[*WwW*, Vol. I, p. 239]

11 Sir Samuel Morton Peto (1809–1889), a partner in the firm of contractors, Grissell & Peto (from 1846 Peto & Betts), undertook considerable railway work during the 1840s including that for the South Eastern, Great Western and Eastern Counties Companies. It was estimated that these contracts amounted to over £20 million. He constructed the Crimean military railway without profit to himself in 1855, and for which he was awarded a baronetcy. A Liberal in favour of extending a franchise to the working classes, vote by secret ballot, and of complete religious freedom for every denomination, he sat for Norwich (1847–54), Finsbury (1859–65) and then was elected MP for Bristol, resigning in 1868.

[*DBB*, Vol. 4 (1985), pp. 644–53; Stenton, *WWMP*, Vol. I p. 309]

12 Farrer Herschell (1837–1899), having been educated at University College London was called to the bar at Lincoln's Inn in 1860. He became a Q.C. in 1872, was Recorder of Carlisle (1873–80), Solicitor General (1880–85), Lord High Chancellor in 1886 and 1892–5. Awarded a peerage in 1886, he also served as Chancellor of London University from 1893.

[*WwW*, Vol. III, p.334.]

13 William Stanley Jevons (1835–1882), born in Liverpool and educated at University College School and University College, was an assayer at the Sydney Mint (1854–9) before becoming a lecturer and then professor at Owen's College, Manchester. He then returned to London to take the post of Professor of Political Economy at University College in 1875–81.

[Negley Harte and John North, *The World of University College London 1928–1978*, London [1979], p. 104; *DNB*, Vol. XXIX, pp. 374–8.]

14 Augustus De Morgan (1806–1871), Professor of Mathematics at University College London, married Sophia Elizabeth, daughter of William Frend, who had been expelled from Cambridge University for expressing heretical opinions. Born in India and educated at Trinity College, Cambridge, he established a considerable

reputation as a teacher and was described by Bellot as having 'a temper of great sweetness and liberality, but the masterful and independent cast of his mind, a love of principle, a keen sense of humour, and an athletic delight in mental agility, made a radical and incisive critic ... Of this fruitful and original mind the eccentricities for which he was famous were part and parcel' (p. 84). His son, William Frend De Morgan (1839–1917), after attending University College School and College, achieved some distinction as an artist, chiefly in stained glass work and ceramics, subsequently becoming a writer of fiction.

[Hale Bellot, *University College London 1826–1926*, London (1929), pp. 80–87; *WwW*, Vol. II, p. 278.]

15 Edmund Ashworth (1800–1881) had two elder brothers Henry (1794–1880) and John (1796–1879), and one younger brother Thomas (1802–1870). Their father John Ashworth (1772–1855) had built the New Eagley Mill in 1793 on the Eagley Brook between Bolton-le-Moors and Turton, for the manufacture of coarse cotton fabrics. He was also a land agent involved in farm and estate work, becoming in 1802 secretary of the Manchester Agricultural Society. Although his sons Henry (responsible for the purchase of Egerton Mill in 1829) and Edmund both entered the family cotton spinning business, both John and Thomas chose to become land agents, initially in partnership with their father. Thomas Ashworth later became agent for Lord Vernon's collieries. Like Waterhouse, they were brought up in the Quaker religion.

[Rhodes Boyson, *The Ashworth Cotton Enterprise 1818–1880*, Oxford (1970, pp. 1–5, 13, 24.]

16 Charles Kingsley (1819–1875), educated at King's College, London, and Magdalene College, Cambridge, became a cleric and then a university lecturer. Best known for the *Water Babies* (1863) and *Alton Locke* (1850), he was reformist rather than revolutionary and believed in the possibility of reconciling religion and science.

[*DNB*, Vol. XXXI, p. 175.]

17 James Edward Coleman, like Turquand, had established a considerable reputation as a City accountant, and was often appointed by the Bank of England to investigate the solvency of suspect enterprises, such as Trueman & Cook, colonial brokers. Coleman, giving evidence to the Select Committee on the Bank Acts, recorded that his 12 largest insolvency cases in 1857 had liabilities totalling £6,726,840. In that year his firm, J. E. Coleman & Co., had merged with Turquand, Youngs & Co. to form one of the largest partnerships in Britain. The success of Coleman was recalled by Ernest Cooper (1848–1926) who added 'I am not sure that I ever saw him, but he was reported to be living in a park as a Buckinghamshire Squire' [*Institute of Chartered Accountants in England and Wales, Proceedings of the Autumnal Meeting* London (1921) 'Fifty-seven years in an Accountants office', p. 46].

[*DBB*, Vol. 5 (1986), p. 582; Jones *Accountancy and the British Economy, op. cit*, pp. 34, 35, 42, 46.]

18 Henry James, Lord Hereford, (1828–1911), educated at Cheltenham College, was called to the Bar at the Inner Temple; he became Solicitor-General in 1873, and Attorney-General 1873–4 and 1880–5. A Liberal M.P. for Taunton (1869–85) and Bury (1885–6), he sat as a Liberal Unionist for Bury from 1886 to 1895, when he entered the House of Lords, (see also pp. 99, 140).

[*WwW*, Vol. 1, p. 373.]

19 David Chadwick (1821–1895), a Manchester accountant, developed a considerable reputation as a company promotor and was responsible for the flotation of many major industrial enterprises, including Bolckow, Vaughan & Co., Charles Cammell & Co., John Brown & Co., the Patent Nut & Bolt Co. and Vickers, Sons & Co. His wide circle of friends and acquaintances in Manchester and Salford provided a core of potential investors to whom he could turn when a new enterprise sought limited liability. Waterhouse is correct in his recollection that Chadwick's involvement in this type of work declined after the financial crisis of 1866, but this was because he devoted more time to a political career (becoming M.P. for Macclesfield in 1868) and because during the 1870s his firm broadened their activities dealing in a wide range of securities including American land sales, shares in overseas mining, telegraph and tramway companies as well as domestic, commercial and public utility companies. He was a founder Council member of the Institute of Chartered Accountants and first president of its Manchester branch.

[*The Accountant*, Vol. XXI, No. 1086, 28 September 1895, pp. 771–2; *DBB*, Vol. 1 (1984), pp. 625–32; P. L. Cottrell, *Industrial Finance 1830–1914*, London (1979), pp. 113–14, 153.]

20 The collapse of Overend, Gurney & Co., the largest discount house in London, on 11 May 1866, created the worst panic in the City since 1825. They failed with liabilities of £18 million and the day became known in financial circles as 'Black Friday'. The Bank of England paid out nearly £4 million on that day to support liquidity. Overend & Gurney, having underwritten much doubtful commercial paper, had been unsound for some years and the general crisis of 1866 finally brought them down. R. P. Harding (p. 224) and William Turquand (p. 212) were appointed joint liquidators. Such was the scale of the collapse that the insolvency work continued for 28 years and in total Harding's firm alone earned £43,205 in fees from this failure.

21 John Ball (1808–1879) began his accountancy career as a clerk in the office of Peter Harris Abbot and when in 1833 the latter was appointed an Official Assignee in Bankruptcy, decided to set up in partnership with a fellow clerk, William Quilter (see p. 217). Insolvency formed the backbone of their practice, which flourished during the commercial crisis of 1847–8. By 1849 Quilter could state that their practice was the most extensive in Britain, and was only rivalled in terms of its fee income by Coleman & Co. Both Coleman and Ball gave evidence to the Select Committee on the Bank Acts in 1858 which included summaries of the cases they had handled in 1857. For Quilter, Ball & Co. the total liabilities of their biggest cases amounted to £4,496,000, though the twelve largest insolvencies dealt with by Colemans attained the figure of £6,726,840.

[*DBB*, Vol. 4 (1985), pp. 791–5.]

22 Edward Aldam Leatham (1828–1900), educated at University College

London, of which he became a Fellow and took an M.A. in 1851, became a banker at Wakefield and Pontefract. A Liberal M.P. he sat for Huddersfield (1859–65 and 1868–86).

[Stenton *WWMP*, Vol. I, p. 231.]

23 Sir Moses Montefiore (1784–1835) amassed a fortune as a stockbroker and retired in 1824, becoming a philanthropist and advocate of the Jewish cause: in 1855 he founded a girls school and hospital at Jerusalem and in 1860 raised funds for Jewish and Christian refugees at Gibraltar.

[*DNB*, Vol. XXXVIII, p. 279.]

24 John Fowler (1826–1864), having been apprenticed at the age of 16 to a corn merchant in Melksham,. persuaded his father to allow him to pursue a career in engineering. Taking advantage of the family's Quaker connections, in 1847 he joined Gilkes, Wilson, Hopkins & Co. of Middlesbrough as an apprentice. In the early months of 1850 Fowler formed a partnership with another Quaker, Albert Fry, a member of the Bristol family of chocolate makers, and began the manufacture of carts, wagons and carriages at Lawrence Hill in that city. Fowler left in 1856, wishing to concentrate his resources on the production of steam-powered agricultural machinery. He designed several mole draining ploughs, and a balance plough, and in April 1859 formed the Steam Plough Royalty Company and, in conjunction with William Hewitson, another Quaker, set up a factory in Leathley Road, Hunslet, Leeds. The strain imposed on Fowler by establishing the business resulted in his suffering a nervous breakdown in 1864. On his doctor's advice he sold his Leeds home and moved to Prospect House in the village of Ackworth. During his recuperation while out hunting he was thrown from his horse, which then rolled on top of him. Although treated by a local doctor and apparently recovering, John Fowler suffered from lockjaw and died, thereby cutting short a promising career as an engineer and entrepreneur. In July 1857 he had married Elizabeth Lucy Pease, daughter of Joseph Pease of Darlington, having met her while an apprentice there.

[Michael R. Lane, *The Story of the Steam Plough Works, Fowlers of Leeds*, London (1980), pp. 7–10, 19, 26, 56–7.]

25 William Hopkins Holyland (1807–1882) was born on 25 December 1807 and was 58 years of age when the partnership of Price, Holyland & Waterhouse was formed in 1865. A member of the City warehousing firm of Rogers, Lowrey, Holyland & Co., he then became clerk with Coleman, Turquand, Youngs & Co. Two possible explanations offer themselves for his comparatively late elevation to the status of partner: that he had not been sufficiently wealthy to afford the premium for training, or that he was not an accountant of Waterhouse's abilities and ambition. Holyland retired on 18 March 1871 some two years before the expiry of the partnership agreement on 30 June 1873. Nevertheless, he retained a room at 13 Gresham Street in order to complete personal commissions, including the Commercial Bank of India, a circumstance which led to him being defrauded of £300 (p. 117). From 1874 he practised under his own name, rather than that of the firm, until his death on 20 January 1882.

He was a Fellow and Trustee of the Institute of Accountants in London and was admitted to a Fellowship of the Institute of Chartered Accountants in 1880, on its foundation.

[G. E. Richards, 'History of the Firm, The First Fifty Years, 1850–1900' (Price Waterhouse & Co. typescript, 1950) pp. 3, 5.]

26 By 1865 Samuel Lowell Price (1821–1887) had been in practice as an accountant for at least 17 years. The son of Charles Price, a pottery manufacturer of Bristol, he decided not to follow his elder brothers in the family business. In 1848 S. L. Price joined William Edwards (d. 1884) who, remarked *The Accountant*, in 1885, starting on his own in 1843, had been responsible for training 'a considerable percentage of the chartered accountants now in practice in London' [*The Accountant*, Vol. XI, No. 527, 10 January 1885, p. 15]. The firm, known as Edwards & Price, was at 5 Gresham Street. Nevertheless, it was short lived and Price left to set up on his own in December 1849, though he remained a life-long friend. Price continued to occupy the same offices in Gresham Street (on the south side and a few yards east of Wood Street) until he was joined by Holyland and Waterhouse, the demands of space forcing them to move to 13 (now 44) Gresham Street.

Price was a moving spirit in the formation of the Institute of Accountants, founded in 1870, an important precursor of the Institute of Chartered Accountants. He was a council member from its foundation and proposed William Quilter to its presidency. On its establishment in 1880 Price became a council member of the Institute of Chartered Accountants, retaining his post until 1887.

On 19 May 1887, at the age of 66, S. L. Price died leaving a daughter and a widow. His relatives reported that he had been a tall, handsome man; that he wore a velvet coat and that in his later years bad attacks of lumbago resulted in his needing help to travel home from the office. A professional colleague said that he had a perfect manner for a practising accountant. Edwin Waterhouse described him as 'a large-hearted and Christian man' (p. 82).

[*The Accountant*, Vol. XIII, No. 651, 28 May 1887, p. 312; G. E. Richards, 'History of the Firm 1850–1900' (Price Waterhouse & Co., typescript, 1950), pp. 2, 6, 7.]

27 Sir Philip Frederick Rose (1848–1919), educated at Harrow School, entered the family firm of parliamentary solicitors, Baxter, Rose & Norton. He was for many years legal advisor to the London, Brighton & South Coast Railway.

[*WwW*, Vol. II, p. 907.]

28 Samuel Laing (1812–1897), educated St John's College, Cambridge, and called to the Bar at Lincoln's Inn in 1837, served as Liberal M.P. for Wick (1852–57, 1859–60 and 1865–68) and Orkney and Shetland (1873–85). Appointed a railway commissioner in 1846, Laing was subsequently Financial Secretary to the Treasury (1859–60) and Financial Minister in India (1860–65).

[*WwW*, Vol. 1, p. 406.]

29 William Quilter (1808–1888), in partnership with John Ball (see p. 215), was one of the foremost accountants in the mid-nineteenth century. Although his reputation was based on insolvency work, he did, as Waterhouse noted, have an expertise in railway accounting. The collapse of the railway mania in 1847 resulted in his being commissioned by shareholder auditors to investigate the accounting manipulations which had been used to sustain dividends. Among the best known of his enquiries was that into George Hudson's frauds at the Eastern Counties Railway Co., while others included the South Eastern, the Midland and the London, Chatham & Dover Railway companies. In his obituary Quilter was credited with the invention of the double account system (by which capital and revenue expenditures were separated), which was made compulsory for railway companies under an Act of 1868. In fact, the system had been in operation before Quilter's personal involvement with railway companies, though he may well have advised the government on the final form adopted. His estate at death was the largest known of any Victorian accountant, amounting to £580,934.

[*The Accountant*, Vol. XIV, No. 728, 17 November 1888, p. 754; *DBB*, Vol. 4 (1985), pp. 791–5; *History of the Institute of Chartered Accountants, op. cit.*, pp. 248–9.]

30 Sir Edward William Watkin (1819–1901) began his career as a merchant in Manchester but left the family business to become secretary of the Trent Valley Railway, subsequently joining the L.N.W.R. where he served as assistant to the general manager, Captain Mark Huish. He then became general manager of the Manchester, Sheffield & Lincolnshire Railway. After a period in Canada,

Notes

Watkin returned to Britain and within two years he was elected to the board of the G.W.R. (1863–7) and the M.S. & L.R., of which he became chairman in 1864. In the following year he joined the South Eastern Railway and was elected chairman in 1866, at the instigation of a group of Manchester shareholders. In 1872 he agreed to join the Metropolitan Railway (p. 93) as their chairman once more at the request of Manchester capitalists, who were worried about lax management. Watkin also served as the Liberal M.P. for Yarmouth (1857–58), Stockport (1864–68), and Hythe (1874–95).

[*DBB*, Vol. 5 (1986), pp. 682–5; *WwW*, Vol. 1, pp. 745–6.]

31 George Harvey Jay, as Edwin Waterhouse relates, was an elderly accountant of considerable experience. On his admission to the partnership in July 1868 the firm's style became Price, Jay, Holyland & Waterhouse; however, the experiment proved unsuccessful and Jay departed on 31 December of the same year, the practice reverting to its original name. He had originally worked as a clerk in the office of Quilter, Ball & Co. (p. 215) but, when the commercial crisis of 1847–48 increased the volume of their insolvency work, both Jay and W. Crosbie were made partners. For what reason Jay departed is not known, though it may have been to set up on his own account.

[Richards, 'History of the Firm', *op. cit.*, p. 4; *DBB*, Vol. 4, (1985), M. Bywater, 'William Quilter', p. 792.]

32 John Wigham Richardson (1837–1908), the second son of Edward Richardson of Newcastle upon Tyne, was like Waterhouse a Quaker. He

too, had attended University College London, but his studies were ended abruptly in 1857 when the Northumberland & District Bank (in which his family were large shareholders) failed. Robert Hawthorn (1796–1867), a friend of his father, agreed to allow Richardson to work in his machine drawing office at the Forth Banks Work. Subsequently he went into partnership with C. J. D. Christie (1830–1905), a Scotsman, and in 1860 they commenced business at the Neptune Yard as shipbuilders. In 1898 2000 were employed in the yards which had a capacity for 30,000 gross tons of shipping and 30,000 i.h.p. of marine engines. Wigham Richardson, a bibliophile, was of a scholarly temperament and a considerable linguist, fluent in French and nearly so in German. Interested in architecture, he designed several houses.

[*DBB*, Vol. 4 (1985), pp. 904–5.]

33 Thomas Whitwell (1837–1878), the distinguished engineer and metallurgist, was a partner with his brother, William, in William Whitwell & Co., Thornaby Ironworks, Stockton-on-Tees. He was responsible for designing a hot-blast stove (to heat the air before it entered the blast furnace and so raise the efficiency of the process of converting iron ore into metal) which incorporated the principles of regeneration (that is using hot waste gases to heat the brick checker work within the stove). Unfortunately Whitwell was killed by an exploding mill furnace at his own works 1878.

[Carr and Taplin, *British Steel Industry, op.cit.*, p. 51; *Journal of the Iron & Steel Institute*, Vol. 15, pp. 604–8.]

34 Jeremiah Head (1835–1899) was born in Ipswich and articled to Robert

Stephenson's Forth Street Locomotive Works in Newcastle, where he served three and a half years in the pattern making, fitting and erecting shops, and one and a half years in the drawing office. While erecting a compound mill engine for Henry Pease & Co. at Darlington, he met John Fowler (p. 215), who was impressed by his abilities, and appointed him as the first works manager at his Steam Plough Works in Leeds. However, Head appears to have encountered difficulties with the abrasive David Greg, Fowler's deputy, and left to join Theodore Fry in Middlesbrough. Fox, Head & Co. prospered and soon employed 600 men and produced over 400 tons of rolled metal per week. He was elected President of the Institution of Mechanical Engineers in 1885.

[Lane, *Steam Plough Works, op. cit*, pp. 19, 44; *The Engineer*, Vol. 87, p. 395.]

35 Henry Selfe Page Winterbotham (1837–1873), the son of Lindsay Winterbotham of Stroud, a banker. He was educated at Amersham School and University College London. Called to the Bar at Lincoln's Inn in 1860, Winterbotham sat as the Liberal M.P. for Stroud from 1867 and in March 1871 was appointed an Under-Secretary of State for the Home Department.

[Stenton, *WWMP*, Vol. 1, p. 415.]

36 Sir David Dale (1829–1906), whose father died at sea before his first birthday, was brought up by his mother in the Quaker faith, though, like Edwin Waterhouse, he resigned from the Society of Friends in later life. Educated privately in Edinburgh, Durham and Stockton, he began work in the offices of the Wear Valley Railway in 1846. Showing a flair for finance, he became a partner in the Shildon Locomotive Works, near Darlington, and later, in 1881, became a director of the North Eastern Railway.

However, business fame was achieved by Dale as an iron and steel maker rather than as a railway manager. In 1858 he had been appointed by the creditors of the insolvent Derwent Iron Co. to inspect the Consett Works. Matters did not improve and when in April 1864 the Consett Iron Co. was formed, Dale became one of the joint managing directors, and from 1884 served as its chairman until his death. It became one of the most profitable steelworks in the country, supplying plate to shipbuilders at home and abroad.

His reputation as an industrial conciliator was considerable. In 1866, after a costly six-month strike, Dale proposed the formation of an arbitration board and in 1869 under his presidency such a body was established for the iron trade in the North of England. A man of patience, even temper and great concentration, he became a successful diplomat, and was asked to assist in the setting up of the Conciliation Board of the Durham Coal Trade in 1895. In 1872 Sir Joseph Pease (p. 227) had taken Dale into his colliery partnership (Joseph Pease & Partners and his iron ore and limestone mines (J. W. Pease & Co.). When these concerns became a private limited liability company, Pease & Partners, Dale became the managing director and later chairman. He also served as vice president of the Durham Coal Owners' Association.

[*DBB*, Vol. 2, (1984), A. Christie and C. Shaw, 'Sir David Dale', pp. 1–5.]

Notes

37 Sir Richard Moon (1814–1899), like Edwin Waterhouse the son of a Liverpool merchant, was educated at St Andrews University (though he did not take his degree) and entered the family business. Having retired from the shipping firm, Moon increasingly devoted himself to the affairs of the London & North Western Railway; in 1855, for example, he headed a committee of investigation which led to the establishment of a committee of 13 directors to supervise traffic operations, and became increasingly identified with a reformist faction within the company. Moon was elected chairman in June 1861 a post he retained until February 1891 (p. 132). By this time the L.N.W.R. was already the largest railway company in Britain, so it was a considerable achievement by Waterhouse to have obtained the post of accountant to the auditors. The care that he took over the preparation of the accounts impressed Moon for whom frugality and careful housekeeping were high priorities. The latter missed only one half-yearly general meeting throughout his chairmanship and in his single-minded commitment refused all other positions apart from directorships of L.N.W.R. subsidiaries. The company grew steadily, if unspectacularly under Moon's control (partly because he discouraged the growth of commuter services and trains on Sundays) and the dividend rose from 4.25% in the year of his appointment as chairman to 7.25% when he retired. An Anglican and a Conservative, Moon appears to have represented something of a father-figure for Edwin Waterhouse; a businessman for whom he held the greatest respect.

[*DBB*, Vol. 4 (1985), M. C. Reed, 'Sir Richard Moon', pp. 301–6.]

38 Sir Edward Lawrence (1825–1909), a Liverpool merchant, in 1853 married Jane Harrison, daughter of Giles Redmayne of Brathay Hall, Ambleside and brother of G. T. Redmayne (below). A director of the British and Foreign Marine Insurance Co. from 1863, he was Mayor of Liverpool (1864–65) and chairman of the council of University College, Liverpool (1891–3).

[*WwW*, Vol. 1, p. 415.]

39 George Tunstall Redmayne (1840–1912), born in Highgate, was the son of Giles Redmayne, who owned an established silk business in London. However, after the birth of George, his youngest child, he purchased Brathay Hall, Ambleside, and moved there. After attending Tonbridge School, George was articled to Alfred Waterhouse in Manchester and married Edwin's elder sister, Katharine Waterhouse (1836–1898), by whom he had three sons and a daughter. Redmayne then practised on his own account in the city, where his designs included an office for the Scottish Widows Fund, Albert Square (1874) and the College of Art at Chorlton-on-Medlock (1880–1). 'He was never greedy for multiplicity or magnitude of work', observed Paul Waterhouse (1861–1924), architect son of Alfred, 'his personal thought and personal labour entered every detail of his designs and he was exceptionally careful in making sure that nothing would appear in his work that was meaningless or nugatory. His comparatively small list of executed works is, therefore, not by any means to be attributed solely to lack of opportunity'. Edwin Waterhouse commissioned him to design his county home, Feldemore (pp. 103–4, 106, 107, 109, 127,

Notes

131) and the various extensions to it, in preference to his more able brother, Alfred. His other major house was Whitton, Herefordshire, for Richard Green.

[*Journal of the R.I.B.A.*, Vol. XIX, 28 September 1912, Obituary by P. Waterhouse, p. 723; *The Builder*, Vol. CIII, No. 3626, 11 October 1912, p. 422.]

40 George Edmund Street (1821–1881), born in Woodford, Essex and having been a pupil of Owen Browne Carter of Winchester, in 1844 found employment with Sir George Gilbert Scott, and in 1856 set up on his own account in London. Primarily a church architect, he also successfully entered the competition to design the Law Courts (1866–70) in The Strand. The house to which Edwin Waterhouse refers was 'Holmdale' (1873–80) situated in the immediate south of Holmbury St Mary. The village church, St Mary's (1877–79), had also been designed by Street (Edwin Waterhouse was one of the churchwardens there) and was where he chose to be buried. The Waterhouse family graves are also in the churchyard. Having won the Royal Institute of British Architects' Gold Medal in 1874, Street served as its president in 1881.

[*The Builder*, Vol. XLI, No. 2029, 24 December 1881, pp. 777–9; Roger Dixon and Stefan Muthesius, *Victorian Architecture*, London (1978), p. 266.]

41 Henry Davis Pochin (1824–1895), was largely concerned with the coal and iron trades (being a director and subsequently deputy chairman of the Patent Nut & Bolt Co. in Smethwick) and was an Alderman of Salford, where he was also Mayor in 1866–7

and 1867–9. Pochin was briefly M.P. for Stafford (December 1868 to March 1869). As a radical Liberal, he advocated educational reforms, the complete disestablishment of the Irish Church, the reduction of public expenditure, especially on the Royal Navy, the creation of life peerages, and was firmly opposed to every form of protection. In 1866 he published *A Plan of Parliamentary Reform* which advocated the enfranchisement of the working classes.

[Stenton, *WWMP*, Vol. 1, p. 314.]

42 Hon. Edward Frederick Leveson Gower (1819–1907), after graduating from Christ Church, Oxford, was called to the Bar at the Inner Temple in November 1845. A Liberal and a supporter of Gladstone, he entered Parliament in May 1847 as M.P. for Derby and subsequently for Stoke-on-Trent (1852–57) and Bodmin (1859–85). He had worked very briefly as a precis writer in the Foreign Office, and was a magistrate for Surrey.

[Stenton *WWMP*, Vol. 1, p. 162.]

43 Gladstone, as the Hon. Frederick Leveson Gower related in his memoirs, *Bygone Years* (1905), dined with the latter at his country home, 'Holmbury'. They had met at house parties at Cliveden and Chiswick given by his relative, Harriet, Duchess of Sutherland. Gladstone admired the scenery in the Holmbury district and was particularly taken with the trees that grew there, but also took pleasure in cutting them down, one of his hobbies.

[The Hon. F. Leveson Gower, *Bygone Years, Recollections*, London (1905), pp. 291–2.]

Notes

44 Frederick Siemens (1826–1904) helped his more famous elder brother Sir (Charles) William Siemens (1823–1883) invent the open hearth method of steelmaking. He had come to England in 1848 and was responsible for suggesting that the regenerative principle (that is using hot waste gases to heat absorbent refractory bricks which in turn can warm currents of cold air and gas) might be applied to furnaces generating great heat. He patented the application which the brothers believed could make great savings in the melting of metals and other materials such as glass.

[J. C. Carr and W. Taplin, *History of the British Steel Industry* Oxford (1962), p. 31.]

45 In 1870 Theodore Waterhouse had purchased an estate of 120 acres at Bowsey Hill, near Twyford, Berkshire. He lived at his country home, 'Upcroft', until 1890 when in a sudden decision the house was sold.

[Edward Fry, Editor, *Theodore Waterhouse, Notes of His Life, op. cit.*, pp. 62, 105, 173.]

46 George Sneath (1842–1921), the son of a yeoman farmer, was born at Baston, Lincolnshire; joining a firm of solicitors in Leicester, he became increasingly involved in estate accounting. To advance his career Sneath travelled to London and entered S. L. Price's office as his clerk, where he became experienced in insolvency work, and played a major part in the various bank amalgamations which occurred in the latter part of the nineteenth century. He made many visits to America for Price,

Waterhouse & Co., having become a partner in 1875. A rapid worker with an uncanny memory and a facility for marshalling and analysing figures, Sneath finally retired on 30 June 1913. He had been a member of the Institute of Chartered Accountants, serving on its council from 1896 to 1914. In about 1899, his brother, H. G. J. Sneath, who also worked for Price, Waterhouse & Co., was asked by Fowler (p. 223) to go to America to undertake a brewery investigation. Although the task was expected to take only two months, he remained there for almost a year. One of George Sneath's sons, William Cecil Sneath, was attached to the Chicago office in 1897 and in 1907 received a partnership in the London firm, retiring in 1934. Another son, Rupert Sneath, after serving his articles and gaining experience in the City, joined the South American firm of which he became senior partner.

[*The Accountant*, Vol. LXVI, No. 2476, 20 May 1922, p. 702; Richards, *op. cit.*, pp. 6–7, 8, 11.]

47 William James Pirrie, Viscount Pirrie (1847–1924), educated at the Royal Academical Institution, Belfast, entered Harland & Wolff in 1862 as an apprentice. He became a partner in the shipbuilding firm in 1874, and following the flotation of the business in 1885 and Sir Edward Harland's death in 1895, Pirrie was the undisputed head of the company and its chairman. Under his leadership Harland & Wolff built up a world-beating specialism in large passenger liners, culminating in the completion of such vessels as the *Olympic* and *Titanic* (both 46,400 tons) and the *Britannic* (50,000 tons).

Notes

Price Waterhouse & Co. were appointed auditors of Harland & Wolff in 1901 to comply with the requirement of the 1900 Companies Act, the commercial manager, John Bailey, having until then performed this task. In 1902 William Tawse, who had trained with Price, Waterhouse, was appointed the company's accountant, having understudied Bailey.

[*WwW*, Vol. II, p. 841; Michael Moss and John R. Hulme, *Shipbuilders to the World, 125 years of Harland and Wolff, Belfast 1861–1986*, Belfast (1986), pp. 105, 111; *DBB*, Vol. 4, D.S. Johnson, 'William James Pirrie', pp. 702–10.]

48 Joseph Gurney Fowler (1856–1916) was one of three brothers who had served their articles with Price, Waterhouse & Co. Having been recently admitted to the Institute of Chartered Accountants, he became a partner on 1 July 1887. Fowler was a powerfully built man keen on sport and gardening; he bred orchids and in 1915 was awarded the Lawrence medal by the Royal Horticultural Society. At the time of his death he was acting as advisory accountant to the government in relation to the compensation payable to the railways under state control, and was a member of the board of referees appointed in connection with Excess Profits Duty.

[*The Accountant*, Vol. LIV, No. 2161, 6 May 1916, pp. 535–6; Richards, *op. cit.*, pp. 7–8, 11.]

49 Lewis Davies Jones (1859–1899) and William James Caesar (1859–1917) in the United States. The investment of an increasing volume of British capital in American enterprises resulted in a growing demand for the services of City accountants whose expertise was required to assess the viability of projected companies and to audit those in existence. George Sneath (p. 222) made several trips across the Atlantic for this purpose and in 1889, when he was accompanied by J.G. Fowler (above) to investigate the Bartholomay breweries prior to their amalgamation and subsequent flotation on the London Stock Exchange, the decision was taken to open an office in New York. In 1890 L.D. Jones, who had been employed by the firm in Gresham Street since February 1877, was selected to open an office at 45 Broadway as Price, Waterhouse & Co.'s agent. In the following year W.J. Caesar, a member of the Society of Accountants in Edinburgh, who had joined the London staff in 1890 having worked on the Continent and in America, joined Jones in New York, but in 1892 moved to Chicago to open an office there.

Jones, of Welsh parentage, took a deep interest in the embryonic professional organizations that were being established in America, while Caesar, the son of a Scottish Presbyterian minister, took no part in this movement. During the five years up to January 1895, and the formation of the partnership of Jones, Caesar & Co., they sent papers and draft reports to 44 Gresham Street for review. Among the British-financed concerns which they examined were breweries, packing houses and stockyards (all funded by the City of London Contract Corporation), insurance companies and other ventures including International Okonite, Liptons, and J. & P. Coats (Pawtucket). The firm was also appointed auditors of the

Notes

Chicago Junction Railways and Chicago Union Stock Yards Co. Virtually all the assistants working for Jones and Caesar were sent to them from London, the first being M. E. Pavey, engaged in 1889 for the brewery audits and who remained until 1893, when he became secretary of the United States Brewing Co.

However, on 1 January 1895 Jones and Caesar set themselves up in partnership agreeing with Price, Waterhouse & Co. that they should act as their American agents. The firm prospered and grew and the arrangement continued until November 1898, when Jones sailed for London with a view to pooling work and profits. A scheme was worked out in principle, and though Jones died aged only 40 on his return, the union of the two practices was effected in 1899 (see also pp. 226, 231).

[*The Accountant*, Vol. XXV, No. 1267, 18 March 1899, Obituary L.D Jones, p. 323; C. W. DeMond, *Price, Waterhouse & Co. in America*, New York (1951), pp. 13–18, 27–8, 43 5.]

50 Frederick Whinney (1829–1916), the son of Thomas Whinney, a licensed victualler turned livery stable keeper, became a clerk in the accountancy offices of Harding & Pullein and in November 1857 was admitted to the partnership. When R. P. Harding (below) retired to take the post of Chief Official Receiver, Whinney became senior partner; a post he retained until 1905. He was both an expert in insolvency and audit work and his clients in the latter category included the Midland Bank (from 1885) and the Equitable Life Assurance Society (1894). Whinney was a director of the London, Tilbury & Southend Railway, his firm being the

auditors from 1892. A founder council member of the Institute of Chartered Accountants, he served as its third president from 1884–88. Ernest Cooper described him as being 'proud of the commanding position his services to our profession had brought him. There was in him a touch of hauteur, derived perhaps from military service' [Cooper, *Proceedings* (1921), *op. cit.*, p. 48]. Whinney had served as a Major in the 3rd Volunteer Battalion of the Middlesex Regiment.

[*The Accountant*, Vol. LIV, No. 2163, 20 May 1916, pp. 582–3; *DBB*, Vol. 5, pp. 766–9; Jones, *Accountancy and the British Economy, op. cit.*, pp. 33–4, 41–2.]

51 Sir Robert Palmer Harding (1821–1893), the son of Robert Harding an auctioneer, appraiser and house agent, reportedly began his business career running a fashionable West End hatters. When this fell into financial difficulties and his books were produced in court, the official complimented Harding on his record keeping and suggested a career in accountancy. He set up on his own in July 1847 and subsequently in partnership with Edmund Pullein (d. 1866). Specializing in insolvency work, the practice grew and in 1857 Frederick Whinney (above) was admitted as a partner. Harding remained as the firm's senior partner until 1883 when, on the point of retirement, he was persuaded by Joseph Chamberlain to take the post of Chief Official Receiver. Among the concerns that he had liquidated were the Marylebone Bank (from 1853), Royal British Bank (1856), National Alliance Assurance (1859) and Overend, Gurney & Co. (1866), the last being administered

jointly with Turquand (p. 212). Harding was a founder member of the Institute of Accountants in London, and of the Institute of Chartered Accountants, serving as the latter's second president in 1882–83.

[*DBB*, Vol. 3, pp. 32–6; Jones, *Accountancy and the British Economy, op. cit.*, pp. 33, 41–2, 49; *The Accountant*, Vol. XIX, No. 995, 30 December 1893, p. 1093.]

52 William Lawies Jackson, Lord Allerton (1840–1917), was Conservative M.P. for Leeds North (1880–1902) and served as Financial Secretary to the Treasury (1885–86, 1886–91) and Chief Secretary for Ireland (1891–2). He was also chairman of the Great Northern Railway Co.

[*WwW*, Vol. II, p. 17.]

53 Reginald Earle Welby, Lord Welby (1832–1915), educated Eton and Trinity College, Cambridge, entered the Treasury in 1856, becoming Assistant Financial Secretary (1880), Auditor of the Civil List (1881) and Permanent Secretary of the Treasury (1885–94). He was also a Commissioner of the Great Exhibition of 1851.

[*WwW*, Vol. I, p. xiv.]

54 Sir (William) Gerald Seymour Fitzgerald (1841–1910), educated at Harrow and Oriel College, Oxford, was called to the Bar at Lincoln's Inn in 1865. He was political A.D.C. to the Secretary of State for India.

[*WwW*, Vol. I, p. 247.]

55 Sir Albert William Wyon (1869–1937), the son of an engraver at the Royal Mint, was educated at Clewer House School, Windsor; he entered the City at an early age and was articled to S. L. Price in 1885. Admitted to a partnership in 1895, Wyon became the senior partner in April 1916 on the death of J. G. Fowler (p. 223). During the First World War he was one of the two auditors appointed by the government in connection with the control of the railways and was a member of the Board of Referees set up by the Treasury under the Finance Act of 1915 to judge on questions of liability arising from Excess Profits Duty. Wyon became a Council member of the Institute of Chartered Accountants in 1933. A great lover of nature, who had possibly been introduced to the Lake District by Waterhouse, he subsequently presented a tract of land there (which included Pillar) to the National Trust. He died in office on 1 December 1937.

[*The Accountant*, Vol. XCVII, No. 3288, 11 December 1937, p. 798; Richards, 'History of the Firm', *op. cit.*, pp. 11–12.]

56 The Riverside Trust Co. Ltd was formed by Matthew Gage, who conceived of irrigating six thousand acres of desert in Southern California so that they could grow oranges. Wilson Crewdson, Edwin Waterhouse's nephew, visited Riverside in 1889 and was favourably impressed by the scheme, as was Theodore Waterhouse who had been introduced to Gage. Later in the year when the company came into being (the flotation being handled by Price, Waterhouse's American firm); Wilson Crewdson and his friend Arthur Lowes Dickinson (p. 231) joined the board, Edwin serving as chairman. Dickinson, a graduate of Cambridge University, had achieved a high placing in the

Institute of Chartered Accountants' final exams. A partner in the relatively small London firm of Lovelock, Whiffin & Dickinson, he had acquired some knowledge of American business. Dickinson made several visits to Riverside in connection with the orange groves and reported to Waterhouse on his return. Accordingly when Price, Waterhouse were looking for a senior partner to replace W. J. Caesar (p. 223), who in 1900 had announced his intention to retire, they offered the position to Dickinson, then aged 40. He sailed for New York in April 1901 (see also pp. 231).

[C. W. DeMond, *Price, Waterhouse & Co. in America*, New York (1951), pp. 17, 47; *Theodore Waterhouse, Notes of His Life, op. cit.*, p. 165.]

57 Sir Samuel Canning (1823–1908), a civil engineer, was responsible for the laying of cables across the Atlantic in 1865–66 and 1869 and of cables between Land's End and Alexandria.

[*WwW*, Vol. I, p. 117.]

58 Howard Lloyd (1837–1920) was the son of Isaac Lloyd (1801–1883), who began the private bank of Christy, Lloyd & Co. in 1824 at Stockport. Although Isaac was able to retire from the partnership in 1830 with a handsome settlement, his success as a banker was eclipsed by that of his son, Howard, who worked for Lloyds Bank during a time of great growth.

[Humphrey Lloyd, *The Quaker Lloyds in the Industrial Revolution*, London (1975), p. 286.]

59 Rt Hon. William St John Fremantle Brodrick, Earl of Midleton (1856–1942), educated at Eton and Balliol College, Oxford, was Conservative M.P. for West Surrey (1880–85) and for the Guildford division of Surrey 1885 to 1906. His political appointments included: Financial Secretary at the War Office (1886–92), Under Secretary of State for War (1895–98), Under Secretary for Foreign Affairs (1898–1900), Secretary of State for War (1900–03) and Secretary of State for India (1903–05).

[Stenton and Lees, *WWMP*, Vol. II, p. 45.]

60 George William Francis Sackville, tenth Duke of Bedford (1852–1893), formerly M.P. for the county of Bedford (1875–85), succeeded to the title on 14 January 1891.

[*Burke's Peerage and Baronetage* (1980), p. 227.]

61 John Belcher (1841–1913) entered his father's architectural firm in London becoming a partner in 1865. He with his chief assistant Beresford Pite (1861–1934) was responsible for the design of Institute of Chartered Accountants' Hall (1888–93) which was opened by Edwin Waterhouse as president. This building, together with the Town Hall at Colchester, established his reputation as an architect. Belcher subsequently became president of the Royal Institute of British Architects (1904–06), was awarded their Gold Medal in 1907 and became a Royal Academician in 1909.

[*The Builder*, Vol. CV, No. 3693, 14 November 1913, Obituary p. 507; No. 3694, 21 November 1913, p. 560; Sir John Squire, *The Hall of the Institute of Chartered Accountants in England and Wales*, London (1937), p. 5; Alastair Service, *Edwardian Architecture*, London (1977), pp. 64–5, 198.]

Notes

62 Lord George Francis Hamilton (1845–1927), after a brief military career, became Conservative M.P. for Middlesex (1868–85), and for the Ealing Division of Middlesex (1885–1906). Amongst other political appointments he was First Lord of the Admiralty (1885–86 and 1886–92) and Secretary of State for India (1895–1903). Hamilton chaired the Royal Commission on the Poor Law and Unemployment (1905–09) and the Mesopotamia Commission (1916–17).

[Stenton and Lees *WWMP*, Vol. II, p. 154.]

63 Rt Hon. William Lidderdale (1832–1902) was a director of the Bank of England from 1870 and appointed Deputy Governor in 1887 and served as the Governor from 1889 to 1892.

[*WwW*, Vol. I, p. 429.]

64 Sir James Francis Garrick (1836–1907), having been called to the Bar at the Middle Temple in 1873 and in Queensland in 1874, became Attorney-General in Queensland (1878–9). Garrick was Agent-General in London for Queensland in 1884–8 and 1890–5.

[*WwW*, Vol. 1, p. 268.]

65 Lord Randolph Churchill (1849–1895) suffered increasingly poor health during the winter of 1892–93, experiencing vertigo, palpitations, numbness of the hands, difficulty in articulation and increasing deafness, the product of advancing syphilis. Once a speaker of audacity and brilliance, Churchill's final appearances in the House of Commons were a grotesque parody of his former self. He was finally persuaded by his doc-

tors to take a world tour in an attempt to recover his health. Whilst visiting Madras his constitution collapsed and he was brought home to Grosvenor Square, where in January 1895 he died.

[Robert Rhodes James, *Lord Randolph Churchill*, London (1959), pp. 361–9.]

66 Sir Joseph Whitwell Pease (1828–1903) was chairman of Pease & Partners Ltd and of the North Eastern Railway Co. and served as Liberal M.P. for South Durham from 1865 to 1885, and subsequently for the Barnard Castle division of Durham. He also owned about 2500 acres of land, and lived at Hutton Hall, Guisborough, Yorkshire.

[*WwW*, Vol. 1, p. 554.]

67 Thomas Henry Ismay (1837–1899), the son of a shipbroker in Maryport, was educated at Croft House School, near Carlisle, and apprenticed to a Liverpool firm of shipbrokers, Imrie, Tomlinson & Co. By 1857 in partnership with a retired sea captain, Philip Nelson, he was the owner of two ships, the latter leaving in 1862. The business expanded rapidly, principally by operating cargo ships to Central and South America. In 1867 Ismay bought the flag and goodwill of the bankrupt White Star Line of sailing clippers to Australia and began operating his own iron ships there and to New Zealand. He became a major shareholder of the Oceanic Steam Navigation Co. on its formation in 1869, and in the following year formed a partnership with his former fellow apprentice, William Imrie Junior, under the style Ismay, Imrie & Co. Ismay also held a directorship of the L.N.W.R. and was deputy chairman of the Royal Insurance Co.

[*DBB*, Vol. 3 (1985), pp. 455–62: *WwW*, Vol. 1, pp. 370–1; *DNB*, Supplement Vol. III, p. 34.]

68 Richard Norman Shaw (1831–1912), born in Edinburgh and articled to the country-house architect William Burn (1789–1870), joined G. E. Street's (p. 221) office as his principal assistant in 1859. Four years later he began his own practice, sharing an office with William Nesfield (1835–88). Together they evolved a style of architecture based on English vernacular buildings, which brought Shaw to prominence as a designer of town and country houses. However, he also designed Gothic churches, and his most famous commission was Scotland Yard (1888–90), London.

[*Journal of RIBA*, Vol. XX (1913), Obituary by R. Blomfeld, p. 55; Dixon and Muthesius, *Victorian Architecture, op. cit.*, pp. 14, 266–7.]

69 Sir Roland Vaughan Williams (1838–1916), educated at Christ Church, Oxford, graduating in 1860, was called to the Bar at Lincoln's Inn in 1861. Becoming a Q.C. in 1889 he served as a judge of the Supreme Court, Queen's Bench Division (1890–7). A neighbour of Edwin Waterhouse, he lived at High Ashe's Farm, Abinger, near Dorking.

[*WwW*, Vol. II, p. 1130.]

70 Alexander Young (d. 1907) was the son of a farmer of Windmill, near Gordonstoun, Moray. His elder brother John (d. 1888) had initially served an apprenticeship in law with Alexander Cooper in Elgin but decided to move to London to enter the accountancy firm of Robert Fletcher & Co. as a junior clerk. In 1840 John Young then set up on his own and was

later joined by his brother. In about 1857 they merged with William Turquand (p. 212) to form Turquand, Youngs & Co., one of the leading City practices. In 1894 Alexander Young succeeded Turquand as the senior partner, by which time the firm had a number of railway companies as audit clients; Young himself was joint auditor of the Caledonian Railway with John Graham of Glasgow. His success as an insolvency expert brought considerable rewards and allowed him to assemble one of the finest collections of Corots, which on his death sold for a record £525,000.

[*The Accountant*, Vol. XXXVII, No. 1707, 24 August 1907, pp. 241–2; Jones, *Accountancy and the British Economy, op. cit.*, pp. 34, 37, 42, 62.]

71 William, seventh Duke of Devonshire (1808–1891), was Chancellor of the University of Cambridge and a senator of London University; he was succeeded in December 1891 by Spencer Compton (1833–1908), the eighth Duke, who held a number of senior political posts including Secretary of State for War (1866, 1882–85) and Secretary of State for India (1866–82).

[*Burke's Peerage and Baronetage* (1980), pp. 797–8.]

72 Cromartie, fourth Duke of Sutherland (1851–1913), formerly M.P. for Sutherland (1874–86), succeeded to the title on 22 September 1892.

[*Burke's Peerage and Baronetage* (1980), pp. 2588–9.]

73 Sir Joseph Lister (1827–1912), educated at London University, became Professor of Surgery at Glasgow University (1860–69) and subsequently at King's College, London (1877–93). He achieved fame for his discovery of an antiseptic system of treatment during surgery. Awarded the Order of Merit, Lister was president of the Royal Society (1895–1900).

[*WwW*, Vol. I, p. 431.]

74 Sir (Richard) Melvill Beachcroft (1846–1926), educated at Harrow, became a solicitor in 1886, becoming a partner in Beachcroft, Thompson & Co. A Conservative, he was an original member of the L.C.C., representing North Paddington in the first Council; subsequently Beachcroft was elected for South Paddington in 1907 and became an Alderman in 1892. Deputy chairman (1896), vice chairman (1897), and chairman (1909–10). From 1903–8 he was chairman of the Metropolitan Water Board.

[*WwW*, Vol. II, p. 70.]

75 Harold John Morland (1869–1939) was a Quaker and like Edwin Waterhouse had been educated at University College London, though he also attended King's College, Cambridge. On leaving university he became a schoolmaster but soon abandoned this for a career in accountancy. After qualifying as a chartered accountant in 1900, he joined Price, Waterhouse, becoming a partner in 1907. He was a prominent member of the Society of Friends and was Clerk (or chairman-secretary) of the yearly meeting from 1927 to 1932. In 1931, as the auditor of the Royal Mail Steam Packet Co., he and his co-defendant, Lord Kylsant, were tried under the 1861 Larceny Act for not declaring the transfer of sums from a secret reserve to improve apparent financial standing of the company. Although Kyl-

sant served a prison sentence, Morland was acquitted early in the hearing of the case. He retired from the partnership in June 1932.

[*The Accountant*, Vol. CI, No. 3384, 14 October 1939, p. 415.]

76 Nathaniel Spens (1850–1933), educated at Glasgow University, became a partner in A. H. & J. Grahame & Spens, chartered accountants and stockbrokers in 1877, but left the firm in 1890. He was chairman of the Stock Conversion and Investment Trust Ltd (1890–1928) and took an active interest in the management and finance of railway companies. Spens was a director of the London, Chatham & Dover Railway and a member of the South Eastern & Chatham Railway's management committee (1904–23). He was a trustee of the London, Midland & Scottish Conversion Trust and a director of the London Scottish American Trust. His relative, Ivan Spens (1890–1964), became senior partner of the London firm of accountants Brown, Fleming & Murray [*The Accountant*, Vol. CL, No. 4649, 25 January 1964, pp. 110–11].

[*WwW*, Vol. III, p. 1272; Jones, *Accountancy, op. cit.*, pp. 161–2.]

77 Sir Felix Schuster (1854–1936), a governor of the Union of London & Smiths Bank (1895–1918) and a director of the National Provincial Bank, was the son of F. J. Schuster, a merchant and banker in the City of London. He served on a number of government inquiries including the Royal Commission on London Traffic (1903–5), India Office Committee on Indian Railway Finance and Administration (1907–08) and the Treasury Committee on Irish Land Purchase Finance (1907–08). Amongst his other appointments he was chairman of the London Chamber of Commerce (1905–06), president and chairman of the Institute of Bankers (1908–09) and governor of University College London.

[*WwW*, Vol. III, p. 1205.]

78 Sir Edgar Speyer (1862–1932), was educated at the Real Gymnasium, Frankfurt-am-Main, and entered his father's business, which comprised the three firms: Speyer Bros (London), Speyer & Co. (New York) and L. Speyer-Ellissen (Frankfurt-am-Main). Having been the resident partner in Frankfurt, in 1887 he took charge of the London office, retiring from the American and German firms in 1914. He was one of the founders of the Whitechapel Art Gallery (see p. 190).

[*WwW*, Vol. III, p. 1272.]

79 Edward Nettlefold (1856–1909), a director of the L.N.W.R., Lloyds Bank, Birmingham Canal Navigations and the North British & Mercantile Insurance Co., owed these appointments to his position as deputy chairman of Nettlefolds Ltd, then the world's largest manufacturer of woodscrews, based in Smethwick. Subsequently, when they became part of Guest, Keen & Nettlefolds, he was appointed to the board of the merged company and held that post until his death. A grandson of the founder of the woodscrew business, John Suttons Nettlefold (1792–1866), he was educated at Mrs Case's non-conformist School in Hampstead and at Christ's and Caius Colleges, Cambridge. In December 1900 on the death of Lord Loch, Edward Nettlefold was appointed to the L.N.W.R. board

and helped to improve the service between London and Birmingham.

[*The Engineer*, Vol. CIII (1909), Obituary, p. 394; Anthony Crofton, *The Nettlefolds, A Genealogical Account*, Lewes (1962), pp. 41–2; Edgar Jones, *A History of GKN, Volume One: Innovation & Enterprise, 1759–1918*, London (1987), Chapter Seven.]

80 Sir George Augustus Pilkington (1848–1916), educated at Guy's Hospital, practised medicine in Southport between 1870 and 1884. He was mayor (Liberal) of Southport (1884–85, 1892–93) before coming M.P. for the Southport Division of Lancashire (1884–85, 1899–1900).

[*WwW*, Vol. II, p. 840.]

81 Sir John Sutherland Harmood-Banner (1847–1927), born at Dingle Mount, Liverpool, and educated at Radley College, entered his father's accountancy firm (see p. 24) in 1865 and became a partner in 1872. He was president of the Institute of Chartered Accountants in 1904–05 and of the Association of Municipal Corporations in 1907. A member of the Liverpool City Council from 1894, he became Lord Mayor in 1912–13. Elected as Conservative M.P. for the Everton division of Liverpool in 1905, he sat until retirement in 1924.

[*Liverpool Express*, 9 February 1905; *The Accountant*, Vol. LXXVI, No. 2726, 5 March 1927, pp. 340–1; Stenton and Lee, *WWMP*, Vol. III, p. 151; *History of Institute of Chartered Accountants, op. cit.*, pp. 236–7; *DBB*, Vol. 3 (1985), pp. 43–7.]

82 By November 1905, when Nicholas Waterhouse crossed the Atlantic,

Notes

Price, Waterhouse & Co.'s American practice had witnessed considerable growth under its new senior partner A. L. Dickinson (below). To add to their offices in New York and Chicago, a branch office was opened in St Louis, Missouri, in November 1901, a city then in the throes of vigorous commercial and industrial growth. It was a considerable coup in 1902 to be appointed auditors of the United States Steel Corporation; the work involved in the examination of its and the various subsidiaries' accounts necessitating the opening of an office in Pittsburgh in the same year. Realising that there were potentially rich opportunities for accountants on the California coast which could not be captured effectively from St Louis or Pittsburgh, Dickinson discussed the possibility of establishing a base in San Francisco with George Sneath (p. 222) during the latter's visit to America in the summer of 1904. In November Dickinson travelled to San Francisco to acquire the business of F. G. Phillips & Co. and the new office was opened under the style of Price, Waterhouse & Co. Fortunately, the staff were widely scattered over the Bay Area when the great earthquake hit the city in April 1906 and all escaped injury.

[DeMond, *op. cit.*, pp. 52, 58–9, 64–5, 73–4.]

83 Sir Arthur Lowes Dickinson (1859–1935) was educated at Charterhouse and King's College, Cambridge, where in 1882 he obtained a first in mathematics; he served his articles with Edwards, Jackson & Browning, being awarded first place in the intermediate examination of the Institute of Chartered Accountants in 1883, and joint first place in the final of

1886. Two years later he became the junior partner in the firm of Lovelock, Whiffin & Dickinson, but in 1901 was approached by Edwin Waterhouse to take charge of Price, Waterhouse & Co.'s practice in America in succession to Caesar (p. 223). At this time there were offices in New York and Chicago, employing 24 professional staff. Ten years later, when Dickinson relinquished the senior partnership, he had succeeded in increasing the number of offices in the United States, Canada and Mexico to eleven, employing 145 professional staff. Among the clients they acquired during this period of growth was the United States Steel Corporation.

Dickinson returned to England in 1913 and remained a partner in the London office until his retirement in 1923. He served on the council of the Institute of Chartered Accountants from 1914 to 1928. During the First World War, he was financial advisor to the Controlled Establishments Division of the Ministry of Munitions and later to the Controller of Coal Mines, for which service Dickinson received a knighthood in 1919. He represented the second generation of university-educated, professionally qualified, and career minded accountants, some of whom were rewarded by the State.

[*The Accountant*, Vol. XCII, No. 3144, 9 March 1935, p. 345; *DBB*, Vol. 2 (1984), pp. 103–5; Richards, 'History of the Firm', pp. 9–12.]

84 'Brantwood', near Coniston, was purchased by John Ruskin (1819–1900) in 1871 and was repaired and remodelled for his occupation the following year. With its uninterrupted views of the fells across Coniston Water, he

was reminded of his beloved Alps. Joan Agnew, Ruskin's cousin and her husband, Arthur Severn, the watercolourist, soon began to use Brantwood as their second home, and the house was extended to accommodate them and their family and servants. The Severns continued living there after Ruskin's death, Joan dying in 1924 and Arthur in 1931.

[*Brantwood, John Ruskin's Home 1872–1900.*]

85 Fawe Park (1856–58), designed by Alfred Waterhouse for James Bell, a Quaker M.P., was occupied in the summer of 1903 by Rupert Potter, the landscape photographer, and his children Beatrix (1866–1943), the writer and illustrator of children's stories, and Bertram, a barrister.

[*The Discovery of the Lake District, op. cit.*, pp. 132–4.]

86 Kenneth Grahame (1859–1932), educated at St Edward's School, Oxford, entered the Bank of England as a clerk in 1879, rising to become its secretary (1898–1908). His publications included *The Golden Age* (1895), *Dream Days* (1898) and *Wind in the Willows* (1908).

[*DNB 1931–40* (1949), pp. 357–8.]

87 Edward Sholto, third Baron Penrhyn (1864–1927), succeeded to the title on the death of his father in March 1907.

[*Burke's Peerage and Baronetage* (1980), pp. 2095–6.]

88 Sir William Edgar Horne, M.P. (1856–1941), educated at Westminster School, became deputy chairman of the Prudential Assurance Co. (1917–28) and its chairman (1928–41). He was president of the Surveyors' Institution. As a Conservative Unionist, Horne unsuccessfully contested the Barnstaple division of Devon in 1906 but was elected for the Guildford division of Surrey in January 1910, and sat until he retired in October 1922.

[Stenton and Lees, *WWMP*, Vol. III, p. 174.]

89 Col Richard Hamilton Rawson, M.P. (1863–1918), educated at Eton and Brasenose College, Oxford, served in the 1st Life Guards and commanded the Sussex Yeomanry (1908–14). A High Sheriff for Sussex in 1899, he unsuccessfully contested the Reigate division of Surrey in 1906 as a Conservative Unionist, but was elected there in 1910, sitting until his death.

[Stenton and Lees, *WWMP*, Vol. II, pp. 297–8.]

90 Sir Philip Magnus (1842–1933), educated at University College London, and Berlin University, became Superintendent of the Technology Department of the City and Guilds of the London Institute. Involved in education he was president of the College of Preceptors and chairman of the Secondary Schools Association, serving on the Royal Commission on Technical Instruction (1881–84). A member of the Senate of London University, he was elected as Unionist M.P. for London University in 1906 and sat until retirement in 1922.

[Stenton and Lees, *WWMP*, Vol. III, p. 233.]

91 Sir Frederick James Mirrielees (d. 1914), who resided close to Edwin Waterhouse at 'Pasture Wood', Holmbury, had lived in Russia, Switzerland and Germany, before moving to London in 1879 to join the firm of Donald Currie & Co., having married

Sir Donald Currie's eldest daughter in that year, where he remained until his retirement in 1912.

[*WwW*, Vol. II, p. 495.]

92 The 'Laycock of Sheffield' referred to by Edwin Waterhouse as a guest on the R.M.S. 'Balmoral Castle' was probably William Samuel Laycock (1841/42–1916), head of W. S. Laycock Ltd, manufacturers of railway carriage fittings (roller blinds, seats ventilators, heating equipment, couplings) and indicator boxes for tramways at the Victoria Works, Millhouses. In 1939 the company was merged with Hardy, Spicer & Co. to form the Birfield Group, which in 1966 was taken over by Guest, Keen & Nettlefolds.

[*The Railway Magazine*, July 1905, T. Booth, 'Firms who Trade with Railways, No. 11, Messrs W. S. Laycock Ltd, Sheffield', pp. 23–32.]

93 Sir Giles Gilbert Scott (1880–1960), a grandson of Sir George Gilbert Scott (1811–1878), entered the competition for the design of the Anglican Cathedral at Liverpool in 1903. The examiners were embarrassed when the extreme inexperience of the winner became known and they appointed G. F. Bodley to act as joint architect. After Bodley's death in 1907, Scott revised his plans in 1910 and produced what was virtually a new design. It proved to be a major undertaking and Scott continued to alter the designs during the rest of his life as the cathedral was built.

[*The Builder*, Vol. CXCVIII, No. 6092, 19 February 1960, obituary, pp. 345–6, 360; Service, *Edwardian Architecture, op. cit.*, pp. 84–6, 207–8.]

94 Sir Lawrence Edward Halsey (1871–

1945) was educated at Haileybury and articled to Price, Waterhouse & Co. in 1890, becoming a partner in July 1900. He was auditor of the London & North Eastern Railway and the Duchy of Cornwall. During the First World War he had served as honorary auditor of the Prince of Wales' Relief Fund, and sat on the Wheat Commission (1918–20). Halsey, described as being of a modest, retiring nature, encouraged the younger members of staff. A keen gardener, he died shortly after his retirement at his home 'Gooserye', Worplesdon, Surrey.

[*The Accountant*, Vol. CXIII, No. 3694, 22 September 1945, p. 146; Richards, 'History of the Firm' *op. cit.*, p. 12.]

95 The first *Price, Waterhouse & Co. Staff War Bulletin* was published in February 1915 and included letters from volunteers serving in the armed forces and news of home developments in the firm. Second and third editions were produced in June 1915 and December 1916. The latter recorded that 109 members of staff (including 22 from overseas offices) were in the forces together with 33 former PW employees. Their letters revealed the horrors of war on the Western Front, while lists of casualties demonstrated its devasting impact. As Nicholas Waterhouse recalled he had tried to enlist as a private soldier but was rejected because of a weak knee which had been further damaged during a soccer match.

[*Price, Waterhouse & Co., Staff War Bulletin*, Nos 1–3 (1915–16); Nicholas E. Waterhouse, 'Reminiscences 1899–1960' (typescript, 1961), pp. 43, 109.]

96 'Mr H' could have been Mr T. C.

Notes

Hutchinson, managing director of the Skinningrove Iron Co. Their steelworks was at Saltburn-by-the-Sea, and a large interest in the company was owned by the North Riding and Durham colliery concern of Pease & Partners Ltd (see p. 227).

[Carr and Taplin, *Steel Industry, op. cit.*, pp. 211, 267.]

97 Sir Gilbert Francis Garnsey (1883–1932), born at Wellington, Somerset, the son of a butcher, was educated at Wellington School. He served his articles with a small firm, Muras, Harries & Higginson of Walsall, but coming first in both the intermediate (1903) and final examinations (1905) of the Institute of Chartered Accountants, Garnsey moved to London on qualification to enter Price, Waterhouse & Co. One of the most able accountants of his generation, he was made a partner in 1913. Ill health prevented his joining the forces in the First World War, when he became Director of Internal Audits and Controller of Munitions Accounts at the Ministry of Munitions, his service winning him the K.B.E. in 1918. Garnsey continued to serve on numerous government committees, including the Metropolitan Water Board (1920), Income Tax Regulations (1932). A prodigious worker he took a leading part in schemes of reconstruction for companies fallen into difficulty, being involved with Armstrong, Whitworth & Co., William Beardmore & Co., and Cable & Wireless. He had paid for his articles in Walsall by playing soccer for Aston Villa second eleven, and was offered employment at Price, Waterhouse by [Sir] Nicholas Waterhouse, who on one occasion at a partners' meeting, thinking of Garnsey's skill in obtaining work for the firm and his sharp mind, referred to him as 'The Card'. Garnsey had read Arnold Bennett's novel and did not take kindly to the nickname. Possibly pressure of work resulted in his premature death in June 1932, at the age of 49.

[*The Accountant*, Vol. LXXXVII, No. 3004, 2 July 1932, pp. 9–10; *DBB*, Vol. 2, pp. 487–9; 'Notes' by Sir Nicholas Waterhouse.]

98 Sir William Barclay Peat (1852–1936), born at Scotstone, Forebank, attended Montrose Academy and was apprenticed to a lawyer in Montrose. However, he did not qualify and in 1870 travelled to London to enter the office of Robert Fletcher, an accountant who had originally practised in Aberdeen. When Fletcher decided to open an office in Middlesbrough in 1877, to be closer to their clients in the iron and steel trade, Peat was appointed partner-in-charge. On the death of Roderick Mackay in 1891, who had become the senior partner in London, Peat took on the entire firm even though it was in some debt. Under his leadership the business expanded. A close professional relationship developed between W. B. Peat & Co. and Price, Waterhouse & Co., helped by the friendship that existed between Sir William Peat's eldest son, [Sir] Harry, and [Sir] Nicholas Waterhouse. Before the First World War a number of joint partnerships were formed overseas, including offices in Cairo, Calcutta, Pretoria and Johannesburg.

[*The Accountant*, Vol. XCIV, No. 3191, 1 February 1936, p. 157; T. A Wise, *Peat, Marwick, Mitchell & Co. 85 years*, United States (1982), pp. 14–16; *DBB*, Vol. 4, (1985) pp. 602–4.]

PAGINATION OF ORIGINAL TEXT

The text of *His Story* appears here
substantially abridged. It would have
been too obtrusive to give the original
manuscript page references for every
paragraph. However, as a general aid to
anyone researching the original text,
given below are the page numbers of
this book, and beside them the
manuscript location of the beginning of
the page concerned.

Book	Original MS	Book	Original MS
49	1	68	56
50	2	69	58
51	4	70	59
52	6	71	61
53	12	72	62
54	16	73	65
55	19	74	69
56	21	75	72
57	23	76	74
58	25	77	78
59	29	78	82
60	31	79	84
61	36	80	86
62	45	81	90
63	46	82	93
64	48	83	97
65	50	84	101
66	52	85	105
67	54	86	108

Book	Original MS	Book	Original MS
87	113	131	385
88	121	132	399
89	122	133	400
90	129	134	407
91	131	135	430
92	132	136	435
93	135	137	438
94	141	138	439
95	145	139	447
96	146	140	448
97	151	141	455
98	154	142	460
99	159	143	473
100	162	144	475
101	166	145	477
102	168	146	494
103	170	147	509
104	184	148	510
105	187	149	512
106	192	150	513
107	197	151	522
108	209	152	544
109	211	153	553
110	221	154	566
111	234	155	576
112	252	156	585
113	256	157	591
114	257	158	611
115	265	159	615
116	285	160	634
117	307	161	635
118	310	162	636
119	320	163	641
120	322	164	642
121	332	165	647
122	333	166	650
123	336	167	653
124	343	168	673
125	344	169	685
126	345	170	698
127	353	171	699
128	365	172	705
129	379	173	717
130	380	174	734

Book	Original MS	Book	Original MS
175	736	193	865
176	739	194	867
177	756	195	877
178	767	196	883
179	778	197	889
180	780	198	894
181	784	199	904
182	784	200	906
183	791	201	921
184	805	202	937
185	808	203	939
186	816	204	948
187	818	205	967
188	826	206	978
189	835	207	987
190	843	208	1006
191	851	208	1010
192	852		

Select Bibliography

BELLOT, H. HALE, *University College London 1826–1926*, London (1929).

BIRD, MARGARET, *Holmbury St Mary, One Hundred Years*, Bromley (1979).

COOPER, ERNEST, *ICAEW, Proceedings of the Autumnal Meeting . . . October 1921*, London (1921).

DE MOND, C. W., *Price, Waterhouse & Co. in America*, New York (1951).

EDWARDS, J. R., *Company Legislation and Changing Patterns of Disclosure in British Company Accounts 1900–1940*, ICAEW London (1981).

   Abacus, Vol. 21, March 1985, 'The Origins of the Double-Account System'.

   DBB, Vol. 5 (1986), 'Edwin Waterhouse'.

FOWLER, LUCY, *Sketch and Recollections of Nicholas Waterhouse*, London (1863).

[FRY, EDWARD, Editor], *Theodore Waterhouse 1838–1891, Notes of His Life and Extracts from His Letters and Papers*, London (1894).

HARTE, NEGLEY and NORTH, JOHN, *The World of University College London 1828–1978*, London (1979).

[HOWITT, SIR HAROLD], *The History of the Institute of Chartered Accountants in England and Wales 1870–1965*, London (1966).

JONES, EDGAR, *Accountancy and the British Economy 1840–1980, The Evolution of Ernst & Whinney*, London (1981).

LEVESON GOWER, THE HON. F., *Bygone Years, Recollections*, London (1905).

MALTBY, SALLY *et al*, *Alfred Waterhouse 1830–1905*, London (1983).

PARKER, R. H., *British Accountants, A Biographical Sourcebook*, New York (1980).

POLLARD, GEORGE B., *A History of Price Waterhouse in Europe 1914–1969*, London (1975).

RICHARDS, ARCHIBALD, B., *Touche, Ross & Co. 1899–1981, The Origins and Growth of the United Kingdom Firm*, London (1981).

RICHARDS, G. E., 'History of the Firm, The First Fifty Years 1850–1900' (typescript, 1950).

Select Bibliography

WATERHOUSE, EDWIN (Editor), *Extracts from the Journals of Mary Waterhouse 1825–1880*, London (1907).

A List of the Descendants of Nicholas Waterhouse of Everton (1910).

WATERHOUSE, NICHOLAS E., 'Reminiscences 1877–1960' (typescript, 1961).

WATT, M. LAIRD, *The First Seventy Five Years, Price Waterhouse Canada* (1982).

WESTBURY, NICOLA, 'The Country Houses of Holmbury St Mary' (B. Arch. thesis, University of Liverpool, 1987).

WISE, T. A., *Peat, Marwick, Mitchell & Co. 85 Years*, United States (1982).

INDEX

Index

Index

Index

Index

Index

Index

Index